WALKING IN THE ENGADINE
– SWITZERLAND

About the Author

Kev Reynolds first visited the Alps in the 1960s, and he has returned there almost every year since, to walk, trek or climb, to lead mountain holidays, devise multi-day routes or to research a series of guidebooks covering the whole range. A freelance travel writer and lecturer, he has a long association with Cicerone Press with whom he has produced more than a dozen books on the Alps, including *The Mountain Hut Book, 100 Hut Walks in the Alps, Walking in the Alps, The Swiss Alps* and *Trekking in the Alps*. He has also written two books on the Pyrenees, several more on Southern England, a series of trekking guides to Nepal, a memoir covering some of his Himalayan journeys (*Abode of the Gods*) and a collection of short stories and anecdotes harvested from his 50 years of mountain activity (*A Walk in the Clouds*).

Kev is a member of the Alpine Club and Austrian Alpine Club. He has been made an honorary life member of the Outdoor Writers and Photographers Guild; SELVA (the Société d'Etudes de la Littérature de Voyage Anglophone), and the British Association of International Mountain Leaders (BAIML). After a lifetime's activity, his enthusiasm for the countryside in general and mountains in particular, remains undiminished, and during the winter months he regularly travels throughout Britain and abroad to share that enthusiasm through his lectures. Check him out on www.kevreynolds.co.uk

Other Cicerone guides by the author

The Mountain Hut Book
100 Hut Walks in the Alps
Abode of the Gods
Alpine Points of View
A Walk in the Clouds
Chamonix to Zermatt:
    the Walker's Haute Route
Écrins National Park
Swiss Alpine Pass Route –
    Via Alpina 1
The Bernese Oberland
The Cotswold Way
The North Downs Way
The Pyrenees
The South Downs Way
The Swiss Alps

Tour of Mont Blanc
Tour of the Jungfrau Region
Tour of the Oisans: GR54
Tour of the Vanoise
Trekking in the Alps
Trekking in the Himalaya
Trekking in the Silvretta and
    Rätikon Alps
Walking in Austria
Walking in Kent
Walking in Sussex
Walking in the Alps
Walking in the Valais
Walks & Climbs in the Pyrenees
Walks in the South Downs
    National Park

WALKING IN THE ENGADINE – SWITZERLAND

BERNINA, ENGADINE VALLEY
AND SWISS NATIONAL PARK

by Kev Reynolds

JUNIPER HOUSE, MURLEY MOSS,
OXENHOLME ROAD, KENDAL, CUMBRIA LA9 7RL
www.cicerone.co.uk

Third edition 2019
ISBN: 978 1 78631 052 1

Second edition 2005
First published 1988

Printed in China on behalf of Latitude Press Ltd
A catalogue record for this book is available from the British Library.

Dedication

For family and friends who have shared Engadine days with me

Updates to this Guide

While every effort is made by our authors to ensure the accuracy of guidebooks as they go to print, changes can occur during the lifetime of an edition. Any updates that we know of for this guide will be on the Cicerone website (www.cicerone.co.uk/1052/updates), so please check before planning your trip. We also advise that you check information about such things as transport, accommodation and shops locally. Even rights of way can be altered over time. We are always grateful for information about any discrepancies between a guidebook and the facts on the ground, sent by email to updates@cicerone.co.uk or by post to Cicerone, Juniper House, Murley Moss, Oxenholme Road, Kendal LA9 7RL.

Register your book: To sign up to receive free updates, special offers and GPX files where available, register your book at www.cicerone.co.uk.

Front cover: In early summer the meadows of Val Tuoi leading to Piz Buin are full of wild flowers (Route 91)

CONTENTS

Mountain safety

Every mountain walk has its dangers, and those described in this guidebook are no exception. All who walk or climb in the mountains should recognise this and take responsibility for themselves and their companions along the way. The author and publisher have made every effort to ensure that the information contained in this guide was correct when it went to press, but, except for any liability that cannot be excluded by law, they cannot accept responsibility for any loss, injury or inconvenience sustained by any person using this book.

International distress signal *(emergency only)*
Six blasts on a whistle (and flashes with a torch after dark) spaced evenly for one minute, followed by a minute's pause. Repeat until located by a rescuer. The response is three signals per minute followed by a minute's pause.

Helicopter rescue
The following signals are used to communicate with a helicopter:

Help needed:
raise both arms
above head to
form a 'Y'

Help not needed:
raise one arm
above head, extend
other arm downward

Emergency telephone numbers
Emergency telephone number: (117 (police) 144 (ambulance)
Swiss Air Search & Rescue (REGA): Tel 1414
Weather report: Tel 162 (in French, German or Italian)

Weather reports
Italy: tel 0165 44 113
Switzerland: tel 162 (in French, German or Italian), www.meteoschweiz.ch/en

**Note: Mountain rescue can be very expensive – be adequately insured
(see Appendix A).**

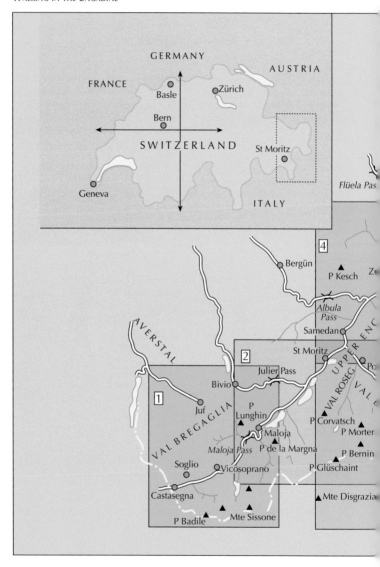

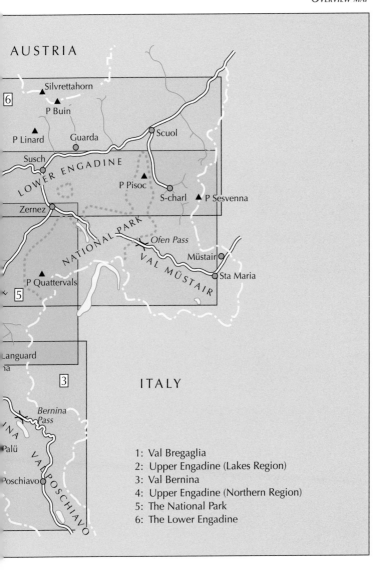

AUSTRIA

▲ Silvrettahorn

▲ P Buin

▲ P Linard ○ Guarda ○ Scuol

Susch

LOWER ENGADINE

▲ P Pisoc

Zernez ○ S-charl ▲ P Sesvenna

NATIONAL PARK

Ofen Pass

VAL MÜSTAIR

Müstair ○

Sta Maria ○

▲ P Quattervals

Languard

na

Bernina Pass

Palü

INA

VAL POSCHIAVO

Poschiavo ○

ITALY

1: Val Bregaglia
2: Upper Engadine (Lakes Region)
3: Val Bernina
4: Upper Engadine (Northern Region)
5: The National Park
6: The Lower Engadine

*From many paths above Pontresina the glimmering snows of
Piz Palü dominate the views (Routes 46 and 47)*

PREFACE

My first view of the Engadine came more than 50 years ago. It was a week before Christmas; snow lay deep, a big moon hung over the mountains, and everything glistened with frost. Next day, as the sun flooded the valley, the intensity of light was almost painful as I ploughed my way across frozen lakes and ducked beneath trees bowed down with hanging baskets of the purest snow I'd ever seen. Smitten by the beauty of an Alpine winter, I imagined no other season could match it. But the Engadine is a valley for all seasons, and working there during the following months I experienced its magic as winter turned to spring, spring to summer, and then autumn transformed the landscape with the Midas touch of gold.

The Engadine has enticed me back many times in the decades since that awakening. No longer having an interest in skiing her slopes, I prefer to walk her paths, cross high passes and stand on a few of her summits; or perhaps wander up to a favourite alp and simply absorb the glories all around me. There's plenty to absorb.

My most recent visits have been to trek the 9-day Tour of the Bernina, and the week-long Tour of the Silvretta, which sneaks into the Lower Engadine. Both these treks stray into neighbouring countries – Italy for the first, and Austria for the second – yet those stages that touch upon the Engadine are full of highlights and would make a fine introduction for newcomers to this corner of the Swiss Alps.

If the routes in this book give you, the reader, as much pleasure as they brought me when walking them, I'll be well satisfied.

Here's a hint: try some of the walks in 'less-obvious' side valleys where you may wander for hours through the most magical of alpine pastures without catching sight of another human being. Give yourself time to sit on a rock and soak in the wonder of it all, and you'll be enriched.

Since my last visit to the Engadine district, a massive rock fall from Piz Cengalo devastated parts of the splendid Val Bondasca (Bregaglia region) and wrought havoc on the village of Bondo below the valley's entrance. Since then the whole of Val Bondasca has been put out of bounds, affecting Routes 15–19 and 23 described in this guidebook. We have decided to retain these as they were when I last walked them, in the hope and expectation that before this edition goes out of print, the valley will be reopened and the two huts (Sciora and Sasc Furä) will be back in business. However, visitors will doubtless find many changes there, although Bondasca will still be one of the loveliest of all valleys and worthy of exploration. (A further warning appears in the relevant sections of this guide.)

My thanks to those friends and correspondents who continue to feed me with essential updates for this guide; to Myrta and Jörg Dössegger of St Moritz, for decades of friendship and hospitality; to hutkeepers, hostel wardens and the staff at various tourist offices throughout the region for patiently answering my questions; to the Swiss National Tourist Office for practical assistance; and to my wife (as ever) for her loving support and for sharing so many Engadine trails with me.

Once again I am grateful to Jonathan Williams at Cicerone for his company on the hut to hut treks we've made together, for the joy of planning new routes with him, as well as the new books and opportunities to revitalise existing titles with his talented team in Kendal. I owe my gratitude to all those at Juniper House who have given life to this latest edition. As I have said on many occasions, creating a guidebook is a team effort – mine is the pleasure of wandering the mountains, while the rest of the Cicerone team do the work! So I thank them all for enabling me to have the world's best job.

Finally, information in this guide is given in good faith, and routes described offered in the hope that users will enjoy many happy days when following them. But I am fully aware that changes occur from time to time, not just to resort facilities, or to roads and huts, but to the landscape too – sometimes through natural causes, but often by the hand of man. It may be that you will discover paths or tracks that have been rerouted, or landscape features altered to such an extent that some of the route descriptions are no longer valid. Should this be the case, I sincerely hope that such changes in no way spoil your holiday, but would appreciate an email giving details in order that I might check them out for future editions. Please write to info@cicerone.co.uk.

Kev Reynolds

Map Key

~~	ridge
⬭	glacier
∿∿∿	road
▪▪▪▪▪▪▪	national park
▬·▬·▬	international boundary
⇧	hut
⅄	col
▲	summit
┼┼┼●┼┼┼	railway/station
⬭	lake/river
— — —	tunnel
= = = = =	train tunnel
●	town
•	village
├——————┤	cablecar

Lago Palü and the Palü glaciers, seen from the Tour of the Bernina (Photo: Jonathan Williams)

INTRODUCTION

The lake at the head of the Bernina Pass (Photo: Jonathan Williams)

Lying in the southeastern corner of Switzerland, the Engadine Valley forms a trench almost 100km long. In it, and on hillsides that flank it, there's something for every walker's taste: gentle valley rambles for a family outing; craggy mid-mountain walks for the more adventurous; high-level routes that lead across glacier, snowfield and rugged pass for the experienced mountain trekker. Dazzling lakes make tempting picnic sites. There are forest walks with deer leaping through the undergrowth; high pastures with ancient haybarns linked one with another by narrow trails, and snow-peaks gleaming as a backdrop.

It's a high valley, a valley of contrasts. In the Upper Engadine between Maloja and St Moritz, several large lakes almost fill the valley floor at an altitude of around 1800m, while snow-peaks of the Bernina Alps rise nearby. Shapely mountains like Piz Palü, Bellavista, Piz Roseg and Piz Bernina spawn glaciers that hang like frozen cascades, or spill into side valleys among lengthy walls of moraine.

In the Lower Engadine, which runs northeastward and gradually loses altitude between Cinuos-chel and Martina, the valley narrows. In places the River Inn squeezes through tight gorges, wild and foaming in cataracts as a fine white-water river. But while the Inn may thunder into these gorges, the valley itself is a green and verdant land, with forests clothing the lower slopes. Flower-rich meadows ease between romantically attractive villages. Some of these are in the valley; others catch the sunshine from a natural terrace on the northern hillside.

The mountains here are quite different to those of the upper valley; mostly bare of snow in summer, grey turrets rising from a world of greenery. But push into some of the northern tributary glens and you'll come up against the Silvretta Alps that display small glaciers and snowfields, and charm those drawn to them with their individuality.

But this guidebook is not limited to the Engadine (although if it were there'd be quite enough walks to justify it). Instead we look at some of its neighbouring valleys too, for each one broadens the walker's opportunities, and adds to the scenic dimension. In the south, for example, at the Engadine's head where the lake of Sils gives way to meadows around the village of Maloja, a sudden drop over the valley's lip shows the Maloja Pass writhing its way with countless hairpins into a deep shaft of a valley filled with the soft air and warmth of Italy. This is Val Bregaglia, still Swiss but running into Italy and absorbing its atmosphere. It's a captivating region with abrupt side glens topped by jagged granite peaks, slabs and walls like those of Piz Badile and Cengalo.

Perched upon hillsides that rise from chestnut woods nearby, unspoilt villages appear to have been built there precisely to capture the most dramatic views. Some of these villages count among the loveliest in all the Alps.

Branching either side of the Upper Engadine, other little valleys are worth exploring: Fedoz, Fex, the narrow wedge of Val Champagna, Suvretta, Val Bever and the seductive Val Susauna. Val Bernina forms a link between Engadine extravagance and modest Val Poschiavo. Like the Bregaglia, Poschiavo too is Italian by nature, lying as it is far below the Bernina Pass and draining across the border into Valtellina. Val Bernina, administered by Pontresina, is the gateway not only to Poschiavo and Valtellina, but – more importantly for us – to the massif from which it takes its name. Access to the Bernina Alps is through either of two tributary glens: Val Roseg or Val Morteratsch. The first is a real gem of a valley, the second dominated by its retreating glacier and an astonishingly beautiful headwall of snow and ice.

The Lower Engadine has its fair share of delightful side valleys, too. Although they may not be as well known as some of those of the upper valley, they're no less rewarding to visit. Val Tuoi behind Guarda is a classic example. At its head the dominant peak is Piz Buin, along whose ridges runs the border with Austria, where Vorarlberg and Tyrol merge in the Silvretta Alps. There's Val Tasna,

The path that runs alongside Lej Vadret eventually climbs to the Coaz Hut (Routes 51 and 52)

flowing parallel to the east of Tuoi, a delight of forest, meadow and running streams, with a wild and stony inner core of glens leading up to the frontier again. Then there's the Val Sinestra, broad and open where it empties into the Engadine, but enticingly mysterious in its upper reaches. There's Val S-charl too, on the south side of the Inn, with the boundary of Switzerland's only national park being drawn along its river.

The national park comprises a number of fine valleys. Contained solely within the Lower Engadine, the park is extraordinarily rich in wildlife, and the sensitive visitor will quickly come to appreciate its unique qualities. Here is a wilderness rarely found in Europe, for the needs of humans are subordinate to those of Nature.

Man has a very low priority, and the natural world is allowed freedom to develop as it will, without his moulding influence. Some of the valleys are out of bounds to walkers, while in those that do have access, one can sense an air of calm, and gain opportunities to observe wildlife grazing or roaming untroubled in a pristine environment. That alone makes a visit to the Engadine worthwhile.

The Engadine is perhaps best known as a winter playground. With international resorts like St Moritz, Pontresina and Scuol, and with such classic ski grounds as those of Corvatsch near Silvaplana, and Diavolezza and Lagalb in the Val Bernina, together with the world-renowned Cresta Run hurtling between St Moritz and Celerina, this is hardly surprising. The international jet set, with all its supposed glitz and glamour, has given St Moritz a reputation it's happy to trade on. But that is not the full story, for as grand as the Engadine may be in winter, it's in summer and autumn that the valley really triumphs. This is when the world of *aprés-ski* gives way to the seduction of winding trails, high pastures and hamlets inaccessible when the snow lies deep. In summer there's colour and fragrance on the hillsides and in the valleys; wild flowers in profusion, marmots bounding across the slopes, mountain lakes and tarns, and tiny pools that reflect distant views. Observant walkers who go quietly among the mountains stand a good chance of being rewarded by the sight of red or roe deer, of chamois, marmot and ibex. There are mountain hares, foxes, and red squirrels among the larchwoods. There are buzzards and eagles and alpine choughs, capercaillie and woodpeckers, and numerous finches to be seen.

Leave your bed or tent early one summer morning, and slip noiselessly through the woods to find a glade where you can observe the valley's wildlife; or bivouac high when the weather's settled, and capture the magic of daybreak spilling over the mountains. Then you'll understand there's even more to the walker's experience of the Alps than the basic joy of wandering through a series of magnificent landscapes.

One of these additional pleasures will be found when visiting bow-walled villages and alp hamlets seemingly unaffected by the passage of time, apparently unmoved by the

Herds of ibex can be found in Val Bernina and many places in the national park, but individuals roam among various corners of the district

The endearing marmot is found throughout the Engadine region

goats and cattle and make cheese as they have done since time immemorial. Plan Vest and Tombal are magnificent examples. Timber and stone constructions with flat slabs of quarried stone on their rooftops, and tiny windows that look out across napkin-sized meadows, out beyond an empty drop of mountainside, to distant peaks like granite teeth on the skyline, often divorced from their roots by wisps and drifts of cloud.

A world above the world, accessible only to the walker.

advance of technology. The Engadine and Bregaglia have their fair share of such villages and hamlets, quite aside from the hybrid abstractions of jet-set resorts. On hillsides remote from the world of fashion houses and discos, trails lead to wonderful belvedere villages like Soglio in the Bregaglia; tiny groups of houses like Blaunca and Grevasalvas above Maloja; Isola, on a spillage of land beside the lake of Sils. There's Guarda, Ardez and Bos-cha in the Lower Engadine, their romantic *sgraffito* patterns etched in the plaster of their walls; old Scuol with its fabulous village square; Tarasp with the brilliance of its window-boxes and a castle atop its rocky knoll. And there's S-charl, tucked away from the world, surrounded by dashing streams and green pastures.

Set high upon some of those pastures, summer-only hamlets still draw a few hardy farmers who graze their

GETTING THERE

By air

The following details were current at the time of writing, but readers should be aware that air travel information is particularly vulnerable to change. Apart from complex fare structures, schedules are often rearranged at short notice, and new routes introduced and as quickly abandoned; new airlines are formed, merged, taken over or cease business with alarming frequency. The best advice is to either visit your local travel agent to check the current situation before booking a flight, or browse the Internet.

The most convenient Swiss airport for visitors to the Engadine is Zürich (Kloten), which has numerous scheduled flights from Britain, with major carriers such as British Airways, Easyjet and SWISS currently dominating the market. Aer Lingus also

MAIN CARRIERS

British Airways: www.britishairways.com currently operates out of London Heathrow and Gatwick, and Manchester

Easyjet: www.easyjet.com flights from London Gatwick, Luton and Liverpool

SWISS International Airlines: www.swiss.com has 42 daily scheduled departures from London Heathrow and City, Birmingham and Manchester

Aer Lingus: www.aerlingus.com flies a regular service between Dublin and Zürich

Online booking agents: www.cheapflights.com – feed your requirements into the search engine and wait for the response

www.skyscanner.net – an easy-to-use interface

www.ebookers.com – accommodation and transport for numerous destinations

Note: Flight tickets can also be arranged through the **Switzerland Travel Centre** in London (Tel 0207 420 4934 https://switzerlandtravelcentre.co.uk)

has regular services from Dublin to Zürich.

Zürich airport is just an escalator ride away from the mainline railway station that will put you in touch with trains for Chur, where you change for the onward journey to the Engadine (see rail details below).

By rail

Currently Eurostar operate up to 19 trains per day between London St Pancras International and the Gare du Nord in Paris. On arrival it's then necessary to transfer to the Gare de Lyon for the TGV departure to Lausanne, where the journey time is around 4½hr.

Change at Lausanne for a direct train to Zürich, and continue from there to Chur. From Chur take the Rhäetian railway to St Moritz (the Upper Engadine railhead), or elsewhere in the valley. There are stations at every village down-valley from St Moritz to Scuol, with another line serving Pontresina and Val Bernina on the way to Val Poschiavo, then to Tirano in Italy. The 19km-long Vereina Tunnel (between Klosters and the Lower Engadine) is a car-carrying rail link that enables motorists to avoid the Flüela Pass, closed by snow in winter.

For up-to-date rail information, contact Rail Europe (www.raileurope.com). Note that the Switzerland Travel Centre can take reservations for Eurostar, TGV, and Swiss rail travel: (Tel 0207 420 4934 or e-mail sales@stc.co.uk).

INTERNET TRAIN TIMES

To work out your rail journey through Switzerland in advance, log on to www.sbb.ch. Feed in details of start and destination (eg Zürich and, say, Guarda) and date of travel, and you'll receive all the information you require, including platform numbers where it's necessary to change trains, plus connecting bus services where relevant.

By road
Should you prefer to drive to the Engadine, please note that a *vignette* (sticker) must be purchased and displayed on your vehicle when travelling in Switzerland. This is, in effect, a motorway tax, the current cost of which is CHF40. Valid for multiple re-entries into the country during the licensed period shown on the sticker, they can be bought at the Swiss border of entry, or in advance from the Switzerland Travel Centre in London (see Appendix A).

The minimum age for driving in Switzerland is 18, and motorists are advised to obtain a Green Card from their insurers to receive the same insurance protection as in the UK.

Roads are well maintained; many high passes are kept open throughout the year, while more and more road tunnels are being created to avoid some of these passes, or to bypass

Piz Bernina towers over the Tschierva Glacier's moraine wall. The path to Lej Vadret and the Coaz Hut sneaks below it (Photo: Jonathan Williams) (Routes 51 and 52)

Autumn colours the hillside above Val Muragl (Routes 46–47)

towns and villages. The interlinking motorway system is good, and journey times from one side of the country to the other are surprisingly low, considering the complex topography. But at peak times expect delays. The motorway speed limit is 120kph (75mph); in built-up areas it's 50kph (31mph), and 80kph (50mph) on other roads unless signed to the contrary.

TRAVEL WITHIN SWITZERLAND

Various incentives are available to visitors to encourage use of either the railways or postbus services. Purchased in advance from the Switzerland Travel Centre (see Appendix A), these incentives are outlined below.

Swiss Pass: This entitles the holder to unlimited travel by postbus, rail or lake ferry for periods of 4, 8, 15 and 22 days, or a month. Discounts are also given on most forms of mountain transport.

Swiss Youth Pass: Advantages are the same as for holders of the Swiss Pass, but young people under 26 can obtain the Swiss Youth Pass at a 25% discount.

Swiss Flexi Pass: Similar to the above, except that validity of the Flexi Pass ranges from 3, 4, 5, 6 or 8 days within a month.

Swiss Half-Fare Card: Valid for one month, the card allows unlimited purchase of train, bus, boat and some cablecar tickets at half price.

Swiss Transfer Ticket: The STT is useful for visitors planning to stay for a period of one month, and gives one free round-trip to any destination in the country. This can start at any Swiss airport or border, and each leg of the journey must be completed on the same day. Holders of the Swiss Transfer Ticket can also claim discounts on most mountain lift systems.

Swiss Card: An extended version of the Swiss Transfer Ticket, the Swiss Card gives the holder a 50% discount on all further train, bus or boat journeys.

Swiss Travel System Family Card: Children under 16 years of age travel free if accompanied by at least one parent in possession of a Swiss Card, Swiss Pass or Flexi Pass. Non-family members between 6 and 16 years old receive a 50% discount. The Family Card is available free of charge from the Switzerland Travel Centre in London.

ACCOMMODATION

A very wide range of accommodation is available within the Engadine and adjacent valleys, from the most basic of campsites to the ultimate in luxury hotels. Outline details are provided within the main body of this guide, but for specific information regarding facilities and prices you are advised to contact the local tourist office, which can usually supply printed lists. Tourist office contact details are given in the introductory section of each main district covered by the guide.

Official campsites

A number of campsites are located in the Bregaglia, Val Bernina, and Upper

Tarasp, near Scuol, is one of the gems of the Lower Engadine

and Lower Engadine valleys. Some of these are rather basic, although the majority have excellent, clean and well-maintained toilet blocks and washing facilities. A few remain open even in winter. Note that off-site camping in Switzerland is officially forbidden. Annual lists of camping and caravan sites are published by the Touring Club of Switzerland (www.tsc.ch) and the Swiss Camping Association (www.swisscamps.ch). Another website that lists campsites throughout the country is www.campingnet.ch.

Youth hostels

Swiss youth hostels (*Schweizer Jugendherbergen*) provide reasonably priced accommodation. Affiliated to Hostelling International, they are primarily open to all young people holding a valid membership card. Small dormitories and family rooms are generally available. There are several hostels within the area covered by this guide, but for a current list visit www.youthhostel.ch or contact the Schweizer Jugendherbergen, Schaffhauserstr. 14, Postfach, CH-8042 Zürich.

Matratzenlagers/Massenlagers

A number of hotels and *gasthofs* in the Engadine district provide low-cost communal dormitories in addition to standard bedrooms. Some have traditional two-tier bunks, while others merely supply mattresses on the floor of a large room. Mention is made where such places exist (where

known); otherwise you are advised, if interested, to contact the local tourist office for specific addresses.

Mountain huts

Since the majority of mountain huts (*chamanna* or *capanna*) are located far from any habitation and in spectacular surroundings, they invariably provide a memorable experience for the first-time (and frequent) user. Most of those in the Engadine region belong to various sections of the Swiss Alpine Club (SAC), although a few are privately owned, but open to all. Mixed-sex dormitories for sleeping accommodation are the norm (take your own sheet sleeping bag; blankets or duvets and pillows are provided), and in a few washing facilities are somewhat primitive. Where a guardian (hut keeper) is in residence during the summer, meals and refreshments are usually available. Outline details are given throughout the guide, but for more information log on to the hut's website where one exists and contact details are given. (See also www.sac-cas.ch)

If you plan to spend several nights in huts during your holiday, it might be worth buying a reciprocal rights card from the British Mountaineering Council (BMC) 177–179 Burton Road, Manchester M20 2BB (www.thebmc.co.uk) to obtain discounts on overnight fees. Members of the UK branch of the Austrian Alpine Club (www.aacuk.org.uk see Appendix A) can also claim a reduction on overnight

At the head of Val Roseg the Coaz Hut makes a fine destination for a day's walk

HUT ETIQUETTE

- As a number of routes in this guide visit huts, a note on hut etiquette may be useful for first-time users. On arrival remove your boots and change into a pair of special hut shoes that you'll find on racks in the boot room or hut porch

Hut shoe options in the Coaz Hut boot room (Routes 37 and 52–54)

- Locate the guardian to book sleeping space for the night, and any meals required

- Meal times are usually fixed; a choice of menu is not always available

- As soon as you're able to go to your dormitory, make your bed; keep a torch handy since the room may be unlit overnight

- Payment should be made in cash the night before departure

An atmospheric dining room at Hotel Roseggletscher (Routes 36, 48, 49 and 51–54)

fees at SAC huts. Discounts are not available for meals.

Holiday apartments
Providing a degree of freedom and flexibility, self-catering apartments (*Ferienwohnungen*) are an option worth considering by families or groups of friends planning to base their holiday in one centre. A large number of Engadine villages have apartments for rent, usually for a minimum period of a week.

Hotels and mountain inns
As mentioned, a huge number and variety of hotels exist throughout the region. In addition, mountain inns and pensions that may not be star-rated are located in some of the villages as well as more remote outlying areas, and many of these provide accommodation that may appeal. There are also a few mountain restaurants that offer good value overnight lodging in bedrooms or dormitories, and these are mentioned in the text where relevant. Details can also be acquired at tourist information offices.

WEATHER

In summer the weather pattern for the Engadine and Bregaglia tends to be somewhat more settled than may be experienced in some of the higher regions of the Western Alps. One feature worth noting in the Upper Engadine, however, is the tendency towards strong winds blowing from the south during the afternoon. These will be felt especially in the lake region between Maloja and St Moritz where the valley is broad and open. These 'Malojawinds' are a sign of settled weather in the Bregaglia, and are welcomed by windsurfers on the lakes.

With a difference in altitude of around 800m between Maloja in the Upper Engadine, and Martina at the extreme northeasterly end of the Lower Engadine, it will be obvious that climatic variations are likely, and that the seasons arrive at different times. Generally speaking, with snow departing the high meadows, June is perhaps the earliest month to contemplate a walking holiday there. (From Easter until the end of May many hotels and tourist facilities are closed.) Even so, it's quite likely that some of the higher routes described will be out of condition until July. But in June the weather is beginning to build its promise, valley meadows are full of flowers, and the mountains still fresh, with their upper slopes dusted with snow.

Being much lower than the Engadine, and influenced by the warmth of Italy, Val Bregaglia is often in better condition for high walks earlier than anywhere in its neighbouring valley.

July and August are the peak season months when temperatures are at their highest, but note that precipitation levels are also at their highest too. When temperatures drop, even in summer precipitation can fall as snow in the Upper Engadine and Val Bernina.

September is often more settled than the high summer, with prolonged spells of fine weather. Night frosts should be expected throughout the region. If blessed with fine weather, October can be truly magical with the larchwoods spilling gold throughout the Engadine, and the Bregaglia's wonderful deciduous forests bewitched with a rich palette of colours.

The above notes are generalisations. In recent years climate change has had a marked effect on the Alps, with extreme weather conditions recording unprecedented high temperatures. These exacerbate glacial recession and begin to thaw the permafrost. There have also been torrential rainstorms causing flash floods

WEATHER FORECASTS ON THE WEB

Frequently updated daily and five-day weather forecasts in English can be located on www.meteonews.ch/en.

and landslides, and avalanches in winter, wreaking havoc on villages in a number of Alpine regions.

As a day-by-day guide to weather prospects, most tourist offices display a two- or three-day weather forecast for the local area in printed form that is easy to understand.

LANGUAGES SPOKEN

The region covered by this guidebook has a wide and complex linguistic range. For most tourist purposes English will be generally understood, but one should not assume that to be true everywhere.

In a country with four official languages (German, French, Italian and Romansch), the Engadine uses three of them: French is the odd one out. Romansch is an ancient Latin-based language spoken by just 1% of the population (70,000 people in Graubünden use it), but it's the traditional language of the valley; a living language in the Lower Engadine where it's taught in the schools, and spoken in the homes. You'll hear people greet one another with *'Allegra!'* and *'Bun di!'* and notice that the names of villages and countryside features are very different to those of German-speaking districts. (A short

Wandering the trail that leads to Lej Vadret and the Coaz Hut is one of the district's many outstanding walks (Routes 51 and 52)

Hotel Roseggletscher, a romantic place to stay in Val Roseg (Routes 36, 48, 49 and 51–54)

glossary of German and Romansch words is given as Appendix C.) German, or rather *Schwyzerdütsch*, is more often heard in regular conversation in the Upper Engadine, while Italian is the dominant language in Val Bregaglia, from Maloja down.

NOTES FOR WALKERS

Most of the routes described in this book have been chosen with a particular viewpoint, lake, alp hamlet, hut or pass as the destination, while the principal objective of each walk is to enjoy a day's exercise among stimulating scenery. In order to gain the most from a walking holiday, one needs to be in reasonably good physical condition on arrival.

If you begin in the Upper Engadine you may find you're affected by the altitude at first, soon getting short of breath and maybe feeling extra tired at the end of the day. This is understandable, for 1800m (valley level) is almost half as high again as the summit of Ben Nevis, Britain's highest mountain! Avoid being too ambitious for the first few days until you're acclimatised and better able to appreciate the Alpine scale of the mountains. A wide range of walks has been chosen for this book, and there should be sufficient routes on offer to enable most walkers to enjoy a good day out at a standard to suit their own ability and ambition.

Walks have been graded into three numerical categories, with the highest grade reserved for the more challenging routes. This grading system is purely subjective and open to argument, but is offered as a rough

Walking routes are signed and way-marked with typical Swiss efficiency

guide of what to expect. Moderate walks (Grade 1) should appeal to most active members of the family, while the majority of walks are graded 2 or 3, largely as a result of the very nature of the landscape, which can be quite challenging. A full definition of these grades is given at the end of this Introduction.

Most of the paths followed are well maintained, waymarked and signed at junctions with typical Swiss efficiency. Footpath signs conform to a national standard and are painted yellow. They contain the names of major landmark destinations, such as a pass, a lake, hut or village, or perhaps a name that does not appear on the map, but which has been given for a specific trail junction. An estimation

of how long it will take to reach that destination may also be given in hours (Std) and minutes (min). A white plate on some of these yellow signs announces the name of the immediate locality, and often its altitude too. Rarely do routes described in this book stray onto unpathed territory, but where they do occasional cairns and/ or waymarks act as a guide. In such places it is essential to remain vigilant to avoid becoming lost – especially if visibility is poor. If in doubt about the continuing route, return to the last point where you were certain of your whereabouts and try again. By regular consultation with the map during the walk, it should be possible to keep abreast of your position and anticipate junctions or a change of direction before you reach them.

Waymarks will be either yellow, for easy, or mostly valley walks (the *Wanderweg*); or white-red-white for higher, more demanding trails (the *Bergweg*). A third form of waymarking, using blue and white stripes, is reserved for so-called Alpine routes, which may involve sections that demand some moderate scrambling, or the use of mechanical aid in the form of fixed ropes or sections of ladder.

For safety's sake, do not walk alone on remote trails, on moraine-bank paths or glaciers. If you prefer to walk in a group but have not made prior arrangements to join an organised holiday, the staff at several tourist offices arrange day walks in the

SAFETY CHECKLIST

- Before setting out on a mountain walk check the weather forecast (see above) and be aware that all Alpine areas are subject to rapidly changing conditions. When on a long walk watch for tell-tale signs and be prepared for the worst by having adequate clothing.

- Study route details beforehand, noting any particular difficulties and the amount of time needed to complete the route. Make sure you can be back safely before nightfall.

- On a full day's walk carry food (and emergency rations such as chocolate or dried fruit) with you, and at least 1 litre of liquid per person to avoid dehydration

- Leave details of your planned route and expected time of return with a responsible person

- Be vigilant when crossing wet rocks, scree, snow patches and mountain streams. If you find a section of path safeguarded by fixed rope or chains, check that they have not worked loose before relying on them.

- Do not stray onto glaciers unless you have experienced companions and the necessary equipment to deal with crevasse rescue. Keep away from icefalls and hanging glaciers.

- Avoid dislodging stones onto others who might be below you

- Never be reluctant to turn back in the face of deteriorating weather, or if the route becomes hazardous. In the event of being unable to reach the place where you were expected, try to send a message.

- Carry map and compass (and GPS if you have one) – and know how to use them

- Always carry some first aid equipment, as well as a whistle and torch for emergencies. The emergency telephone number for rescue is 117. Try not to use it!

- Make a note of the International Distress Signal printed at the front of this guide: six blasts on a whistle (and flashes with a torch after dark) spaced evenly for one minute, followed by a minute's pause. Then repeat until an answer is received and your position located. The answer is three signals followed by a minute's pause. Be insured against accidents (rescue and subsequent medical treatment), for although mountain rescue is highly organised and efficient in Switzerland, it can be extremely expensive for the casualty. (See Appendix A for a list of specialist insurers.)

• Finally, please help keep the mountains and valleys litter-free

company of a qualified leader. These take place throughout the summer months and are often free of charge to guests staying in the organising resort. Enquire at the local tourist office for specific details.

SUGGESTED EQUIPMENT LIST

Experienced mountain walkers will have their own preferences, but the following list is offered as a guide for newcomers to the Alps. Some items will clearly not be needed if you envisage tackling only low valley routes.

Clothing
• Walking boots – must be comfortable, a good fit, have ankle support and plenty of grip in the soles
• Trainers or similar for wear in hotels and villages
• Wind- and water-proof jacket and overtrousers
• Warm hat and sunhat
• Gloves
• Fleece or sweater
• Shirts – 2 or 3 for a fortnight's holiday

• Warm long trousers (not jeans which are cold when wet and take ages to dry)
• Shorts (optional)
• Socks
• Underwear

Miscellaneous
• Rucksack – with waterproof liner and/or cover
• Sheet sleeping bag (if you intend to sleep in huts)
• Bivvy bag – in case of emergencies
• Collapsible umbrella – excellent rain protection, especially useful for spectacle wearers
• Trekking pole(s) – highly recommended
• Headtorch plus spare battery and bulb
• Water bottle – 1 litre minimum
• Sunglasses, suncream/sunblock and lip salve
• First aid kit
• Map and compass (and GPS if available)
• Whistle
• Watch
• Guidebook

Left to right: Almost before snow melts from the meadows, the tassle-headed soldanella makes its appearance; The alpine pasque flower (Pulsatilla alpina) appears in springtime

- Penknife
- Camera
- Altimeter
- Binoculars

RECOMMENDED MAPS

The Swiss National Survey maps (*Landeskarte der Schweiz*) that cover the Engadine region at 1:50 000 are beautifully produced, with immaculate attention to detail. By clever use of shading, contours and colouring, the line of ridge and rockface, the flow of glaciers and streams, all announce themselves with clarity. The yellow/orange-covered *Wanderkarte*, whose sheet number carries the letter T, indicates the fact that major walking routes have been outlined in red to make them easy to identify. Postbus stops are also shown, and mountain huts circled. Although the 1:25,000 series shows greater detail, the 1:50,000 scale should be perfectly adequate for most walkers' needs. Six separate map sheets cover the Engadine region: 268T Julier Pass, 278T Monte Disgrazia, 258T Bergün, 259T Ofenpass, 269T Passo del Bernina and 249T Tarasp.

The commercial publisher Kümmerly + Frey also covers the Engadine with their Wanderkarten, but at a scale of 1:60,000. These too have walking routes outlined in red, and in addition clearly highlight the location of mountain huts. Just two sheets are needed for the whole of the region covered by this guide: Oberengadin, which includes the Bregaglia, Val Bernina and Val Poschiavo, and Unterengadin. For an overall picture of the region, the same publisher has produced a 1:120,000 sheet that covers the whole canton. Graubünden could be very useful for planning purposes.

Map suppliers are listed in Appendix A. Note that some local tourist authorities produce their own Wanderkarten to show local walking routes, and these are on sale at the tourist information offices.

USING THIS GUIDE

Times quoted for each walk are approximations. They refer to **actual walking time only and make no allowances for rest stops or photographic interruptions** – such stops can add considerably to the overall time you're out for (add 25–50% to times quoted), so bear this in mind when planning your day's itinerary. Although such times are given as an aid to planning, they are, of course, entirely subjective and each walker will have his or her own pace which may or may not coincide with that quoted. By comparing your times with those given here, you should soon gain an idea of the difference and be able to compensate accordingly.

Distances and heights are quoted throughout in kilometres and metres. Details were taken directly from the map where shown, but in attempting to measure the actual distance of each walk it has been necessary to make an estimation, for with countless zigzags on many routes it's impossible to be precise.

ABBREVIATIONS

These are used sparingly, but some – of necessity – have been adopted. While most should be easily understood, the following list is given for clarification:

hr	hours
km	kilometres
LS	Landeskarte der Schweiz (maps)
m	metres
min	minutes
PTT	Post Office (Post, Telephone & Telegraph)
SAC	Swiss Alpine Club
VTT	Trains à Grande Vitesse

GRADING OF WALKS

Walks in this book have been chosen with the express intention of helping you to make the most out of a holiday in the Engadine region. Since it is hoped that walkers of all degrees of commitment will find something useful here, a grading system has been adopted to direct you to the standard of outing best suited to your individual requirements. As mentioned above, routes have been graded into three

The painter Giovanni Segantini wrote of Soglio as being on 'the threshold of paradise' (Routes 7–9 and 12–14

categories, but since the grading of walks is not an exact science, each of these categories will cover a fairly wide spectrum. Inevitably there will be variations and, no doubt, a few anomalies, which may be disputed by users of the book. But they're offered in good faith and as a rough guide only.

Grade 1: Suitable for family outings; mostly short distances or walks along gently graded paths or tracks with little altitude gain.

Grade 2: Moderate walking, mostly on clear footpaths with a reasonable amount of height gain. Walkers should be adequately shod and equipped.

Grade 3: More strenuous routes on sometimes rough or unclear paths. Some modest scrambling or use of fixed ropes and so on may be involved in rare instances. A good head for heights may be called for. On some of these routes there will be passes to cross and some screes to negotiate. On rare occasions glacier travel will be involved, but this will be clearly marked in the text. There will be steep ascents and descents, and fairly long distances involved: in short, true Alpine walking. Walkers attempting such routes need to be fit and well equipped.

37

INFORMATION AT A GLANCE

Currency: The Swiss franc (CHF); 100 centimes/rappen = CHF1. Although Switzerland is not in the Euro zone, some hotels and retail outlets accept payment by Euro, but change will be given in Swiss francs.

Formalities: Visas are not required by holders of a valid UK passport, or other EU nationals. Visitors from other countries should enquire at their local Swiss Embassy.

Health precautions: Be aware of the powerful high altitude sunlight, and use a broad spectrum suncream (factor 30+) as protection against harmful UV rays that can cause sunburn and lead to skin cancer. Note too, that Switzerland – along with much of Central Europe – harbours the *Ixodes* tick, whose bite causes TBE (tick-borne encephalitis). Risk is seasonal, from March to September, and visitors who take part in outdoor activities may be vulnerable. An injection of TBE immunoglobulin gives short-term protection; ask your medical practitioner for advice. As there is no state health service in Switzerland, any medical treatment must be paid for; make sure you have adequate insurance cover that includes personal accident, sickness and rescue. (See Appendix A for specialist insurers.)

International dialling code: When dialling Switzerland from the UK, dial 0041. To phone the UK from Switzerland, the code is 0044, then ignore the initial 0 of the area code that follows.

Languages: German, Italian and Romansch are all spoken in the Engadine region, but English is widely understood.

Tourist information: Switzerland Travel Centre, 30 Bedford Street, London WC2E 9ED (Tel 0207 420 4934 https://switzerlandtravelcentre.co.uk) Graubünden Vacation, Alexanderstr. 24, CH-7001 Chur, Switzerland (www.graubuenden.ch) Swiss National Park, Planta-Wildenberg Castle, CH-7530 Zernez, Switzerland (www.nationalpark.ch)

VAL BREGAGLIA

Lägh da Cavloc in Val Forno (Routes 1–3)

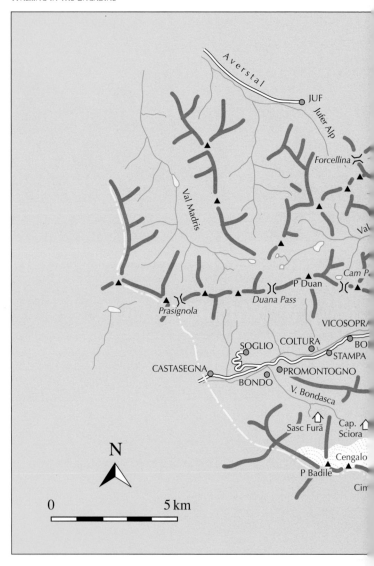

VAL BREGAGLIA

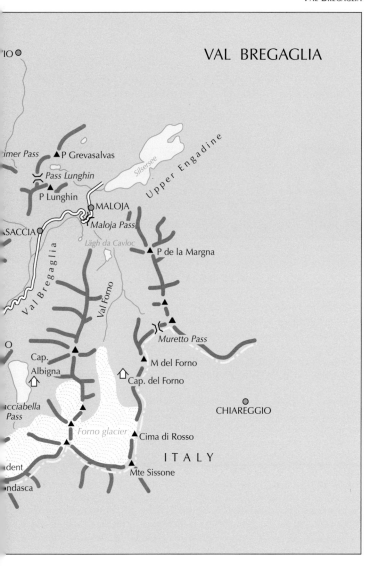

'IO ●

imer Pass

▲ P Grevasalvas

Pass Lunghin

Silsersee

▲ P Lunghin

U p p e r   E n g a d i n e

● MALOJA

Maloja Pass

SACCIA ○

Lägh da Cavloc

▲ P de la Margna

V a l   B r e g a g l i a

Val Forno

▲

)(▲

Muretto Pass

○

Cap. Albigna

▲

▲ M del Forno

⬆ Cap. del Forno

⬆

acciabella Pass

▲

● CHIAREGGIO

▲ *Forno glacier*

▲ Cima di Rosso

I T A L Y

dent

▲ Mte Sissone

ndasca

*Along the classic Sentiero Panoramico, the way
leads across the alp of Durbegio (Route 9)*

VAL BREGAGLIA

Draining into Italy by a series of natural terraces from the saddle of the Maloja
Pass, the Bregaglia (or Bergell) is the smallest of the southern valleys of canton
Graubünden, yet it has given its name to a whole district of rugged mountains and
seductive glens that straddle the border. In this guide we concentrate on the Swiss
Val Bregaglia and its tributaries; the high alps and romantic stone-walled villages;
the chestnut woods in the deep valleys; as well as chaotic moraines and glacial
slabs lying under the headwall of remote cirques and granite peaks that rival any
in the Alps for scenic wonder and climbing challenge. Mountain paths go to all
these places, and reward those who tread them with the very special atmosphere
that enriches this southern slope of the Alpine watershed.

Wild and unspoilt sums up the character of the Swiss Val Bregaglia. As you
descend the countless hairpins of the Maloja Pass, so you exchange the shim-
mering lakes and open aspect of the Upper Engadine for a very different world.
The Bregaglia is low, narrow, steep-walled, washed with the balmy warmth of
Italy, suffused with a soft and lucid light. Down there stuccoed villages may have
the neat orderliness of Switzerland, but the architecture is distinctly Italian, with
Italian names to the streets and houses, Italian voices in the shops and surrounding meadows. Italian breezes stir the leaves in the chestnut trees, and bring with
them a flavour of the Lombardy plain.

It doesn't feel like the Alps. At least, not like the showy Bernina Alps whose snowy massifs spill long tongues of glacier into the valleys. But look up onto the north-facing mountain wall and you'll see magnificent peaks of granite wearing the last draperies of ice and snow, whose melt dashes through the side valleys in wild torrents and cascades of spray to water the lower meadows and woodlands.

Only 23km separate the Maloja Pass from the Italian border at Castasegna, but there's an altitude difference of more than 1100m, and a whole new world of culture, tempo and atmosphere. Tranquillity is the essence of this valley, for Bregaglia is gracious with its time, its warmth, colour and old-world sense of calm. You become aware of it in the villages as you tread rough cobbles that pave each street and shadowed alleyway beneath flower-bright balconies; you can feel it on the hillsides where peasant farmers swing their scythes with that timeless rhythm that has been carried through numberless generations of hay-makers and goatherders. High on the steep green hillsides, tiny alp hamlets harvest staggeringly beautiful views; hamlets of ancient stone-based, timber-walled chalets and granaries, they belong to the mountainsides as surely as the angular pines and weathered boulders stained by lichen and moss. Up there, on the north slope, far, far above the valley bed, there's a wonderland of tree, shrub, flower and impossibly steep pasture broken now and then by a ribbon of stream, a brief levelling of meadow with a huddle of barns and chalets, and a traversing path unrivalled for its glorious panoramas. Across unseen depths of the valley, where the woods of chestnut, beech and walnut grow, there ripples a skyline formed by what Freshfield (in *Italian Alps*) described as 'a coronet of domes and massive pinnacles carved out of grey rocks'.

By contrast with the north side of the valley, Bregaglia's southern wall bursts out of the forested darkness of its lower slopes with such abruptness that few alps can claim a toehold. Hidden behind this wall of mountains runs Val Forno, a lengthy ramp of grey moraine debris and glacial highway rimmed with granite peaks fretted and carved by both time and ice.

Between Forno and Bregaglia comes the savage little Albigna glen, although all you see of this from the valley is a huge dam wall which effectively blocks its secrets from the outside world. With Val Forno to the east, the Albigna glen is effectively wedged between two magnificent tributaries, for on its west lies the finest of them all – Val Bondasca, in turn sliced by the shaft of the Trubinasca glen. As Hubert Walker proclaimed, on turning into that glen: 'He must be very dull of soul indeed who could not see without a catch of his breath the sudden upward surge of the Bondasca peaks of Badile and Cengalo' (*Walking in the Alps*).

This, then, is the Swiss Val Bregaglia, and there's no better way to explore it than on foot, following paths that lead step by step into a landscape of immense beauty.

ACCESS AND INFORMATION	
Location:	Southwest of Maloja and reaching to the Italian border at Castasegna
Maps:	LS 268T Julier Pass & 278T Monte Disgrazia at 1:50,000; Kümmerly + Frey 28 Oberengadin at 1:60,000 and Graubünden at 1:120,000
Bases:	Maloja (1815m), Vicosoprano (1067m), Stampa (994m), Promontogno (821m), Castasegna (697m), Soglio (1097m)
Information:	Bregaglia Engadin Turismo, Strada principale 101, CH-7605 Stampa (www.bregaglia.ch)
	Maloja Tourist Information, Strada principale, CH-7516 Maloja (www.engadin.stmoritz.ch/maloja)
Access:	Val Bregaglia is served by postbus which runs between St Moritz and Chiavenna on the Italian side of the border, visiting most villages en route. A special short-wheel-base postbus links Promontogno with Soglio.

MAIN BASES

MALOJA (1815m) is a straggling village, well situated as a base for exploring the upper reaches of Val Bregaglia, and especially for walks in Val Forno. Although it appears to all intents and purposes to belong to the Engadine, politically Maloja is the main village of the Bregaglia. There are several hotels graded up to 3-star, numerous holiday apartments and a campsite at the southern end of the lake (Camping Plan Curtinac www.camping-maloja.ch). Maloja has restaurants, post office, limited shopping facilities, and a helpful tourist office in the heart of the village with lots of useful information including accommodation lists covering the whole Bregaglia region.

VICOSOPRANO (1067m) is one of the best valley bases in the Bregaglia proper, with a number of fine old houses. There are three hotels – the Corona, Piz Cam and the Crotto Albigna – plus several apartments and a campsite with good facilities located a short distance outside the village to the northeast (Camping Mulina Tel 081 822 10 35 www.campingbregaglia.ch). Vicosoprano has a few shops, a bank, post office and a dairy, and an indoor climbing wall.

STAMPA (994m) huddles astride the old road on the south side of the valley midway between Vicosoprano and Promontogno. This, the birthplace of the painter Augusto Giacometti and his sculptor son Alberto, has three hotels: the Stampa (which also has 12 dormitory beds), Val d'Arca and Walther. There's both a post office and the valley's tourist office, but few other facilities – apart, that is, from the Bregaglia museum in the former home of the Giacomettis, the Ciäsa Granda (open daily July–October, 2–5pm), and the impressive Palazzo Castelmur in nearby **COLTURA**.

PROMONTOGNO (821m) and neighbouring **BONDO** (823m) crowd at the mouth of Val Bondasca, offering accommodation in just two hotels – the Bregaglia and Hotel-Pension Sciora – plus a few apartments and a campsite (closed until further notice). Apart from a small supermarket and a post office, other tourist facilities are non-existent, although Promontogno does have the valley's hospital (Tel 081 838 11 99). In August 2017 Bondo was badly damaged by an outwash of debris caused by a major rock fall from Piz Cengalo. See note on p74.

CASTASEGNA (697m) is located on the border with Italy. With less obvious charm than previously mentioned villages, it does at least have access to better facilities over the border at Chiavenna. Castasegna has two hotels, the Locanda Rocca Bella and Ristorante-garni Post, each with just eight beds. The village also has two banks and a post office. (See www.bregaglia.ch/en/castasegna)

The perfection of Soglio lies as much in its setting as its closely gathered buildings (Routes 7–9 and 12–14)

SOGLIO (1097m) is without question one of the most attractively situated villages in the Alps, with one of the most dramatic outlooks. Painter Giovanni Segantini called it 'the threshold of paradise' – and so it is. Reached by postbus via a narrow, tightly twisting road from Promontogno, it occupies a projecting shelf of hillside among meadows and haybarns, with a direct view across the Bregaglia to Val Bondasca, Piz Badile and the Scioras. There are five hotels or pensions and about 18 apartments for holiday let. Soglio has restaurants, two grocery stores and a post office, and memorable views at practically every turn.

OTHER BASES

Elsewhere in Val Bregaglia accommodation can be found at **CASACCIA** (1458m), where both beds and dormitory accommodation are available at the Hotel Stampa (Tel 081 824 31 62 www.hotelstampa.ch); at **PRANZAIRA** (1232m) near the Albigna cablecar – again, both beds and dormitory accommodation at the Pranzaira hotel (Tel 081 822 14 55 www.pranzaira.ch); and at **SPINO** (793m) near Bondo, in the Pension Fanconi (beds and dormitory Tel 081 822 18 55 www. hotelfanconi.ch).

MOUNTAIN HUTS

Four mountain huts, each owned by the SAC, are located on the south side of the valley.

CAPANNA DEL FORNO (2574m) Privately built under the supervision of the great Engadine guide Christian Klucker in 1889, the Forno Hut was enlarged and given to the SAC in 1920. Standing high above the east bank of the Forno Glacier, the hut can now sleep 80. Reached by a walk of 4hr or so from Maloja (including a glacier crossing), it is manned, with meals provided, from mid-March to mid-May, and from July to end September (Tel 081 824 31 82 www.fornohuette.ch).

CAPANNA DA L'ALBIGNA (2336m) Located just above the east bank of the dammed Albigna lake, this hut is very popular with day visitors thanks to ease of access via the Pranzaira cablecar. Manned from mid-June to end September, when there's a full meals service, it has 94 places, and is reached in 35–40min from the upper cablecar station, or by a walk of 3½hr from Vicosoprano. For reservations Tel 081 822 14 05 www.albigna.ch.

CAPANNA DI SCIORA (2118m) At the head of Val Bondasca, about 4hr walk from Promontogno or Bondo, the Sciora Hut stands on an old moraine slope at the foot of the jagged Sciora group. With places for 42, and a guardian on duty from July to end September (meals provided), it's owned by the Hoher Rohn section of the SAC (Tel 081 822 11 38 www.sachoherrohn.ch).

CAPANNA SASC FURA (1904m) Gained by a very steep approach walk of 3–3½hr from Promontogno or Bondo, this hut is situated on a promontory below Piz Badile's North Ridge in the Trubinasca cirque. Usually manned with full meals service between July and end September, the hut has places for 45 (Tel 081 822 12 52 www.sascfura.ch). A very fine route – for experienced mountain trekkers only – links this with the Sciora Hut by way of the Colle Vial.

Note that due to the danger of further rock fall from Piz Cengalo, both the Sciora and Sasc Füra huts will be closed until they are deemed to be safe. See note on p76. As this edition goes to print it has just been announced that the Sasc Furä hut will reopen in the summer of 2019. A new approach route has been created – details as yet unknown. All other Val Bondasca routes remain closed until further notice.

VAL FORNO WALKS

The Forno glen wears three faces. As you wander into it from Maloja the first impression is one of a green and pleasant valley, unassuming with gentle meadows bright in early summer with flowers and shrubs. A broad track winds among forested slopes to the Lägh da Cavloc (Cavolocciosee), a popular tarn that mirrors the neighbouring mountains. South of the tarn the valley grows a little wilder. It forks at Plan Canin: southeast towards the Muretto Pass and Italy, southwest into a granite heartland.

Continuing deeper into Val Forno, one enters a desolate region of grey moraine boulders and rocks, the milky glacial stream tumbling from ice-fields out of sight. But as the glaciers retreat, so the wilderness is being slowly transformed into a garden. Flowers, dwarf shrubs and wispy trees have begun to establish themselves among the grit and rocks left by the departing ice, and wandering through this raw landscape is to understand the power of nature's tireless industry. Then the moraine wilderness is left behind, and Val Forno's third face is revealed. This is the snow-and-ice world of the Forno Glacier; an arctic basin rimmed with jutting peaks, slabs and bastions of granite that create an amphitheatre of impressive dimensions.

ROUTE 1

*Maloja (1815m) – Lägh da Cavloc
(Cavolocciosee) (1907m) – Maloja*

Start	Maloja (1815m)
Distance	7km (4.3 miles)
Height gain	92m (302ft)
Height loss	92m (302ft)
Grade	1
Time	2hr
Location	South of Maloja

An hour's walk from Maloja leads to an utterly charming, partially tree-fringed lake in the lower reaches of Val Forno. Lägh da Cavloc is justifiably popular as both a destination for a family outing and as a picnic site. The route to it follows a modestly graded track among open meadows, shrubs and trees. In the early summer masses of pink primulas colour the banks, while in September there are bilberries in vast quantities. At the southeastern end of the lake a restaurant enjoys a view across the water to Piz Lagrev, while the southern view looks beyond the low buildings of Alp Cavloc to Monte del Forno. This walk makes a circuit of the lake and a varied return to Maloja.

Just over the Orlegna stream an alternative path breaks right to Lägh da Biterbergh (1854m) in 20min, then 1hr uphill to the viewpoint of Motta Salacina (2150m) – fine views of the Bregaglia and Engadine lakes.

Walk along the main road towards the Maloja Pass, and when it curves to the right take a service road cutting ahead – a sign indicates the way to Lägh da Cavloc, Plan Canin and so on. Passing a few houses the road ends, and is replaced by a track which, in turn, becomes a footpath. This is part of the Sentiero Segantini, and as you progress along it you'll pass a few information panels depicting scenes from the artist's work.

The path angles down through meadows, passes between houses, and comes onto a service road/track where you turn left to cross the Orlegna stream moments later. ◀

Lägh da Cavloc (the Cavolocciosee) is easily reached in an hour from Maloja (Routes 26–28)

GIOVANNI SEGANTINI (1858–99)

The artist, who came to live in Maloja and is buried there, was largely self-taught, but his portrayal of Alpine life in the 19th century ensures that his reputation lives on. Scenes from both the Engadine and Val Bregaglia feature largely in his work, and a visit to the Segantini Museum in St Moritz-Bad is recommended. See www.segantini-museum.ch

This track goes all the way to the lake, but has a few obvious footpath short cuts to avoid some of the bends. There are also several alternative paths cutting away, mostly to the right, but the recommendation is to remain with the track as it rises above a gorge and then passes along the eastern side of the **Lägh da Cavloc**. At the earliest opportunity go through the trees beside the track and complete the walk to the restaurant on the lakeside path (about 1hr from Maloja.)

Just beyond the restaurant the way divides – left to Plan Canin, Passo Muretto and the Forno Hut; right for a circuit of the lake. Follow the lakeside path round the tranquil west side, among little grassy bays and rocky promontories, until you reach the northern end where the path forks. Take the left branch, a path of stone slabs rising through a wooded gully. On gaining a highpoint you then descend with views of Maloja ahead.

Another option is to take the unmarked footpath, which descends across the track and provides an alternative route back to Maloja.

When the path forks again, with the route straight ahead signed to Lägh da Biterbergh, descend to the right below crags, then among larch, pine, alpenrose and juniper, and about 10min from the junction come onto the service road/track used on the way to the lake. Turn left and retrace your steps to **Maloja**. ◄

ROUTE 2

Maloja (1815m) – Lägh da Cavloc (1907m) – Passo del Muretto (2562m)

Start	Maloja (1815m)
Distance	7km (4.3 miles) one way
Height gain	747m (2450ft)
Grade	3
Time	3–3½hr
Location	Southeast of Maloja

Standing on the Swiss-Italian border, the Muretto Pass is the divide between the Bernina and Bregaglia Alps. It's part of an old trading route, used since the 14th century, linking Maloja with Chiesa in the Italian Val Malenco (8–9hr), and it is also used by climbers moving from one side of the district to the other. Chiareggio, a small village at the very head of Val Malenco which makes a good walking/mountaineering centre, lies directly below the pass and is reached from there by a jeep track in about 2hr. The way up to the pass on the Maloja side is a little rough in places, and with some avalanche danger early in the season. The Italian slope offers wonderful views across to the ice-clad Monte Disgrazia (3678m), the dominant mountain of the Bregaglia Alps.

Take Route 1 as far as **Lägh da Cavloc** (1hr), then continue up-valley across the pasture of Alp Cavloc. Passing the low alp buildings to your left the path soon goes through a rocky cleft and eases downhill among pine and larchwoods towards the stony river bed. Rising again you come to a small hut, and moments later the way forks at **Plan Canin** (1975m), about 20min from the lake.

A short distance from Lägh da Cavloc stand the low stone buildings of Alp Cavloc

MONTE DISGRAZIA

Seen from the Italian side of the pass, the 3678m Monte Disgrazia is the highest of the Bregaglia Alps, a mountain that stands alone, unsurpassed as to grace of form and classic proportions. First climbed in 1862 by E.S. Kennedy, Leslie Stephen and T. Cox, with Melchior Anderegg as guide, connoisseurs reckon it to be one of the most beautiful mountains in the Alps.

Leaving the Forno Hut path (which goes ahead), descend to a footbridge over the Orlegna stream, then up, fairly steeply, on the left (east) side of the **Val Muretto**. There is nothing difficult about the route, but as you gain height, so it becomes rougher as you pick a way across slopes of scree and large rocks. It's quite possible that there will be old slips of snow to cross too, coming from a scoop between Piz dei Rossi and Monte del Forno above to the right, although the path seeks to avoid this by climbing above it to the left. You will notice there are two cols. The one to aim for is that on the left, which you gain about 2hr from the Lägh da Cavloc.

Allow at least 2hr for the return to **Maloja**.

ROUTE 3
Maloja (1815m) – Capanna del Forno (2574m)

Start	Maloja (1815m)
Distance	10km (6.2 miles) one way
Height gain	759m (2490ft)
Grade	3 (includes a glacier crossing)
Time	4hr
Location	South of Maloja

This approach to the Forno Hut makes a splendid introduction to a high mountain environment. As you progress from Maloja so you make the transition from a landscape of meadow, lake and woodland, to one of arctic sterility. It's a very fine walk, but a tough one, for beyond Plan Canin the inner Val Forno is uncompromisingly rough, the path picking its way over a chaos of rocks and boulders before you reach the snout of the Forno Glacier. The way across the glacier is usually marked with poles, but there are crevasses to avoid, and normal safety precautions should be taken. (If unsure, do not go onto the glacier, but turn back here.) Once across the glacier a very steep ascent is made of an unstable moraine – **caution: danger of stonefall**. Once at the hut, you gaze over a wild but magnificent scene.

Follow Routes 1 and 2 as far as the path junction at **Plan Canin** (1975m/1hr 20min) where a sign gives 2½hr to Capanna del Forno. Here you gain a first view of Val

Forno's wild splendour, and from this point blue and white waymarks (indicating an Alpine route) direct the continuing path into the inner valley, almost at once passing a small stone building and a weir. Picking a route over a jumble of rocks on the west side of the glacial stream, the stark nature of the valley is relieved only by a few low-growing shrubs and spindly larch trees. Huge granite slabs soar overhead, and as you draw nearer to the glacier, so you have increasingly fine views of the rocky peaks that carry the Italian frontier at its head.

On reaching the snout of the **Forno Glacier** (Vadrec del Forno), the way forks: slightly right ahead to the Casnil Pass (for the Albigna Hut), left ahead to the Forno Hut. Marker poles direct a way onto the glacier, at first on the right-hand (west) side, then angling southeastward across the ice. The glacier being fairly level at this point, major crevasses should not be a problem although **safety precautions should be taken.**

The icy highway of the Forno Glacier has cut a long deep trench between the mountains

The Forno Hut stands high above the glacier, four hours from Maloja

Leave the glacier at about 2330m, then follow paint marks and cairns that lead steeply up the unstable moraine bank. There is **potential danger here from stonefall**, so study the route above before committing yourself, and take care to avoid dislodging stones onto anyone below. After a height gain of about 80m, the way swings to the right to make a southward traverse before looping up the final slope on a well-defined path to reach the hut.

THE FORNO HUT

This popular hut is used by the SAC as a base for climbing courses. Perched almost 200m above the glacier it has the feeling of an eyrie with tremendous views of the rock-rimmed basin to match its situation. With a resident guardian during the summer months (July to end September) meals and refreshments are usually available. The hut can accommodate 75 in its dormitories. For reservations Tel 081 824 31 82 www.fornohuette.ch

Allow about 3hr for the return to **Maloja** by the same route.

BREGAGLIA NORTH WALKS

The north flanking wall of Val Bregaglia has paths winding along it that present some of the most spectacular walking of the district, and some of its finest views. It's a green and lush series of hillsides with deciduous woods, pine forests and pasture. There are high sloping terraces dotted with alp chalets and haybarns remote from traffic and tourism, but immensely inviting to those with a map and an eye for a winding trail. Above the uppermost pastures, grey mountains linked by dipping ridges have a few accessible cols that lead into hidden valleys. By using these cols one can branch out on long walks and tours that visit far-off villages and quiet corners of other mountains. Best of all are the dreamy panoramas seen from remote alp hamlets; scenes that catch your breath with wonder, fill you with exhilaration, and remain fresh in memory long years after.

ROUTE 4

Maloja (1815m) – Pass Lunghin (2645m) –
Septimer Pass (2310m) – Casaccia (1458m)

Start	Maloja (1815m)
Distance	13km (8.1 miles)
Height gain	830m (2723ft)
Height loss	1187m (3895ft)
Grade	2
Time	5½–6hr
Location	North and west of Maloja

By walking from Maloja to Casaccia an interesting link may be made between the Upper Engadine and Val Bregaglia proper. It begins with a broad view of the Engadine lakes, and ends with the deep and narrow Bregaglia sweeping before you. Between these two extremes there's much wild country to enjoy; historic, geographically important country in which there's a distinct possibility of sighting marmots and chamois. As postbuses run a regular service across the Maloja Pass, it's feasible to return to Maloja from Casaccia at the end of the walk.

The route begins near Hotel-Restaurant Longhin in Maloja's main street, and is signed to Pass Lunghin. A narrow path at first, it climbs steeply then emerges onto a track at a hairpin bend. Walk up the track to the farm buildings of Pila, then take a path on the right which descends steps to a stream before working a way up through a short rocky gorge. Before long you come to a signed junction (**Plan di Zoch**, 1945m) and take the left branch.

The upward route is persistent but clearly marked, and about 2hr from Maloja it brings you into a desolate basin of scree and boulders in which there lies **Lägh dal Lunghin** (2484m), birthplace of the River Inn which gives the Engadine its name. South of the lake stands Piz Lunghin; to the north Piz Grevasalvas rises with bands of steep rock interspersed with sloping shelves of scree and daubs of grass. The path goes round the left (south) side of the tarn, then climbs another 160m to the obvious saddle of **Pass Lunghin** (2645m/2½hr).

THE LUNGHIN PASS

The Lunghin Pass is a major watershed. On its east side the Inn drains into the Engadine and flows by a devious route to the Black Sea. On the west slope a meagre little brook, unseen from the pass, becomes the Maira which flows down to the Bregaglia and out to the Mediterranean, while northwest of the Lunghin Pass flows a tributary of the Gelgia which in turn joins several larger streams to become the Rhine. This, of course, empties into the North Sea.

Between the Lunghin and Septimer passes the path works leftward among rocks round the head of a valley that eases out to the north. Marmot and chamois can often be seen here. About 40min or so from Pass dal Lunghin come onto the **Septimer Pass** (2310m, 3½hr) to meet a broader track which began in Bivio at the foot of the Julier Pass. Descend left into a tight little valley to pass a couple of neat buildings and stables. After this the path narrows, crosses to the left bank of the stream and loses height with some very steep zigzags in order to reach the confluence with Val Maroz (1799m). Remaining on the left bank of the stream the way continues down, with Val Bregaglia now coming into view. More zigzags, but less steep than previously, eventually bring you into the village of **Casaccia**.

ROUTE 5
*Casaccia (1458m) – Septimer Pass
(2310m) – Bivio (1769m)*

Start	Casaccia (1458m)
Distance	12km (7.5 miles)
Height gain	852m (2795ft)
Height loss	541m (1775ft)
Grade	2
Time	4½–5hr
Location	West and north of Casaccia

Used by the Romans, the Septimer Pass (Pass da Sett) is one of the oldest of Alpine trade routes whose importance only diminished with the opening of the Gotthard railway in the late 19th century. Sections of Roman paving can still be seen on the way down to Bivio. During the Middle Ages the Septimer crossing was frequently used in conjunction with the Muretto Pass as a way of linking Chur with the Valtellina (now in Italy), since the whole route lay within the jurisdiction of the Bishop of Chur. Walked from Casaccia to Bivio this historic route makes an interesting day out on a straightforward path. The way up to the pass is quite steep in places, but the descent on the far side is both long and gradual. Bivio is on a regular postbus route, which runs between Chur and St Moritz across the Julier Pass.

Opposite the post office at the southern end of Casaccia's main street, take a back street heading down-valley where you come to a large open meadow. Here you turn right along a lane signed to the Septimer Pass (among other destinations). The way leads through the lower Val Maroz, and about 1hr from Casaccia brings you to the alp buildings of **Maroz Dora** (1799m). A short distance beyond these the way forks. The Septimer route is to the right, now becoming steeper as you climb through a narrow defile, which eventually opens towards the pass.

It takes about 2½hr to reach the **Septimer Pass** (2310m) from Casaccia, and the continuing route on the north side is clearly defined with a good track sloping all the way down to Bivio. In the valley's lower reaches a number of side streams join the main river, which has been accompanied by the track from just below the pass. Here the track crosses to the left bank, and before long cuts away to the northwest through pastureland in order to reach **Bivio** (2–2½hr from the pass).

BIVIO

Said to be the only village on the northern side of the Alpine watershed to have an Italian-speaking majority, Bivio has a regular postbus service with both Chur and St Moritz (to return to Maloja or Casaccia change at Silvaplana). It also has shops, a post office and 250 hotel beds – tourist info: Tel 081 684 53 23.

ROUTE 6

Casaccia (1458m) – Septimer Pass (2310m)
– Forcellina Pass (2672m) – Juf (2126m)

Start	Casaccia (1458m)
Distance	13km (8.1 miles)
Height gain	1214m (3983ft)
Height loss	546m (1791ft)
Grade	3
Time	6½hr
Location	Northwest of Casaccia

A rather strenuous walk, this route crosses a region of wild and remote country around the Forcellina Pass, before descending to the Jufer Alp at the head of the Averstal, to reach Europe's highest permanently inhabited village. Some 25km from Andeer on the Thusis-San Bernadino road, Juf (sometimes referred to as Avers-Juf) sits at the lonely roadhead; it has pension and youth hostel accommodation, and postbus link with Thusis.

Follow Route 5 as far as the **Septimer Pass** (2½hr), where you bear left and, past a little tarn, trace a path which takes you up the side of a ravine to a saddle found on the north side of **Piz Forcellina** (1½hr from the pass). ▶

Once over the saddle you look into the Averstal. Descend gently at first to the right, skirting rocky slopes to a point a little below Fuorcla da la Valletta. Here the way zigzags leftward, dropping to the pastures of the Jufer Alp at the headwaters of the Jufer Rhine, eventually coming to the cluster of farmhouses that comprise the village of **Juf**.

A diversion from the saddle to the summit of Piz Forcellina (2936m), taking about 1½hr, is said to reward with a very fine view.

EXTENDED ROUTE

To make a multi-day circuit, wander 6km down-valley to Avers-Cresta (1959m). After a night spent there continue to Cröt (the next village) where you turn south into the Madrisertal. After 8 or 9km the valley forks. Take the right branch, **Val Prassignola**, heading roughly south, and climb for about 2hr by a well-made path to gain **Forcella di Prassignola** (2724m). On the south side of this pass descend steeply to **Soglio** where you can catch a post-bus to Promontogno, and from there return to Casaccia.

ROUTE 7

Casaccia (1458m) – Val Maroz – Val da Cam (2433m) – Soglio (1097m)

Start	Casaccia (1458m)
Distance	16km (9.9 miles)
Height gain	975m (3199ft)
Height loss	1336m (4383ft)
Grade	2–3
Time	6½hr
Location	West and southwest of Casaccia

Making a high traverse of Val Bregaglia's north flank, this outing is one of the classic 'middle mountain' walks of the district. It's a long day's walk, but is full of interest and variety, and with some very fine vantage points along the way. Keep your camera handy to capture some truly spectacular panoramic views. It should be noted that the paths are not as clearly defined as most hereabouts, and concentration may be needed to stay on track.

Follow Route 5 out of Casaccia and into Val Maroz for 1hr, to reach the alp buildings of **Maroz Dora** (1799m). Shortly after these the way divides. Bear left, cross the stream and enter the main stretch of Val Maroz where another 1hr will bring you to the upper alp, **Maroz Dent** (2035m), which consists of a small dwelling and a long cattle byre in a lovely setting. Beside it there's a pentagonal walled sheepfold, with the stream below.

The path descends to the stream and crosses by a wooden bridge. The way forks and you take the left branch to climb the steep hillside ahead. There are in fact two paths that come together just below the false saddle that gives access to Val da Cam; the easier option picks a line left of the stream tumbling down the hillside, while the alternative path climbs more steeply on the right of the stream. Both are led by paint flashes, and at the head

of the ascent you gain a saddle marked by a group of lofty cairns. Beyond lie the pastures of **Val da Cam**.

Wander through this gentle valley keeping more or less to the centre, and climb a grassy step at the far end. This brings you to the next level, with the continuing path winding among hillocks that obscure the pass through which you gain the hillside above Val Bregaglia.

Once you go through the rocky 'gateway' of **Pass da Cam** the Bregaglia begins to open out to reveal its unique charm. The path loses height, then heads to the right on a westward descending traverse way above the valley bed. ▸

On the far side of the Bregaglia the mountain wall teases your concentration, dragging your eye away from the narrow trail. Come to a water trough constructed of huge slabs of stone with, below it, the isolated farmstead of Plan Lo. Our path continues westward, losing itself among boulders, but coming clear again with a marker post that directs the route along the hillside.

In places the trail is extremely narrow, with a substantial drop to one side. Now and again it rises to cross a bluff, sometimes it loses height; but mostly maintains

Above the alp of Maroz Dent a cairn-marked saddle gives access to Val da Cam

An alternative path drops steeply from here on a knee-crunching descent to Vicosoprano.

a steady traverse among wild and rampant vegetation. **Cadrin** is a deserted alp with decaying buildings (2127m). Just beyond it the path from Val da la Duana (see Route 8) meets ours. The next alp is **Löbbia**, a meagre collection of dwellings and barns with a stream nearby; but the best of all is **Plän Vest** (1821m), a string of alp chalets and haybarns tucked against the steep hillside with a sloping apron of pasture before it, and an amazing view of the Sciora aiguilles, Piz Cengalo and Badile stabbing at the sky at the head of Val Bondasca.

The continuing path crosses the pasture, then plunges down through pinewoods in steep zigzags to spill out at **Tombal**, another alp with jaw-dropping views and an air of pure enchantment. The path heads south past old buildings and on across the pasture before swinging right in more woodland on a tiring descent to the utterly charming village of **Soglio**. From here you can take a postbus down to Promontogno for the return to Casaccia.

ROUTE 8
Casaccia (1458m) – Val Maroz – Val da la Duana
– Pass da la Duana (2694m) – Soglio (1097m)

Start	Casaccia (1458m)
Distance	16km (9.9 miles)
Height gain	1236m (4055ft)
Height loss	1597m (5240ft)
Grade	2–3
Time	8hr
Location	West and southwest of Casaccia

This is a variation of Route 7; an alternative high route to Soglio which gives similar spectacular views but tackles even more remote country.

Tucked against the wooded slope 450m above Soglio, the few alp buildings of Tombal are visited on several walks

Follow Route 7 to the bridge which crosses the stream just below the alp buildings of **Maroz Dent** (2035m/2hr), then continue up-valley on a marked trail leading to the Val da la Duana. The way goes through this valley passing a small tarn, then veers left at a fork to gain **Pass da la Duana** (2694m/4½hr). ▸

Pass da la Duana is 567m above **Cadrin**, and it will take about 1½hr for the descent to that deserted alp where you join the path of Route 7 down to **Tombal** (another 45min), and then to **Soglio**.

East of the pass stands Piz Duan (3131m), said to be gained easily enough from Pass da la Duana (2hr). Somewhat detached from its neighbours, it has the reputation for being a charming viewpoint.

ROUTE 9

Casaccia (1458m) – Roticcio (1268m) –
Durbegia (1410m) – Soglio (1097m)

Start	Casaccia (1458m)
Distance	14km (8.7 miles)
Height gain	142m (466ft)
Height loss	503m (1650ft)
Grade	2
Time	5hr
Location	Southwest of Casaccia

Known as the Sentiero Panoramico, this is one of the classic walks of Val Bregaglia. To German-speaking Swiss it's famed as the Panoramahöhenweg, although it's not a high route in quite the same way as the previous two routes. However, it climbs way above the valley bed (much more so than the height statistics might indicate) and offers a number of fine views to the southern wall of mountains. In its early stages the walk visits villages and alp hamlets, but for much of the way it weaves a route among mixed woods that screen the views. In those woods ancient barns and chalets are crumbling into the hillsides.

On the west side of the road opposite Casaccia post office a sign gives directions to Roticcio, Durbegia, Parlongh and Soglio. Turn left along a back street that leads directly to a large open meadow. Walk ahead with views south to the Pranzaira dam blocking the entrance to Val Albigna, but coming to a crossing track by a large pylon, turn right, cross the Maira stream and follow its right bank down-valley After passing a small electricity building continue above a reservoir, beyond whose dam the way remains on the right bank, but forks at the entrance to a meadow in which stand two buildings. Take the left branch, easing downhill. About 35min

from Casaccia another track cuts left to Röivan and Vicosoprano, but the Sentiero keeps ahead.

The way soon rises gently with lovely views across the valley. Then you come to a fork by a house and take the lower branch. This leads to **Roticcio** (1268m/1hr) which you reach at a hairpin bend. Walk down the road for 2min, then when it forks go up a little side street which runs through the village among a mixture of old and new houses. Leaving Roticcio you gain a view onto Vicosoprano's campsite (Roticcio's service road passes alongside this). Take a grass path which cuts into an indent, crosses a stream, and shortly after begins to climb the wooded hillside.

Making height by a series of long twists, reach a point at about 1400m where the angle eases for a brief contour, before losing height again, then contouring once more. An open stretch with a bench seat provides a bird's-eye view onto Vicosoprano, while Borgonovo and

The southern wall of Val Bregaglia, as seen from the Sentiero Panoramico

65

Stampa can be seen further down-valley. Now descend a few steps, and a few minutes later come to a short chain-assisted passage down an easy rocky ramp. Thereafter the way progresses through attractive woodland running with small streams, and comes to a path descending to **Vicosoprano**.

Continue ahead, and 3min later come to a second junction where the upper path is signed to Plan Lo and Val da Cam. Keep to the lower option which leads to a track, and wander up it, soon leaving the woods behind to reach the open alp of **Durbegia** (1410m/2hr) with its scattered barns and lovely views, the best of which are seen looking back to mountains walling the Albigna cirque. A small *ristoro* has been set up here to provide drinks and refreshments for passing walkers – the only possibility between Roticcio and Soglio.

The track returns to woodland, and 10min later narrows to a footpath, soon crosses a gully cut by landslide, then over a stream to rise once more. The next stream crossing has wooden handrails, and it is here that you gain a first view of the glacier at the head of Val Bondasca. A few minutes after this there's another stream crossing

Soglio looks directly across the Bregaglia to Val Bondasca

below a showering cascade, with yet another soon after – this crossing is made on stepping stones.

The path takes you past some dilapidated buildings before sloping down to barns at the **Parlongh junction** (1274m/4hr) where a sign indicates that the route left offers a way down to Muntac and Coltura in 1hr, while the way ahead gives a rather generous 1hr to Soglio. Between here and Soglio there are many sections of ancient stone paving – large stone slabs too, that make fine stairways – part of an old Roman route. Views are impressive for much of the way now, and after one fairly long paved section, you turn a bend to discover that **Soglio** lies just below. ▸

Soglio offers refreshments and accommodation. There are food stores, and a postbus ink with Promontogno, connecting with other postbus services throughout Val Bregaglia.

ROUTE 10
Casaccia (1458m) – Barga (1368m) – Val Furcela (2369m) – Maroz Dent (2035m) – Casaccia

Start	Casaccia (1458m)
Distance	14km (8.7 miles)
Height gain	1001m (3284ft)
Height loss	911m (2989ft)
Grade	2–3
Time	6hr
Location	South and west of Casaccia

This route is one of the Val Bregaglia's recommended circuits, and is marked in red on the LS 1:50,000 sheet, Julierpass, as well as the Kümmerly + Frey Oberengadin sheet. Reversing parts of Route 7, the way is mostly well marked and utterly delightful, but it makes a demanding, albeit stimulating day out.

Follow directions for Route 9 as far as the fork by a house between the Röivan turn-off and the hairpin bend above Roticcio (45–50min from Casaccia). This is marked as **Barga** (1368m) on the map. While the Sentiero Panoramico takes the lower branch, for the Val Furcela it's necessary to take the upper option. Angling across the steep wooded hillside, the way rises into the narrow valley, whose stream descends through Roticcio, and about 1hr from Barga you come to the alp of **Nambrun** (1611m). The way now steepens, twisting up to Alp Furcela, and continues from there to the head of the hanging **Val Furcela** at a saddle of 2369m, gained about 2–2½hr from Nambrun.

Heading briefly west you enter Val da Cam (see Route 7) not far from a group of lofty cairns, then turn right (north) to descend steeply into Val Maroz. Cross the stream at the foot of the slope and go up to the alp buildings of **Maroz Dent** (2035m/5hr). Now above the left bank of the Maira, wander down the trail to **Maroz Dora**, reached in another 40min, and continue all the way to **Casaccia**.

ROUTE 11

*Vicosoprano (1067m) – Borgonovo
(1043m) – Stampa (994m)*

Start	Vicosoprano (1067m)
Distance	4km (2.5 miles)
Height loss	73m (240ft)
Grade	1
Time	1hr
Location	West of Vicosoprano

This is an easy meadow and woodland walk which remains in the valley throughout, and links three of its lovely old villages.

From the village square near the church walk along a side road which takes you across the river, where you then turn left. There are tennis courts nearby. Take the next road right, then head left by apartments. Thereafter a path leads across meadows and into woodland, remaining on the right bank of the Maira all the way, although mostly keeping some distance from the river. In a woodland section timber boards carry the path across a boggy stretch, and you later twist among huge boulders on a track which then swings left and brings you to a charming old stone-built humpbacked bridge, across which you enter **Borgonovo** (about 40min).

Vicosoprano is the largest of Bregaglia villages, and a good base for a walking holiday

For the continuing walk to Stampa, return to the right bank of the Maira and head to the left on a track which curves right then left through open meadows. Come to a narrow crossing lane and turn left along it. (The continuing path leads to Coltura.) The lane very shortly brings you to a double-arched bridge spanning the Maira. Cross this into **Stampa**.

ROUTE 12

Stampa (994m) – Coltura (999m) – Soglio (1097m)

Start	Stampa (994m)
Distance	4.5km (2.8 miles)
Height gain	103m (338ft)
Grade	2
Time	1½hr
Location	West of Stampa

The distance and height gain of this walk belie its true nature, for it's uphill most of the way, and in the deciduous woods above Caccior there's an amazing stairway of stone slabs to carry this historic route.

Leave Stampa by crossing the double-arched bridge over the Maira, then turn left and wander along the lane that leads to **Coltura**. At the western end of the village, shortly

The twin-turreted Palazzo Castelmur is the most eye-catching building in Coltura

after passing the colourful Palazzo Castelmur in the square, the way curves right and soon forks. Take the left branch rising steadily between woods and meadows and eventually you will reach the hamlet of **Caccior** (933m).

Go through the hamlet, and when the track curves left towards Promontogno, leave it to go ahead on a path through meadowland, passing old barns, then on a footbridge across a stream and past more barns or granaries. In woods of chestnut, beech, oak and birch the path, known as the Sentiero Storico, winds uphill on a steady gradient. There are several sections of paved stairway – some of the slabs must weigh a ton – and one flight amounts to more than 80 stone slabs. It's a remarkable path, which emerges at last from the woods to an open grass area from which you gain wonderful views across the valley to Val Bondasca and its walling mountains. Turning a bluff **Soglio** lies just ahead.

ROUTE 13
Soglio (1097m) – Tombal (1547m)

Start	Soglio (1097m)
Distance	2km (1.2 miles) one way
Height gain	450m (1476ft)
Grade	2
Time	1¼hr
Location	Northeast of Soglio

Tombal is one of those truly magical alps, perched on a brief grassy shelf high above the Bregaglia. With stunning unhindered views it's well worth making the effort to walk up the steep path from Soglio to discover it. There are no refreshment facilities, so you're advised to choose a clear day, take a picnic lunch and a flask of drink, and treat yourself to several hours of relaxation on what seems to be the lip of the world. The panorama is one you're unlikely to forget in a hurry.

Soglio's buildings are so close to one another their rooftops almost overlap

From the village square in Soglio in front of Hotel Palazzo Salis, take a narrow cobbled alley to the left of the hotel where there's a sign to Cadrin, Val da Cam, Casaccia and so on. Waymarks guide you through the alleys and out of the village onto a path rising steeply between drystone walls. This leads onto a road where you walk ahead for about 200m, then take a path on the right signed to Tombal, Plan Vest and so on.

Climbing the steep wooded slope in numerous zig-zags, the path then makes a longish rising traverse to the right and emerges onto a crossing stony track. Cross the track straight ahead to climb some stone steps. The way then resumes its steep ascent through woods before making another rightward traverse, at the end of which there's an unmarked fork. Take the upper branch to twist uphill again before emerging on the edge of an open sloping pasture. A bench seat here gives a bird's-eye view onto Soglio's rooftops.

Wander up and across the pastures, and at the end of the second building (a stone barn) veer left – there's a sign to Plän Vest. In a few minutes you will reach the delightful row of old stone dwellings and haybarns that represent **Alp Tombal**, one of the most magical places in all the Alps, with one of the most awesome of views. Allow 45min for the descent to **Soglio** by the same route. ▶

Some 270m/about 1hr above Tombal is another splendid little alp, Plän Vest: magnificent views and worth visiting. The path – extremely steep – rises into woodland behind the main buildings.

ROUTE 14

Soglio (1097m) – Parlongh (1274m) – Muntac (1043m) – Coltura (999m) – Stampa (994m)

Start	Soglio (1097m)
Distance	5km (3.1 miles)
Height loss	145m (476ft)
Grade	2
Time	2hr
Location	East of Soglio

This descent to Stampa adopts the finest section of the Sentiero Panoramico (see Route 9), with memorable views not only of the Bondasca peaks, but also of the upper Val Bregaglia stretching to the northeast. It's a surprisingly energetic walk with plenty of ups and downs, and a steepish descent from Parlongh to Muntac. For an alternative, and shorter, descent to Stampa, see Route 12 which may be reversed.

Facing Hotel Palazzo Salis take the cobbled lane on the right where a sign gives directions to Stampa, Borgonovo, Vicosoprano and so on. A few paces along this lane branch left on the Sentiero Panoramico signed to Casaccia. At first this is another narrow cobbled alleyway, but you shortly leave it by climbing some stone steps on the left (waymarks) whose continuing path rises alongside drystone walls, gaining about 40m before easing among trees.

In and out of trees the path climbs intermittently, sometimes on stone steps, sometimes using enormous stone slabs; a remarkable undulating mule trail of historic origin. Now and then bird's-eye views are afforded onto villages far below; often it's the Sciora peaks and Piz Badile that hold your attention. The way takes you past old haybarns, crosses minor streams, and after 50–60min brings you to a junction of trails by a couple of barns. This is **Parlongh** (1274m).

Leave the Sentiero Panoramico here and take the right branch descending past more buildings. The path is steep in places, and you lose height quickly, coming to the small village of **Muntac** where you pass to the right of a water fountain, then walk through the village and down the road beyond. Coming to a road junction veer slightly left and soon you will arrive on the outskirts of **Coltura**. Take the street to the left to walk through the village (passing Palazzo Castelmur on the right) and continue between meadows before coming to the double-arched bridge that spans the Maira. Across this lies **Stampa**.

Other walks from Soglio

Most walks from Soglio are steep either in ascent or descent, but practically all are visually stimulating. Some of the paths tend to be bullied by vegetation in summer, yet waymarking is reasonably good. The following is just a small selection of possible routes.

- Beginning by the church, a very pleasant descent path weaves a way through the chestnut woods and brings you down to **Promontogno** in about 1hr.
- Two possible descent routes lead to **Castasegna**: one breaks away from the Soglio–Bondo road; the other leaves Soglio at its western edge and works a way through meadow and woodland – another 1hr walk.
- Taking Route 8 in reverse, **Casacca** can be reached via the **Pass da la Duana** and Maroz Dent in a tough walk of about 8hr. It begins by visiting Tombal as described in Route 13.
- A slightly shorter route to **Casaccia** (7hr) goes via **Val da Cam** by reversing Route 7. This too first visits Tombal and Plän Vest.

- A very long and demanding walk of 9hr from Soglio crosses the 2724m **Forcella (or Pass) di Prassignola** and descends to **Cröt** in the Averstal; a classic crossing; from Cröt it's possible to catch a bus to Thusis.

VAL BONDASCA WALKS

Without question, Val Bondasca is the loveliest, most romantic and certainly the most dramatic of the side glens feeding into the Maira. A small valley at the southwest end of Val Bregaglia, it rises steeply from a riot of sub-tropical vegetation to a bold savagery of granite spire and vast slab wall, from ferns as high as a man's shoulders to a world of scree, lichen and fast-shrinking glacier. Thick woods clothe slopes that mask the valley's entrance behind Bondo and Promontogno. Here Bondasca is a narrow gorge, steep-walled and dark with shadow, but as you delve deeper into its recesses, so it opens a little to reveal small pockets of pastureland. On the west flank the mysterious Trubinasca glen offers a challenge, but beyond it the upper Val Bondasca spreads into one of the most enchanted of cirques. Bounded by the huge walls of Cengalo and Badile on one side, and the craggy Cacciabella ridge on the other, there rise (in the words of J. Hubert Walker) 'the flamelike outlines of the fantastic Sciora peaks': Sciora di Fuori, Punta Pioda, Ago di Sciora, Sciora Dadent. Wonderful peaks, these are, appearing sharp as a

Coltura, one of many stone-built villages set among the meadows of Val Bregaglia

Granite blades of the Sciora aiguilles form fence posts at the head of Val Bondasca, dwarfing the SAC's hut, seen at their feet

knife blade, smooth-walled and a great temptation to rock climbers. From the walker's point of view, they form a backdrop to dreams and the horizon within which days of pleasure may be spent.

But the path which leads there has its own special appeal. Gaston Rébuffat wrote of it in his *Starlight and Storm*: 'Wild gorges open up on either side: deep and twisted, worn and polished smooth each spring by the avalanches, they are sprinkled with dead trees tossed among the bushes that are reborn each summer. It is a romantic scene. Here you are tempted to sit and gaze and drink it in. The air is laden with a delicious scent of grass, of resin and of the keen breeze. Here a man forgets everything, even that he has come to climb.' Or to walk.

Note: As mentioned in the Preface, in August 2017 a massive rock fall from Piz Cengalo (estimated at 2 million tonnes) devastated parts of Val Bondasca and wrought havoc on the village of Bondo at its entrance. As a consequence the whole of this valley has been CLOSED until further notice. This affects Routes 15–19 and 23. When it is considered safe to re-enter the valley a note will be added to this guidebook's update section on the Cicerone website.

ROUTE 15

Promontogno (821m) – Val Bondasca
– Capanna di Sciora (2118m)

Start	Promontogno (821m)
Distance	6.5km (4 miles) one way
Height gain	1297m (4255ft)
Grade	2
Time	3½–4hr
Location	Southeast of Promontogno

The Sciora Hut sits among old moraines immediately below the Sciora peaks, and looks out across the length of the Bondasca valley to hillsides on the northern side of Val Bregaglia where you can just make out the buildings of Soglio, Tombal and Plän Vest. With savage mountain scenery at every turn, it's a wonderful situation for a hut, and the approach walk, although fairly steep and demanding, is both varied and scenically interesting.

Note: An approach from Bondo is also described.

Opposite Hotel-Pension Sciora in Promontogno's narrow main road, a cobbled side street cuts back towards Bondo. Walk along this to a stone bridge that spans the Bondasca torrent. Immediately before this bridge take a signed path climbing steeply to the left. Rising among woods this eventually comes out onto a dirt road/track overlooking the **Bondasca gorge** (30min). Cross this track, which is used by walkers coming from Bondo, and continue on a stony path signed to Sasc Furä and Sciora.

The stony path is merely a short cut, for it soon brings you onto the track again. Now remain on the track to its end (1hr), passing on the way a very fine view into the

ALTERNATIVE START FROM BONDO

From the small parking area on the southern edge of Bondo, take a grass path which angles briefly up to a dirt road/track, and follow this as it winds uphill through woodland, passes through two short rock tunnels, and curves into the mouth of Val Bondasca. After about 30min the track crosses the very narrow **Bondasca gorge**, a few paces beyond which you turn right on a stony path, thereby joining the route from Promontogno.

Trubinasca cirque where Piz Badile looks especially dramatic. A footpath continues and forks in another 10min. The right branch goes to the Sasc Furä Hut (see Route 16), but the left-hand option is the one for the **Capanna di Sciora**. The path is clearly signed and waymarked and it remains to the left of the stream. Wild raspberries are there for the picking in late summer; there are rough little pastures, and straggling vegetation, while the path picks its way among boulders and trees before zigzagging steeply among rocks. Finally you come onto the moraine wall to reach the hut.

SCIORA HUT

With places for 42 and a guardian in residence from July to end September, the Sciora Hut belongs to the Hoher Rohn section of the SAC. It's very much a climber's hut with a wonderland of rock routes nearby. The original hut was burnt down during World War II; the present building dates from the late 1940s. For reservations Tel 081 822 11 38 (www.sachoherrohn.ch)

ROUTE 16

Promontogno (821m) – Capanna
Sasc Furä (1904m)

Start	Promontogno (821m)
Distance	6km (3.7 miles) one way
Height gain	1083m (3553ft)
Grade	2–3
Time	3–3½hr
Location	Southeast of Promontogno

The path to Sasc Furä is a magical one. It's also steep and demanding, but on emerging in the little mountain glade where the hut, backed by soaring walls of rock, gazes onto a scene of great beauty, you will know without a glimmer of doubt that you've arrived at a very special belvedere.

Despite its modest altitude (1904m), the Sasc Furä Hut has a 'high mountain' atmosphere

Take Route 15 as far as the path division some 10min beyond the end of the track in Val Bondasca (1hr 10min). This is marked as **Laret** (1360m). Taking the right branch, the path weaves among trees then crosses the **Bondasca torrent** on a wooden footbridge. On the south side of the valley now the way rises very steeply through mixed woods, then works its way up a narrow rock rib where timber-braced steps and fixed cable handrails provide aid in the most exposed places. Above this rib, cross a stream and go up the edge of a gully, beyond which the way swings to the right, crosses a little bridge and another small stream, then climbs steeply again among trees. Shortly after this you emerge from the trees just a few paces from the **Sasc Furä Hut**, with Piz Badile's North Ridge soaring behind it; a most dramatic spot. ◄

Experienced mountain trekkers might consider extending the walk over Colle Vial to the Sciora Hut (see Route 17).

A return to Promontogno or Bondo by the same route of ascent will take about 2–2½hr.

SASC FURÄ HUT

This SAC hut is usually manned during the main summer period of July to mid/late September, when meals and refreshments are normally available. It has room for 45, but just 5 places in the winter room. For reservations Tel 081 822 12 52 www.sascfura.ch. Not surprisingly the Sasc Furä Hut is used mainly by climbers aiming for Piz Badile.

Note that after a two-year closure following the 2017 rockfall, the Sasc Furä hut is due to reopen in the summer of 2019. Its approach has been rerouted.

ROUTE 17

Capanna Sasc Furä (1904m) – Colle Vial
(2266m) – Capanna di Sciora (2118m)

Start	Capanna Sasc Furä (1904m)
Distance	4km (2.5 miles)
Height gain	362m (1187ft)
Height loss	148m (486ft)
Grade	3
Time	3½hr
Location	East of the Sasc Furä Hut

A natural route linking the two Bondasca huts, this crosses the rocky spur extending from Piz Badile's North Ridge and drops to the glacial debris fanning below Piz Cengalo. It's a route that should only be attempted in settled weather, and by experienced mountain trekkers.

Paint flashes signal the route up the smooth slabs immediately behind the Sasc Furä Hut, then a vague trail of markers and occasional signs of a path head steeply south towards the ridge of Piz Badile. Once the few trees and shrubs have been left behind the way leads up granite boulders keeping right of the spur. About 30min from the hut you'll come upon cairns that take the route up towards the crest, now aiming leftward. In 45min reach the **Colle Vial** (2266m); a notch in the granite crest marked by a cairn and paint marks. The view down the eastern side is sobering, for it drops very steeply by way of a series of ledges to the rocks and moraine of the Cengalo Glacier. The red-shuttered Sciora Hut can be seen upon the moraine mound in the east, with the jagged Scioras rising like granite fence posts behind it.

Descend with caution on a narrow gritty path that soon turns to a 'ladder' of ledges slanting right, down which you climb with the wall of the ridge leaning

On the crossing of Colle Vial between the Sasc Furä and Sciora Huts, a sudden view reveals the Sciora aiguilles across the receding Cengalo Glacier

towards you. It's an exposed descent, but safe enough when taken with care. At the foot of the wall cairns and paint flashes lead through a boulderfield and up to a moraine cone being colonised by vegetation. Beyond this the route crosses a number of glacial slabs with streams running down them. Take great care when crossing these. There follows more boulder chaos, more moraines, more streams; but the route is marked throughout, although should mist or low cloud descend over this part of the route, you'll need to exercise great caution. The final

CHRISTIAN KLUCKER'S TOUR

In his eminently readable autobiography, *Adventures of an Alpine Guide*, Christian Klucker describes a circular tour he made in 1906 with his great friend Theodor Curtius, in which he crossed the Colle Vial in the opposite direction to that suggested here. He writes: 'The passage from the Sciora Hut over the Cengalo Glacier to the Viale is far from simple. The small but awkward glacier and its three treacherous moraines offer anything but an agreeable *Wanderung*.' The glacier has, of course, receded considerably since Klucker's time.

approach to the hut is across more old glacial moraine with the magnificent Sciora needles looking foreshortened above.

ROUTE 18

Promontogno (821m) – Capanna Sasc Furä (1904m) – Colle Vial (2266m) – Capanna di Sciora (2118m) – Promontogno

Start	Promontogno (821m)
Distance	16.5km (10.2 miles)
Height gain	1445m (4741ft)
Height loss	1445m (4741ft)
Grade	3
Time	9hr (2 days)
Location	Southeast of Promontogno

Making a tour of Val Bondasca, this is a magnificent, albeit quite tough, circuit for fit and experienced mountain trekkers that links the previous three routes (nos 15 in reverse, plus 16 and 17). High mountain scenery is just one of its themes; the two huts visited on the way add their own character to the route, while the trails themselves demand plenty of attention – especially from the head of the track in Val Bondasca to the Sciora Hut via Sasc Furä and Colle Vial. Refreshments are available at both huts, and although fit walkers could complete the circuit in a long day's activity, it's preferable to take your time and spend a night in one or other of the huts in order to absorb the atmosphere of this splendid wild region.

For the first stage of the walk as far as **Capanna Sasc Furä**, a description of the route will be found under Route 16. Beginning in the low, often steamy warmth of the lower Val Bregaglia, it's a demanding 3–3½hr trek with some very steep and exposed sections, which brings you up into a rugged cirque dominated by the great Northeast Ridge of Piz Badile.

The next stage (described as Route 17) demands concentration for the crossing of **Colle Vial**, the descent from which is exposed and with one or two potentially tricky moves if the ledges are covered with grit. Below this the route weaves a course over glacial debris and old moraines before reaching the **Sciora Hut**.

From Capanna di Sciora back to Promontogno through **Val Bondasca** will take a couple of hours or so (Route 15 in reverse). The first section is the steepest, but the scenery is always very fine, and you'll no doubt keep stopping to look back at the lofty ridge of ragged peaks behind you. Once you reach the motorable track below Alp Laret, you're faced with an easy jog down to the Bregaglia.

ROUTE 19

Capanna di Sciora (2118m) – South Cacciabella Pass (2897m) – Capanna da l'Albigna (2336m)

Start	Capanna di Sciora (2118m)
Distance	6.5km (4 miles)
Height gain	779m (2556ft)
Height loss	561m (1841ft)
Grade	3
Time	4½hr
Location	Northeast of the Sciora Hut

The crossing of the Cacciabella ridge, that separates the Bondasca and Albigna glens, is one that is often made in summer by climbers and experienced mountain trekkers. There are two passes; one on either side of the spiky rock tower of Pic Eravedar (2934m), the easiest of which is the southern and higher option which has been in use by local chamois hunters for at least 200 years. The way is well marked on both sides of the ridge with cairns and the blue and white stripe that indicate an 'Alpine route'.

Note: Before proceeding, two warnings should be heeded: i) do not set off unless the weather is clear; ii) take extra care on the upper section of the route to the pass, for if there is no snow, the rocks can be loose and dangerous, especially if others are above you.

The route to the Cacciabella Pass is signed from the Sciora Hut. Heading northeast across rough slopes of boulder and scree, the way then veers round to the right (east) on the north side of a spur projecting from the ridge. An old moraine leads up to a small snowfield, then continues up a broad snow couloir, which could possibly be bare loose rock by mid-season (**caution needed here**). There then follows a steep zigzag route with fixed cable near the top, before angling left to the small nick of a pass, gained about 3hr from the Sciora Hut.

On the Albigna side you look onto the East Ridge of Piz Eravedar a little north of the pass. To cross this ridge, first descend a short, narrow gully, then work onto the ridge to reach a saddle at about 2800m. A path now descends northeastward over grass slopes, crosses a ravine and then cuts below the Northeast Ridge of the rocky **Piz Frachiccio**. The trail eases northward above the Albigna lake and comes onto the dam wall. Cross to the eastern side and continue on a clear path that curves to the right over boulder slopes to gain the **Albigna Hut**. ▸

To descend to Val Bregaglia, either ride the cablecar down to Pranzaira, or follow a good path descending below the cableway to reach the valley in 1½hr (Route 20 in reverse).

ALBIGNA HUT

Capanna da l'Albigna is a very busy hut. With 94 places it is manned from mid-June to end September when meals are available. For reservations Tel 081 822 14 05 (www.albigna.ch).

VAL ALBIGNA WALKS

From the Val Bregaglia the full impact of the Albigna region is hidden by the vast wall of the dam which blocks the upper glen from view, and spreads in an immense sheet of concrete from one natural rock wall to the other. Behind this dam lie the icy waters of the lake, created by holding back the streams draining glaciers at the southern end of the valley. It's a bleak scene when compared with that of Bondasca. Its vegetation is limited, and under a cloudy sky the landscape appears almost monochrome. But the spiky peaks jutting from the valley's containing ridges have an appeal all their own, and the shrinking glaciers and snowfields contrast the lush greenery of both Val Bregaglia and Bondasca. In that there's a subtle charm.

An approach to the Val Albigna will normally be made either from Vicosoprano or, more frequently, from Pranzaira (2km northeast of the village) where there's a cableway originally provided for maintenance staff working at the dam. Not surprisingly this cablecar is used by walkers and climbers who wish to avoid the uphill walk from Vicosoprano. There is also a woodland path leading from Pranzaira that joins the Vicosoprano trail. This would have been very different in the days before the dam was built, for it led to the waterfall of the Cascata dell'Albigna, described in an early Baedeker as 'a fine fall in a wild ravine, near the foot of the Albigna Glacier'. That ravine is now dominated by the massive concrete wall which towers overhead. As for the Albigna Glacier, this is now several kilometres south of its former snout, and shrinking towards the frontier peaks of its birth.

Val Albigna is a raw land of rock and water, with old snow drapes and glacier remnants at its head

ROUTE 20

Pranzaira (1195m) – Capanna da l'Albigna (2336m)

Start	Pranzaira (1195m)
Distance	7km (4.3 miles)
Height gain	1141m (3744ft)
Grade	2
Time	3–3½hr
Location	South of Pranzaira

The Pranzaira cablecar takes about 15min to whisk passengers from the valley to the dam. To walk from one to the other demands more than 3hr of effort, but if you're not burdened with a heavy rucksack it's a walk to be recommended. This is a route full of botanical interest; in the woods there's life and fragrance and plenty to interest anyone with a love of nature. The path is steep, and the close-growing trees restrict some of the views, but such an approach to a wild region will bring out the full impact of the mountain world's rich diversity. In short: it's a walk worth tackling for itself.

At Pranzaira there's plenty of parking space and a post-bus stop. About 300m beyond the cablecar station, on the way to the Maloja Pass, a broad track turns away from the main road heading to the right. Follow this through woods to a stream and cross by a footbridge. The track continues among lofty conifers, winding in long sweeps through the forest before shrinking to path-size. Shortly after this the path is joined by another from the right coming from Vicosoprano (Route 21). Later you come to a sign where you leave the main path to join another which climbs steeply to the right. This now leads in a consistently steep and lengthy haul up the rib that forms the western wall of the **Albigna ravine**.

On gaining the foot of the dam, cross below it to the eastern side by a continuing path, climb to the head of the wall at 2165m (about 3hr from Pranzaira), and find the hut path which leads from the lakeside. It ascends rough boulder slopes heading right, and reaches the hut, set below **Piz dal Päl**, in about 35min from the dam.

ALBIGNA HUT

This commands a wild panorama of grey rocks and glaciers; snagged peaks above and cold-looking lake below. Owned by the Hoher Rohn section of the SAC it is manned from mid-June to end September when meals are available. For reservations Tel 081 822 14 05 (www.albigna.ch).

ROUTE 21
Vicosoprano (1067m) – Capanna da l'Albigna (2336m)

Start	Vicosoprano (1067m)
Distance	8km (5 miles)
Height gain	1269m (4164ft)
Grade	2
Time	3½hr
Location	Northeast and south of Vicosoprano

This route is an alternative to Route 20, and is recommended for its more leisurely initial approach.

The path begins on the south side of the main valley road which bypasses Vicosoprano, where the village road joins it at its western end. It leads steadily up-valley through forest, soon taking a course on the true left bank (south side) of the **Albigna river**, until deserting it to climb among pines and eventually joining the path of approach from Pranzaira (30min) which comes from the left. Now follow directions given under Route 20 all the way to the hut.

ROUTE 22

Capanna da l'Albigna (2336m) – South Casnil
Pass (2941m) – Capanna del Forno (2574m)

Start	Capanna da l'Albigna (2336m)
Distance	5.5km (3.4 miles)
Height gain	849m (2786ft)
Height loss	611m (2005ft)
Grade	3 (with glacier crossing)
Time	5hr
Location	East of the Albigna Hut

The crossing of the ridge wall that divides the Albigna and Forno valleys has long been a popular excursion for both climbers and experienced mountain trekkers, for it is the most obvious linking route between the two huts. As with the Cacciabella ridge (on the west side of the Albigna glen), there are two Casnil passes. Being more direct when approached from the Albigna Hut, the northern pass was formerly the most frequented, but conditions have changed, and now the southern pass has become the more popular of the two.

Note: Descent on the east side of the pass is steep and, towards the foot of the slope, you should beware of loose rock; standard safety precautions should be taken when crossing the Forno Glacier.

Leave the Albigna Hut on a clearly defined path heading east (a sign on a boulder nearby marks the start of the trail). It soon forks left, heading northeast to zigzag over a rough grassy spur east of Piz dal Päl to reach a couple of little tarns lying in a small plateau. Veer right, cross a stream and work your way up the hillside to a ridge extending west from the main **Casnil ridge**. On gaining this ridge wander along its crest heading east almost as

far as a nameless peak of about 3039m. It is this peak
which divides the two passes. Bear right over boulder
slopes and traverse across the south side of the nameless
peak and come onto the pass in about 2½hr from the hut.

Descend with care, heading northeast down the remnants of a small glacier to below the northern pass, then
zigzag steeply down towards the **Forno Glacier** – taking great care not to dislodge rocks onto anyone below.
There is much loose rock. At the foot of the slope head
down-valley towards the snout of the glacier, to find a
marker pole which directs the way onto the ice.

A whole series of marker poles signals the route
across the glacier, but although the ice is fairly level,
there are crevasses which can usually be stepped across
without difficulty. However, **standard safety precautions
should be taken.** The way angles southeastward, and
leaves the glacier at about 2330m. Paint marks and cairns
now lead steeply up the unstable moraine bank where
there is **potential stonefall danger**. Study the onward
route before committing yourself, and beware of dislodging stones onto anyone below. After gaining about 80m
of height, the way swings to the right, makes an easy
traverse, then loops up the final slopes on a well-defined
path to gain the **Capanna del Forno**. ◄

For the 3hr walk
down to Maloja,
see Route 3, which
should be taken
in reverse.

FORNO HUT

This stands almost 200m above the glacier and enjoys a tremendous overview of the upper Forno valley – and practically the whole route of descent
from the Casnil Pass. The hut has 100 places and a guardian in residence
from July to end September. For reservations Tel 081 824 31 82 www.
fornohuette.ch.

ROUTE 23
A Bregaglia Circuit

Distance	65km (40.3 miles)
Height gain	4878m (16005ft)
Height loss	4878m (16005ft)
Grade	3 (some glacier crossing involved)
Time	6–7 days
Location	A counter-clockwise circuit beginning and ending at Maloja

By linking a number of routes described earlier, a magnificent high-level circuit of the Bregaglia district can be achieved by experienced mountain trekkers. Depending on weather, fitness of the individual trekker, and condition of the passes, the circuit could be achieved in less than six days. But this long-distance outing deserves to be taken at a leisurely pace with time to study the flowers as well as the views, the old stone granaries, to stray perhaps onto an accessible summit, and to absorb the essence of this unique corner of the Alps. The best time to tackle it is from mid-July to late September; the later the better when huts and hotels will be less crowded and you can have the trails more or less to yourself.

It's a challenging route and one that should not be taken lightly. There are several high passes to cross, stretches of glacier to negotiate, one or two places where there's potential rockfall danger, and plenty of wild terrain with which to come to terms. Good conditions are essential. But throughout the views are enticing, ever varied and alive with interest. First of all the Bregaglia's north wall is traversed from east to west with that wonderful panorama of jagged peaks opposite as a backdrop; with alp hamlets near at hand; and the deep shaft of the valley far below. Then, after leaving Soglio, the way drops into the Bregaglia to ascend the lovely Val Bondasca. Keeping high the way journeys across the southern glens, glaciers and mountains before descending through Val Forno back to Maloja.

WHERE TO STAY

Overnight accommodation will be found in Maloja, Casaccia, Soglio and Promontogno, and in the SAC huts of Sasc Furä, Sciora, Albigna and Forno. Supplies may be bought in Maloja, Soglio and Promontogno; meals are normally available in huts when the guardians are in residence (details are given with the individual routes described above).

Begin the circuit in **Maloja**, and follow directions for Route 4 via the Lunghin and Septimer passes to **Casaccia** near the foot of the Maloja Pass. Next day go back up the valley towards the Septimer Pass, then turn off at the alp of **Maroz Dora** to make the splendid high route to **Soglio** via Maroz Dent, Pass da Cam and the exquisite alps of Plän Vest and Tombal described as Route 7.

From Soglio's magical shelf descend through the chestnut woods to **Promontogno** (not described but clearly signed), then go up into Val Bondasca to the **Sasc Furä Hut** (Route 16), and over Colle Vial to **Capanna di Sciora** (Route 17).

Between the Sciora Hut at the head of Val Bondasca, and Capanna del Forno, the Bregaglia Circuit has two rugged passes and a glacier to negotiate. The first section goes over the **South Cacciabella Pass** to the **Albigna Hut** (Route 19), the second has to cross the 2941m **South Casnil Pass**, followed by descent into Val Forno and the crossing of the Forno Glacier (Route 22). Finally, the return to Maloja descends steeply from the **Forno Hut** to the glacier, then wanders down-valley, exchanging ice for moraine debris, and moraines for woods, meadows and lakes. This is described in reverse as Route 3.

UPPER ENGADINE

Isola, a small hamlet on a spit of meadowland beside the Silsersee (Lej da Segl)

Grevasalvas, with Piz Corvatsch as a backdrop

UPPER ENGADINE

It's 44km from the head of the Maloja Pass (1815m) to the point where the valley becomes known as the Lower Engadine at Punt Ota just above Brail. In that distance the Upper Engadine (Engiadina Ota, or Oberengadin) loses less than 200m in altitude and changes in character from a broad, flat-bottomed lakeland to a more narrow, river-cut region of pasture and forest. Scenically diverse, the valley's walking potential is tremendous, with routes to suit all ambitions and abilities.

The four extensive river-linked lakes, which fill the valley between Maloja and St Moritz, endow the upper valley with its romantic appeal. It's said to be Europe's highest lake district, and when the sun shines the valley positively glistens. Mountains of 3000m or more rise on either side, their mirror images dancing in the water. In winter these lakes are frozen for months at a time, during which both cross-country skiers and walkers travel across them in the crisp brilliance of snow. Forests of larch and pine come down to the right-bank shoreline, and these are unbelievably attractive when the Midas touch of autumn paints the valley gold; while on the left bank one community after another gazes across the water, their backs to hillsides that carry the long-distance Via Engiadina trail. In winter Piz Corvatsch above Sils Maria is an important ski mountain, but when the snow melts it loses much of its appeal. Nearby, however, and surveying the whole district from its ridge southeast of Maloja, Piz de la Margna – although not a particularly high mountain at just 3159m – has an easily recognised shape which assures its pre-eminence and holds one's attention.

In its early stages the southeast flank of the valley is interrupted by two small tributary glens: the Vals Fedoz and Fex. On the opposite bank above the Silsersee (Lej da Segl) a sloping shelf of pastureland supports two tiny alp hamlets: Blaunca and Grevasalvas. Above and behind Silvaplana the mountainside is cleft by the Julier road pass; east of St Moritz, Val Bernina is the largest by far of the early tributary valleys, acting as gateway to the snowy Bernina massif and, via the Bernina Pass, to the Italianate Val Poschiavo. (See Val Bernina section for details and walks.)

Northeast of the confluence of Engadine and Val Bernina (see section titled Northern Region), the mountains sacrifice individuality for a series of ridges rucked with minor valleys and with forests at their ankles. Only Piz Kesch (3418m) among the Albula Alps above Madulain and Zuoz is of interest to climbers, and that peak is largely hidden from much of the Engadine's view. But although mountains are not the prime interest here, they form an important backdrop to feeder glens and hillsides loud with the warning cry of marmots.

These feeder glens are many and varied. On the left bank the Vals Bever and Alvra both have roads: in the first a short stretch of tarmac accompanies the railway to Alp Spinas where the Rhätische Bahn disappears into a tunnel; the second carries a small amount of traffic over the Albula Pass to Bergün and Chur. Then there's the pastoral hanging valley of Val d'Es-cha which drains the south side of

Piz Bernina (left) and Piz Roseg, the classic view from Fuorcla Surlej

Piz Kesch; the lengthy Val Susauna that digs deep into the mountains just short of Cinuos-chel, enticing walkers with a route leading round to the north side of Piz Kesch, and offering trekkers a way over the mountains to Davos and several other destinations; while the little Val Punt Ota under Piz Vadret is the last of the left-bank tributaries of the Upper Engadine.

ACCESS AND INFORMATION

Location:	Running northeast from Maloja to Punt Ota, between Cinuous-chel and Brail. Includes Val Bernina.
Maps:	LS 268T Julier Pass, 258T Bergün, 259T Ofenpass & 269T Passo del Bernina at 1:50,000
	Kümmerly + Frey Oberengadin & Unterengadin at 1:60,000
Bases:	Maloja (1815m), Sils Maria (1806m), Silvaplana (1815m), St Moritz (1822m), Pontresina (1805m), Samedan (1721m), Zuoz (1716m)
Information:	Verkehrsverein/Ente Turistico, CH-7516 Maloja (Tel 081 824 31 88 www.engadin.stmoritz.ch/maloja)
	Verkehrsverein Sils/Engadin, CH-7514 Sils Maria (Tel 081 838 50 50 www.sils.ch)
	Verkehrsverein, CH-7513 Silvaplana (Tel 081 838 60 00 www.engadin.stmoritz.ch/silvaplana)
	Verkehrsverein, Via Maistra 12, CH-7500 St Moritz (Tel 081 837 33 33 www.stmoritz.ch)
	Verkehrsverein, CH-7504 Pontresina (Tel 081 838 83 00 www.pontresina.com)
	Samedan Tourismus, CH-7503 Samedan (Tel 081 851 00 60 www.engadin.stmoritz.ch/samedan)
	Tourismusverein Zuoz, CH-7524 Zuoz (Tel 081 854 15 10 www.engadin.stmoritz.ch/zuoz)
Access:	The Upper Engadine may be reached by rail (the Rhätische Bahn) from Chur. Trains run as far south as St Moritz, with a branch line through Val Bernina connecting with the Italian rail network at Tirano. There are postbus services from Chur (Julier Route Express) and Lugano (Palm Express). The Engadin Bus serves all villages between Brail and Maloja.

Feeding into the River Inn from the valley's right bank below Val Bernina there's the charming Val Champagna nudging behind the famed viewpoint of Muottas Muragl; the much longer Val Chamuera, some of whose trails cross the mountains into Italy; and Val Trupchun, a major entry point to the Swiss National Park.

Below Samedan most of the villages have been bypassed by the main valley road, and to visit them the tourist must forsake speed for the pleasures of cobbled streets and thick-walled houses leaning one towards another. Madulain has an attractive onion-domed church; Zuoz crowds its streets with ancient buildings built and decorated in traditional Romansch style. And although to drive through some of these villages is a rather tortuous affair, the railway sneaks in and out without difficulty and provides one of the best ways of seeing the valley – apart, that is, from walking.

MAIN BASES

MALOJA (1815m) stands at the very head of the valley and is ideally situated for the exploration of a number of side valleys, hillsides and walks alongside the lake of Sils. It also overlooks Val Bregaglia down the hairpins of the Maloja Pass (see Val Bregaglia section). A rather straggling village, it has most of the usual services: post office, restaurants, tourist information, but limited shopping. There are several hotels graded up to 3-star, numerous holiday apartments, and a campsite at the southern end of the lake, open June to end September (Camping Plan Curtinac Tel 081 824 31 81 www.camping-maloja.ch).

SILS MARIA (1806m) is the larger of the two neighbouring Sils villages, nestling below the mouth of the idyllic Val Fex (Sils Baselgia to the north has glorious views over the Silsersee). A substantial underground car park keeps traffic from its streets, and a free local bus service ferries visitors between Baselgia and Maria to the Furtschellas cablecar station. Horse-drawn 'buses' serve the traffic-free Val Fex daily from June to mid-October, and horse-drawn carriages work a private taxi service into the same valley from the village. For several years Sils Maria was the summer home of philosopher Friedrich Nietzsche, and his house is now a museum. The village has shops, a bank, post office, restaurants, tourist information, and plenty of accommodation in hotels and holiday apartments.

SILVAPLANA (1815m) overlooks the lakes of Champfer and Silvaplana from the left bank of the valley below the Julier Pass. It's a well-contained village, released from much of the valley's traffic by a bypass road that curves round it to the east. A frequent bus service links Silvaplana with other Engadine villages, and across the Julier Pass itself. The village has a choice of shops, post office, restaurants, hotels

With a view of the Silsersee, the few houses of Splüga are visited on Route 29

and apartments. The large 3-star campsite on the shores of Lej da Silvaplauna has first-class facilities and magnificent views across the lake to Piz de la Margna (Tel 081 828 84 92 www.campingsilvaplana.ch), but prospective users should be warned that the site is a very windy one.

ST MORITZ (1822m) has a glitzy reputation that's hard to dodge. Fashion and prices are high, and after more than a century as the cream of resorts, it still attracts the international jet set – but that's in the winter. Happily the summer season is less busy, less pricey, although there's little here for the budget traveller. The village is officially divided between Dorf (above the railway station) and Bad, the spa quarter at the southern end of the lake; but the two have now moulded into one long sprawl. Architecturally St Moritz is a brazen hybrid, short of the elegance it craves. However, it lacks nothing in entertainment, shopping facilities, banks, post offices, restaurants, museums, cinema, casino, indoor swimming pool, sports facilities, and trails for walking. There's a large tourist office; there are funiculars and cablecars; trains to Chur, to Val Poschiavo and Tirano, and down through the valley as far as Scuol in the Lower Engadine. Although the majority of its numerous hotels are in the upmarket scale, there's a youth hostel in St Moritz-Bad (Tel 081 836 61 11 www.youthhostel.ch) and a TCS campsite on Via San Gian (Tel 081 833 40 90) open from mid-May to end September.

PONTRESINA (1805m) is located a short distance inside Val Bernina and is linked with St Moritz by train, bus and footpath. Despite pretensions, it is less glitzy than St Moritz, with which it competes with half a dozen luxury hotels and a few classy shops. Built on a southwest-facing terrace it has an outlook that stretches into the wonderful Val Roseg, and with the Bernina mountains close by has long been a favourite centre for mountaineering. The local mountaineering school and guides' bureau, which is based in the tourist office, is the largest in Switzerland (Schweizer Bergsteigerschule, CH-7504 Pontresina Tel 081 842 82 82 www.berg-steiger-pontresina.ch). The tourist office is located in the Rondo convention centre on Via Maistra. Apart from the upmarket hotels, there are several more modest establishments with 1 or 2 stars, plus pensions, guesthouses, apartments to rent, and a youth hostel by the railway station (Tel 081 842 72 23 www.youthhostel. ch). There are two campsites nearby: at Punt Muragl (open throughout the year except April–May and October–November Tel 081 842 81 97 www.tcs-camping. ch/samedan), and on the way to the Morteratsch Valley, Camping Plauns (open end May to mid-October, and mid-December to mid-April Tel 081 842 62 85). Pontresina has a good range of shops, restaurants, banks, PTT, indoor swimming pool, and in the region of 500km of marked paths.

SAMEDAN (1721m) is the administrative 'capital' of the Engadine, looking across the Inn-Bernina flood plain to the snows of Piz Palü and the Bernina group. A small, workaday town without the glitz and glamour of St Moritz or Pontresina, Samedan has some fine old buildings at its heart. It houses the valley's hospital; it has a selection of shops, restaurants, post office, bank, tourist office, and a number of hotels and apartments. Across the river to the east lies the valley's small airport with its casual use by light aircraft and gliders.

ZUOZ (1716m) claims, with some justification, to be the best-preserved village in the Upper Engadine, with the characteristic vernacular architecture of its build-ings forming a splendid square. Certainly a much quieter place than the tourist towns and villages further up-valley, it has a variety of hotels and apartments. Zuoz has several shops, restaurants, post office, bank and tourist information. Conveniently situated for many walks, and with the national park a short distance away, the village has much to commend it as a valley base for a walking holiday.

OTHER BASES
While those centres listed above are the main valley bases, almost every vil-lage in the Upper Engadine has something to offer the discerning holiday maker, and there are hotels and/or pensions or apartments to rent in most communities. **SILS BASELGIA** (1791m) has less to offer than neighbouring Sils Maria, but there

are a few hotels and apartments, details of which can be obtained from the Sils Maria tourist office (see above). Behind Sils Maria, in **VAL FEX**, hotel and pension accommodation can be found in idyllic and peaceful surroundings (again, details from Sils Maria tourist office).

Between St Moritz and Samedan, **CELERINA** (1724m) has a good choice of accommodation (details from Celerina Tourismus Tel 081 830 00 11 www. engadin.stmoritz.ch/celerina), but its local hillside walks tend to be marred by mechanical clutter left by the ski season.

BEVER (1708m) is located at the junction of the Albula railway and the main valley line; it has more modestly priced accommodation and some good walking country nearby. Further information from Tourismusverein Bever (Tel 081 852 49 45 www.engadin.stmoritz.ch/bever).

Twin villages separated by the River Inn, **LA PUNT-CHAMUES-CH** (1697m) have a modest number of hotels, pensions and apartments. For tourist information see www.lapunt.ch.

MADULAIN (1684m) is an attractive village at the foot of Piz Kesch, claiming to be the smallest in the Upper Engadine. It has hotels, holiday apartments, and a campsite: Camping Madulain open most of the year (Tel 081 854 01 61).

At **CINUOS-CHEL** (1628m) and **BRAIL** at the northeastern limit of the Upper Engadine, there are a few small hotels and holiday apartments, and a campsite with good facilities at the mouth of Val Susauna (Camping Chapella Tel 081 854 12 06 www.campingchapella.ch). There are excellent walking opportunities nearby.

MOUNTAIN HUTS
Several mountain huts are situated either in or within walking distance of the Upper Engadine, the majority of which belong to the SAC. Beginning in the south and working down-valley, these are:

BERGHAUS FUORCLA SURLEJ (Chamanna Fuorcla Surlej: 2755m) This privately owned inn/restaurant sits in the saddle of Fuorcla Surlej below Piz Corvatsch with a classic view across the depths of Val Roseg to Piz Bernina. With places for 55 (including dormitory beds), it is open in summer from July to end September. For reservations Tel 079 791 48 84.

COAZ HUT (Chamanna Coaz: 2610m) Named after the man who made the first ascent of Piz Bernina, this attractive 16-sided hut is situated on the 'Plattas' rock

The SAC's Coaz Hut looks down the length of Val Roseg

on the west side of the Roseg Glacier, from where it has a close view of the glacier's icefall, and almost complete command of Val Roseg stretching away to the north. It is owned by the Rätia section of the SAC, has places for 80 and full meals service, and is wardened from March to mid-May, and from mid-June to the beginning of October (Tel 081 842 62 78 www.coaz.ch).

TSCHIERVA HUT (Chamanna da Tschierva: 2583m) Built on the east bank moraine of the Tschierva Glacier in Val Roseg, this popular hut is often crowded in the high season and at weekends. Reached by a walk of 3–3½hr from Pontresina, it has 100 dormitory places, and restaurant service, and is wardened from the end of March to mid-May, and from mid-June to mid-October. Owned by the St Moritz-based Bernina section of the SAC, for reservations Tel 081 842 63 91 www.tschierva.ch.

BOVAL HUT (Chamanna da Boval: 2495m) Not surprisingly, given its location and splendid approach walk, this is one of the busiest of SAC huts and is owned by the Bernina section based in St Moritz. It stands on a rocky shelf above the left (west) bank of the Morteratsch Glacier, with Piz Bernina to the south, and a vast glacial cirque topped by the Bellavista ridge blocking the head of the valley as a backdrop. The hut has 100 dormitory places, and a full meals service when the guardian is in occupation. This is from late March to mid-May, and from mid-June to mid-October. For reservations Tel 081 842 64 03 www.boval.ch. The approach walk from Morteratsch station takes about 2hr.

BERGHAUS DIAVOLEZZA (29/3m) This privately owned hotel and restaurant, at the upper station of the Diavolezza cablecar, has standard beds and hut-style dormitory accommodation (a total of 170 places). With the most wonderful panoramic views of Piz Palü and the Bernina group, it is open throughout the year except mid-October to end November. For reservations Tel 081 839 39 00 www.diavolezza.ch.

RIFUGIO SAOSEO (1985m) Situated in the tranquil Val da Camp (Val di Campo) southeast of the Bernina Pass, this SAC hut makes an ideal base for walking and ski-touring. Reached by a walk of about 1½hr from Restaurant Sfazù on the Bernina Pass road, the hut can accommodate 80 in rooms and dormitories, and is wardened from mid-February to end April, and from mid-June to mid-October, during which there's a restaurant service. For reservations Tel 081 844 07 66 www.saoseo.ch.

The privately owned Georgy Hut is perched just 76m below the summit of Piz Languard

GEORGY HUT (Chamanna Georgy: 3186m) This small, privately owned hut is perched just 76m below the summit of Piz Languard above Pontresina, and is reached by a steeply climbing path in a little over 3hr (2hr with Alp Languard chairlift). The hut has 20 dormitory places and a full meals service when the guardian is in residence (end June to mid-October). For reservations Tel 081 832 14 06 www.georgy-huette.ch. The panorama from the terrace includes all the Bernina range to the south.

JENATSCH HUT (Chamanna Jenatsch: 2652m) Used by ski-tourers in winter/ spring, and by walkers in summer, the Jürg Jenatsch Hut belongs to the Bernina Section of the SAC. It's situated at the head of Val Bever under Piz d'Err, and may be reached in 5hr from Bever, or in about 3½hr from the Julier Pass by way of the Fuorcla d'Agnel. It has 70 dormitory places, and is manned over the Christmas/ New Year period, from end January to mid-May, and from July to end September. For reservations Tel 081 833 29 29 www.chamannajenatsch.ch.

ES-CHA HUT (Chamanna d'Es-cha: 2594m) Reached by a very pleasant walk of 3hr from either Madulain or Zuoz, or by a shorter approach of 1½hr from the Albula Pass road, this hut is placed on an old moraine below the Southeast Face of Piz Kesch, with a fine distant view of the Bernina group. It has dormitory places for 60, and is wardened from mid-March to mid-April, and from end June to mid-October. For reservations Tel 081 854 17 55 www.es-cha.com.

KESCH HUT (Chamanna digl Kesch: 2632m) Owned by the Davos Section of the SAC, this hut has a direct view of the glaciated North Face of Piz Kesch. The short-est route of approach is from Chants in Val Tuors above Bergün (2½hr), but from Cinuos-chel it's about 5–5½hr through the delightful Val Susauna. The Kesch Hut has 92 dormitory places, and a guardian in residence at Christmas/New Year, in March and April, and from end June to mid-October. For reservations Tel 081 407 11 34 www.kesch.ch.

VARUSCH HUT (Chamanna dal Parc Varusch or Parkhütte Varusch: 1771m) Standing in a small meadow on the edge of the Swiss National Park in Val Trupchun, this attractive hut is reached by a walk of just 45min from the Prasüras car park in the mouth of Val Trupchun, or 1½hr from S-chanf. It has 35 dormitory places and a resident guardian from June to end October. For reservations Tel 081 851 54 54 www.varusch.ch.

A little pool at the Fuorcla Surlej reflects Piz Roseg and snowpeaks at the head of Val Roseg

UPPER ENGADINE –
LAKES REGION

A dazzling region of lake, forest and high mountain, this southwestern, upper section of the Engadine Valley has much to commend it as a centre for walking holidays, with routes to meet everyone's taste and ability set within a landscape of great beauty. Noted for their alpine flora, Engadine meadows will brighten any walker's day. At the head of Val Fex there are glaciers and snowfields, while clear streams run everywhere, and on the hillsides small tarns add much to the charm of the area. The source of the River Inn is in one of those tarns. Below it simple alp hamlets provide a contrast to the major resorts down-valley and represent a very different world where time, it seems, is marked by the slow progress of the seasons, rather than by the hands of a clock. Trails meander along the hillsides, cross easy saddles slung between modest peaks, or skirt the lakes that give the region its most obvious appeal.

By straying briefly from the path between Blaunca and Maloja, a fine view is had along the Upper Engadine's lakes

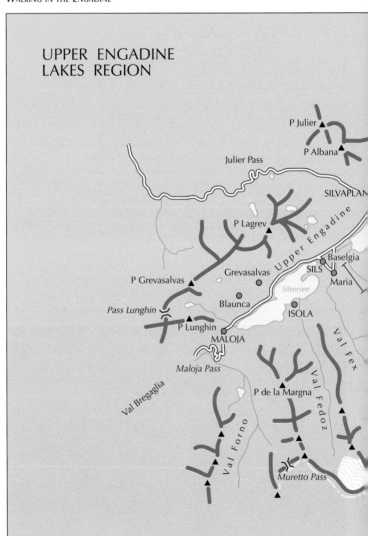

UPPER ENGADINE
LAKES REGION

P Julier

P Albana

Julier Pass

SILVAPLAN

P Lagrev

Upper Engadine

Baselgia

P Grevasalvas

Grevasalvas

SILS

Maria

Silsersee

Pass Lunghin

Blaunca

ISOLA

P Lunghin

Val Fex

MALOJA

Maloja Pass

Val Fedoz

Val Bregaglia

P de la Margna

Val Forno

Muretto Pass

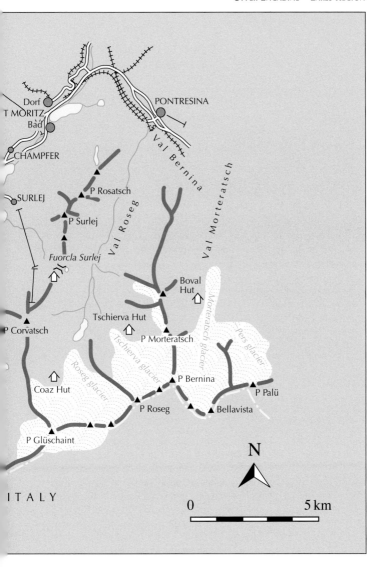

ROUTE 24

Maloja (1815m) – Isola (1812m)
– Sils Maria (1806m)

Start	Maloja (1815m)
Distance	6.5km (4 miles) one way
Height gain	Negligible
Height loss	Negligible
Grade	1
Time	1¾hr
Location	Northeast of Maloja

If you fancy an undemanding stroll in utterly delightful surroundings – this is it. It's ideally suited to families with small children, as well as to anyone who enjoys fine scenery. The path traces the southern shoreline of the largest of the Engadine lakes with larches overhanging in places, and with shrubs and flowers almost everywhere in summer. It's a walk to tackle at any time of the year (including deep winter), although autumn is perhaps the most rewarding season, when the gold of the larchwoods makes an unforgettable scene. Refreshments are available midway between Maloja and Sils, at the little hamlet of Isola.

A broad track leaves Maloja alongside the Schweizerhaus, and brings you eventually to the southern end of the **Silsersee** (Lej da Segl). Another comes from Cadlägh beside the main Engadine road (at the northeastern end of Maloja) and edges the lake heading south to join the track mentioned above. Follow this lakeside track among wooded slopes until you come to **Plan Cunchetta** at the entrance to the campsite. Leave the track here and take the larch-fringed lakeside path from which you have glorious views across the lake to Piz Lagrev. Emerging at an open meadow (Plan Brüsciabräga) with a stream flowing through it, cross a wooden bridge and join a dirt road which leads to **Isola**. The first building is Ristorante Lagrev.

ISOLA

A farming hamlet crowded on a spit of meadowland below Val Fedoz. Attractive in its simplicity and setting, a waterfall gushes behind the hamlet through a gorge at the mouth of Val Fedoz. Views are splendid up, down, and across the valley.

Leaving Isola the path crosses the Fedoz stream (Aua da Fedox), rises a little then forks. Remain on the lower option – the upper path leads to Val Fex. It's an undulating path that for the most part between Isola and Sils Maria remains a few metres above the lake shore, but with several viewpoints from which you look onto tiny islands. Shortly before it reaches the Sils meadows, the path returns to the shoreline, passes a boathouse and forks once more. Now take the right branch and head straight across the meadows to reach **Sils Maria**.

Either return to Maloja by the same path, catch a bus, or walk across the valley to Sils Baselgia where you'll find a bus stop beside the main valley road.

A shoreline path beside the Silsersee (Lej da Segl) gives gentle, but scenically rewarding walks

ROUTE 25

A Circuit of the Silsersee (Lej da Segl)

Start	Silsersee (Lej da Segl)
Distance	15km (9.3 miles)
Height gain	213m (699ft)
Height loss	213m (699ft)
Grade	2
Time	4–4½hr
Location	Northeast of Maloja

Making a highly scenic tour of the Silsersee, this walk has a few surprising uphill and steep downhill stretches, for on the left flank of the valley the way deserts the lake shore to angle up the hillside and over a highpoint to look down on Grevasalvas, a charming little alp hamlet in a secluded pasture-land setting. The walk visits this hamlet, then goes down to an isolated farm before dropping very steeply to an even smaller huddle of buildings on the way back to the lakeside. This last descent path could be troublesome for anyone suffering vertigo. Although refreshments are available in Isola, Sils Baselgia and Maloja, it's worth taking a picnic lunch with you and stopping for a while on one of the many fabulous vantage points in order to absorb the magic of the whole area. Being a circular walk it could, of course, be joined at almost any point, but the most obvious starting places are Maloja, Cadlägh or Sils Baselgia.

Assuming a start is made at either Maloja or Cadlägh, follow directions for Route 24 as far as the boathouse at the northeastern end of the lake (about 1½hr). Just beyond the boathouse the lakeside path forks. Bear left to remain on the lake shore where there are many bench seats placed to exploit the view which from here is directed towards the head of the valley where Piz de la Margna reigns supreme.

Coming to another path junction, one veers right to Sils Baselgia, the other curves left to explore the

tree-crowned isthmus known as Chastè. The latter option is recommended. Taking about 30min it makes a near-circuit of this thumb-like projection, before returning to the path junction, where you then take the branch to **Sils Baselgia** across meadows. Refreshments are available at Pension Chastè in Baselgia.

Near the church of St Lorenz cross the main road with care and take the left-hand of two paths; this one signed to Grevasalvas, Blaunca and Maloja. Angling up and easily across a slope of larch and pine you soon join the Via Engiadina at another path junction. Keep ahead (the left branch) which contours for a while, crosses scree and then rises once more. The way crosses a boggy patch of pasture and comes to yet another junction. The left-hand path descends to the road at Plaun da Lej, but to continue the circuit you take the upper path. Turning a corner, cross below cascades, then rise again under leaning crags, and 2½hr or so from the start, come to a high-point at about 2010m, from which you look down on the hamlet of **Grevasalvas** (1941m).

The way descends steeply to the hamlet, and there you turn left along the track which leads to Plaun da Lej.

Isola and the lake of Sils are clearly seen from the high path near Grevasalvas

Lej da Segl (the Silsersee) is the first of the Engadine lakes when coming from Maloja

A few paces after the track crosses the second of two bridges, break off to the right on an alternative farm track. The way eases into a secluded little valley occupied by the few farm buildings of **Buaira** (1899m). Walk between the buildings, after which a grass path goes across a stream on a footbridge, and winds up the hillside, curving left just below a drystone wall. Go through a gap in the wall and turn left on a narrow crossing path. This takes you down through a rough little meadow, then up a short slope among larch trees to gain a viewpoint from which you look steeply down onto the huddled houses of **Splüga**.

Take care on the very steep descent to these buildings, then pass behind them and cross another boggy meadow beyond which the path eases along the hillside, then slopes down to the road at a small parking area about 200m east of Cadlägh. Cross the road with care and follow a faint grass path along the lake's shoreline, and 5min later draw level with the **Cadlägh** parking area. Here you turn left along the service road that runs along the end of the lake to join the track coming from **Maloja**.

ROUTE 26
Maloja (1815m) – Piz de la Margna (3158m)

Start	Maloja (1815m)
Distance	5km (3.1 miles) one way
Height gain	1343m (4406ft)
Grade	3
Time	4hr
Location	Southeast of Maloja

The ascent of Piz de la Margna is included in this walking guide as it involves little technical climbing ability, and should be within the capabilities of **experienced** mountain walkers undeterred by a little scrambling. Summit views are magnificent, for they include not only the long sweep of lake and valley below, but nearby Bernina snowpeaks, the aloof Monte Disgrazia to the south, the granite spires of the Bregaglia, and the more modest shapes of the Albula Alps to the north.

The amount of snow lying on the mountain should be obvious from the valley; in the early part of the season an ice axe will be useful, if not essential. When most of the snow and ice has gone, do not assume the route will be any easier, for with the melting of ice that had formerly held the mountain together, the rocks – and even the turf on the upper slopes – tend to be unstable. **Caution at all stages is advised**.

Take Route 24 as far as the open meadow of Plan Brüsciabräga where the track forks. Take the right-hand, upper track, which rises into Val Fedoz and brings you to the alp buildings of **Ca d'Sternam** (2024m), from which you have a view across the Silsersee to Piz Lagrev. Immediately beyond the buildings a clear path breaks away to the right, ascending rough grass slopes, steeply at times, to reach scree and slips of snow. A little stream is seen, but just before reaching it you leave the path and head up to the right over a mixture of grass and scree in a steeply sloping hanging valley (**extra caution advised**); there's a vague trail to follow which leads onto a broad saddle in the mountain's northeast ridge. Having gained the ridge, work your way up to the summit.

Allow at least 2½hr for the descent.

ROUTE 27
Maloja (1815m) – Piz Lunghin (2780m)

Start	Maloja (1815m)
Distance	3km (1.8 miles) one way
Height gain	965m (3166ft)
Grade	3
Time	3–3½hr
Location	West of Maloja

Although not so obviously attractive as Piz de la Margna, Piz Lunghin's location on the west side of the Maloja Pass makes it as much a gatepost to both the Engadine and Bregaglia valleys as is Piz de la Margna on the east side of the valley. The summit outlook may not be quite as extensive as that of la Margna's, but it is nonetheless very impressive, for it commands not only the Bregaglia, Engadine and Bernina mountains, but country to the west too, where a sea of converging ridges fold into mysterious hinted valleys. As for the ascent, this should be straightforward under normal summer conditions, with no technical difficulties to overcome.

Follow directions given under Route 4 as far as **Pass Lunghin** at 2645m. This should be gained in about 2½hr from Maloja. At the pass a sign directs the route left, where a trail winds without difficulty up the craggy rocks to gain the summit about 30min from the Lunghin Pass.

Allow 2hr for the descent by the same route.

ALTERNATIVE DESCENT ROUTES FROM PIZ LUNGHIN

1   Descend to Pass Lunghin and bear left to the **Septimer Pass**, then descend southward to Val Maroz through which you continue to **Casaccia** at the foot of the Maloja Pass (3hr: see Route 4), then catch a postbus back to Maloja.

2   From Pass Lunghin continue round to the **Septimer Pass** and descend on the north side to **Bivio** in the Oberhalbstein (2–2½hr: see Route 5), from where you can catch a postbus back to the Engadine.

ROUTE 28

*Plaun da Lej (1805m) – Grevasalvas (1941m)
– Blaunca (2037m) – Maloja (1815m)*

Start	Plaun da Lej (1805m)
Distance	6km (3.7 miles)
Height gain	232m (761ft)
Height loss	222m (728ft)
Grade	1
Time	1½hr
Location	Northeast of Maloja

On the Engadine's left bank a hidden shelf of pastureland supports two small alp hamlets: Grevasalvas and Blaunca. A track links the two, while paths lead away from them to a variety of destinations. This particular walk makes a traverse of the pastureland from which you overlook the Silsersee, its flanking mountains, and a hint of Val Bregaglia. Although rather short, it's a very fine walk, and when taken on a bright summer's day, it will no doubt take much longer than the time suggested above. In any case, this is not a walk to hurry; there's far too much to enjoy for that. Take a picnic lunch with you and make a day of it.

Walk up the narrow private road, which begins beside Restaurant Murtaröl, and wind easily uphill among trees. Footpaths short-cut some of the loops in the dirt road, should you wish to take them. When the track/ dirt road forks on a bend, take the right branch (in effect the main route) – the alternative goes to Splüga. In another 5min it forks again; this time the left-hand option leads to the few buildings of Buaira. Continue on the main track looping uphill and so reach **Grevasalvas** (1941m/30min), its old grey stone buildings nestling among the pastures.

PLAUN DA LEJ

Plaun da Lej, where the walk begins, is an attractive spot halfway along the shore of the Silsersee between Maloja and Sils Baselgia. Served by both post-bus and Engadin Bus, there's a hotel, the Cristallina (www.plaundalej.ch/cristallina.html) and a restaurant (Murtaröl); also ample parking space and access to the lake, across which there are, of course, splendid views.

Grevasalvas is a charming huddle of buildings reached from either Maloja or Plaun da Lej

PIZ GREVASALVAS

In Grevasalvas a signed path breaks away to Fuorcla Grevasalvas, **Piz Grevasalvas** and Pass Lunghin. The ascent of Piz Grevasalvas (2932m) is tempting for experienced scramblers. A path and waymarks direct a route up its east flank in 2½–3hr from the hamlet, while a more demanding route tackles the mountain's Southeast Ridge; this involves grade III/IV climbing to overcome a prominent rock tower. For a route across **Fuorcla Grevasalvas**, see Route 30; for **Pass Lunghin**, see Route 4.

The track continues to rise between pastures, and on the way to Blaunca you gain a splendid, albeit brief, view left to the Forno peaks on the Swiss-Italian border. **Blaunca** (2037m/50min) is an even smaller hamlet than Grevasalvas, a small group of stone buildings at a junction of trails. Passing through, the track narrows to a footpath across a moorland-like stretch, and as you wander along it you gain more hinted views of Val Bregaglia ahead, Piz Badile and Cengalo on that valley's southern wall, and another snatched view of the Forno peaks. ▶

The path begins its descent towards Maloja, and a few paces before coming to a wooden seat there's an unmarked junction. The left-hand path descends to Cadlägh at Maloja's northeastern end, while the continuing trail is the one to take for the centre of Maloja. This leads to a short rocky gorge, at the bottom of which the path swings right to cross a small stream, then up a flight of wood-braced steps to emerge at the farm buildings of **Pila**. Turn left and wander down the farm track, but at a hairpin take a path descending to the right. This brings you to **Maloja** beside Hotel-Restaurant Longhin. Turn right for the village centre.

About 5min from Blaunca it's worth straying left away from the path (there is no sign for this), to gain a rocky outcrop which makes a stunning vantage point overlooking the Upper Engadine. It's one of the valley's great viewpoints.

ROUTE 29

*Maloja (Cadlägh: 1801m) – Splüga
(1880m) – Blaunca (2037m) – Grevasalvas
(1941m) – Plaun da Lej (1805m)*

Start	Maloja (Cadlägh: 1801m)
Distance	5km (3.1 miles)
Height gain	236m (774ft)
Height loss	232m (761ft)
Grade	2
Time	1¾hr
Location	Northeast of Maloja

Reversing a section of the Circuit of the Silsersee (Route 25), this fairly short walk has its demanding moments, but views are first-class almost every step of the way. It's a constantly varied walk with a number of highlights. Both Cadlägh and Plaun da Lej are served by the Engadin bus and postbus routes.

From Cadlägh at the southern end of the Silsersee find a faint path which goes between the road and the lake shore and follow this, heading down-valley. At the road's first minor bend cross the road to a footpath which begins about 50m short of a lay-by. This rises above the road, angles above the lay-by, then contours between rocky bluffs providing lovely views across the lake. About 8min from the road the path forks. Take the upper branch to climb steeply, then cross a boggy meadow to reach the small group of stone buildings known as **Splüga**. Overlooking the Silsersee from a natural shelf, Splüga is reached about 15min from the road.

Passing behind the houses the trail forks again. The lower path gives a direct route to Plaun da Lej, but for Blaunca and Grevasalvas you take the left branch, climbing very steeply to gain a grass-covered bluff from which you look directly down onto Splüga. Now the path eases

among trees, but when it emerges you find yourself in a charming hidden corner of the mountains overlooking the farm of **Buaira**.

Briefly follow a drystone wall, after which the now faint path veers away, weaves among trees and shrubs as it rises again, before contouring across a slope of alpen-rose and juniper – with yet another splendid view of the lakes of Sils and Silvaplana. After this brief contour the way then aims steeply up the hillside, and suddenly improves as you follow a little stream into **Blaunca**. Turn right along a track that winds through pastures to **Grevasalvas**, and continues with a series of loops all the way down to **Plaun da Lej**.

Blaunca, a handful of old stone buildings at a junction of paths

ROUTE 30

*Plaun da Lej (1805m) – Fuorcla Grevasalvas
(2688m) – La Veduta (Julier Pass: 2233m)*

Start	Plaun da Lej (1805m)
Distance	8km (5 miles)
Height gain	883m (2897ft)
Height loss	455m (1493ft)
Grade	3
Time	3½hr
Location	Northeast and north of Maloja

Making a crossing of the mountain wall above the Silsersee, this route turns away from the Engadine and descends into a lonely patch of country in which there's a small lake on the way to the west slope of the Julier Pass. From Gasthaus La Veduta, take a postbus back to the Engadine.

Leaving Plaun da Lej, walk up the dirt road/track to **Grevasalvas** described in Route 28. The hamlet is reached after about 30min. Take the signed path which breaks to the right, and go up the grass slopes (signs at junctions) in a 2hr climb to gain the obvious saddle of **Fuorcla Grevasalvas** (2688m) in a ridge system that links Piz d'Emmat-Dadaint with the rocky Piz Lagrev (the latter being the highest mountain south of the Julier Pass). The *fuorcla* is a great viewpoint, with the icy Bernina massif holding your attention across the depths of the Engadine. ◄

The ascent of the 3165m Piz Lagrev by the broken Southwest Ridge begins at the Fuorcla Grevasalvas and takes 2½–3hr. It is graded 3.

The way descends steadily on the northern side of the pass into a hanging valley in whose lower reaches lies the Lej Grevasalvas, a tarn caught among old moraines at 2390m. This is reached in a little over 30min from the pass. At the northern end of the lake the path forks. Take the right branch with views of Piz Julier ahead, and soon come to **Gasthaus La Veduta** a little below the rather bleak Julier Pass.

VAL FEX WALKS

Traffic-free Val Fex is one of the loveliest of the side valleys feeding into the Upper Engadine, its swathe of pastures leading to tiny remnant glaciers and snowfields at its head. There are no great mountains walling the valley, no dramatic rock walls or hanging glaciers. Instead, it's a gentle, seductive valley, rich in spring flowers, full of pastoral charm. At its head two passes suggest ways over the mountains to the Italian Val Malenco: the first is Fuorcla dal Chapütsch (2929m); the other, lying a little further northeast, is the Pass dal Tremoggia (3014m). Both have been used for centuries by smugglers and chamois hunters, and both are still fairly popular today with climbers and trekkers equipped for glacier crossing.

Just inside the valley the chalets of Fex Platta and Crasta are dotted among the meadows, and the tiny white church, so neat and cared for, makes an attractive picture with mountains rising behind it. In the graveyard lies Christian Klucker (1853–1928), one of the finest mountain guides of his day, who was born in the Chesa Nova farm and lived most of his life within the valley. It was at the age of six that he went to work for his father as a cowherd 'amongst the beautiful flowering pastures of the Fextal' is how he described it in his autobiography, *Adventures of an Alpine Guide*. Cattle will no doubt be seen grazing the pastures of Plaun Vadret (the plain of the glaciers). It's possible that they do not belong to local farmers; a number of herds that spend their summers in the Engadine and adjacent valleys are sent by train from the lowlands of Switzerland in early June, to be tended by Engadine cowherds throughout the snow-free months. Leaving lowland farmers to grow crops, their cattle feed on the high Fex pastures, increasing milk yield from which butter and cheese is made in valley dairies.

ROUTE 31

Sils Maria (1806m) – Val Fex –
Plaun Vadret (2122m)

Start	Sils Maria (1806m)
Distance	8km (5 miles) one way
Height gain	316m (1037ft)
Grade	1
Time	3hr
Location	South of Sils Maria

This gentle walk makes a fine introduction to the Val Fex, for it goes beyond the chalets of Platta and Crasta, beyond the farm road that ends at Curtins, and up into the pastures near the head of the valley. Refreshments are available in several places along the way. When planning to tackle this walk, please bear in mind that you'll need to allow at least 2hr for a return to Sils by the same route.

Begin in Sils village square by the tourist office, where horse-drawn carriages wait to ferry passengers up the road into Val Fex. A sign here indicates a path, which edges alongside a small meadow on the left of the Fedacla – the stream that drains Val Fex. This path soon goes through a timber gallery in the Fex gorge, then rises on a series of wood-braced steps among trees, to emerge at an open meadowland. Across this you soon come to the chalets of **Fex Platta** (1890m) about 30min from Sils Maria. Among the buildings here is the Pensiun Chesa Pool whose restaurant provides refreshment for visitors (Tel 081 838 59 00 https://chesapool.swiss-hotels-stmoritz.ch).

A minor service road takes you past several houses, then a footpath continues, crosses the stream and rises up a slope to join the valley road at **Fex Crasta** (1951m/45min). Next to the attractive little church here stands Hotel Sonne where again refreshments are available (Tel 081 826 53 73 www.hotel-sonne-fex.ch). There's also a restaurant just to the right immediately beyond the church. ▸

Continue up-valley along the road, but then take the first path, which leaves it on the right-hand side; this is signed to Curtins and Muott Ota. The path twists among larches up the west flank of the valley, passes a solitary house on the edge of a small meadow, and about 8min from the church comes to a junction. Keep ahead, the path now contouring along the hillside, and about 20min from Crasta it forks again. The right-hand trail climbs to Muott Ota, but our route continues ahead with the hamlet of Curtins now seen in the valley below. Shortly after, the path descends to the stream, which is crossed by a wooden bridge, and you walk through a farmyard to the head of the valley road. (To the left stands Hotel Fex, Tel 081 832 60 00 www.hotelfex.ch)

Turn right and make your way up-valley once more, now on a footpath. Before long cross the Fedacla again on another bridge and continue towards the head of the valley. The pastures here can be rather marshy. The way curves round an old moraine, shown on the map as Muot-Selvas, where there's a small tarn with a hut beside it at 2070m. Ahead lie the pastures of **Plaun Vadret**, with streams draining the last glacial remnants, and the wall of mountains which closes the head of the valley being topped by the Chapütschin on the left, Piz Tremoggia, and Piz Fora. Walk as far as you feel comfortable, then retrace your steps to **Sils Maria**.

The pretty little Romanesque church in Fex Crasta makes a worthwhile diversion. It contains some very old murals, and the grave of mountain guide Christian Klucker lies just outside the church, near the gateway.

DIRECT RETURN TO SILS

Keep to the farm road as far as **Fex Crasta**, then take the footpath used on the outward route across the meadows to **Platta** and down through the gorge. However, a longer and more varied alternative return leaves the valley bed at **Curtins** and slants across the right-hand hillside to the **Marmorè** viewpoint – this is described as Route 32 below.

Silvaplana and the Silsersee are on show from the high path that eases along the hillside above Sils Maria (photo: Jonathan Williams)

ROUTE 32

Sils Maria (1806m) – Curtins (1973m)
– Marmorè (2199m) – Sils Maria

Start	Sils Maria (1806m)
Distance	8km (5 miles)
Height gain	393m (1289ft)
Height loss	393m (1289ft)
Grade	2
Time	3–3½hr
Location	South of Sils Maria

Making a circular walk, this route provides an alternative return to Sils Maria to that suggested by the previous walk, visiting the viewpoint of Marmorè which overlooks the toy-like houses of Fex Platta and Crasta below, and gains a view of the Engadine lakes. The return path goes through a flowery stretch of hillside, especially rich in primulas and dwarf azaleas that form a lush carpet. The descent from Marmorè to Sils, although not difficult, is steep, and care is needed should the path be wet.

Follow Route 31 directions as far as **Hotel Fex** (1¼–1½hr), then wander down the farm road to the little hamlet of **Curtins**, reached a few minutes later. At the entrance to the hamlet, just beyond a small stream, take a signed path on the right. This mounts the hillside, then veers left to make a gentle rising traverse towards a rocky gateway. About 10min or so from Curtins there's a path junction. One trail descends to Fex Crasta, another cuts back to the right and climbs to Lej Sgrischus (2618m), but the Marmorè path continues ahead, still rising and gaining views of the Silsersee in the Upper Engadine.

Ten minutes from the last junction, come to another on a rocky corner at 2130m. The lower path here descends to Sils via a small group of buildings known as Vanchera, but we take the upper trail, which leads directly to a third junction. This is **Marmorè**, a belvedere on top of a cliff with splendid views. A path breaks away here to the Furtschellas cablecar, to give an easy alternative return to Sils, while the recommended descent path goes straight ahead, losing height through lush vegetation, then among trees in a series of zigzags that eventually brings you to **Sils Maria**.

Other walks in Val Fex

The following are a small selection of walks in Val Fex.

A pleasant circular route of about 2½hr can be made by walking from Sils Maria to **Fex Crasta** (as per Route 31), then branching right by the church to meet a path which descends to **Isola** beside the Silsersee. From Isola to Sils Maria simply follow the lakeside path to the north-eastern end of the lake, where you then continue across meadows to the village.

The west wall of the valley slopes upward from just above Isola to the summits of Piz Salatschina, Piz Led, Piz Güz and Piz Fora. The northern end of this rising crest, known as **Muott Ota**, makes a splendid viewpoint. The Isola path, mentioned above as starting at Fex Crasta, has another which breaks from it, and this climbs onto Muott Ota without too much effort. Once there follow the ridge southward between Vals Fex and Fedoz. Shortly after crossing the highpoint of 2449m, descend into Val Fex, reaching the valley bed a short distance south of Curtins, then walk back through the valley to reach Sils Maria, making a 4–4½hr tour.

By using the Furtschellas cableway, access is given to a path which ascends the slopes of Piz Corvatsch to reach the **Lej Sgrischus** tarn (2618m). The path then curves away from the tarn's northern end and ascends the little 2689m Piz Chüern, before descending to Sils Maria by one of several routes. This walk will take from 4–5hr, depending on which descent trail is used.

ROUTE 33
Sils Maria (1806m) – Chastè – Sils Baselgia (1799m)

Start	Sils Maria (1806m)
Distance	3.5km (2.2 miles)
Height gain	Negligible
Height loss	Negligible
Grade	1
Time	1½hr
Location	West and northwest of Sils Maria

Sils Maria and Baselgia are separated by a marshy plain drained by two rivers. To the west lies the great Silsersee (Lej da Segl), and projecting into it roughly midway between the two communities is the narrow wooded promontory of Chastè. A footpath circles this (see Route 25), affording as it does some delightful views across and along the lake to its walling mountains. This path is a popular one for it can be enjoyed by young and old alike. There's practically no height to gain, but there are red squirrels scampering among the trees overhead, the scent of pine, the gentle lapping of the wavelets, and the shapely Piz de la Margna casting its reflection in the water. This is a walk to savour early on a summer's morning before a breeze disturbs the lake, or perhaps after dinner one balmy evening when shadows are stretching through the valley and swifts darting low over the water. Then you'll share the stillness with only fishermen gazing at their lines statue-like from a mid-lake rowing boat, but probably have the paths to yourself.

Take the path from Sils Maria which cuts down to the northeastern end of the lake, then bear right and follow the shoreline path (there are several bench seats) towards the **Chastè isthmus**. On coming to a junction turn left, and follow the trail round the edge of the promontory until it brings you back to the junction. Now bear left and walk across the meadows to **Sils Baselgia**.

ROUTE 34
*Sils Maria (1806m) – Crap da
Sass – Silvaplana (1815m)*

Start	Sils Maria (1806m)
Distance	7km (4.3 miles)
Height gain	negligible
Height loss	negligible
Grade	1
Time	2¼hr
Location	Northeast of Sils Maria

Between Sils and Silvaplana the Silvaplanasee (Lej da Silvaplauna) is the second largest of the Engadine lakes and, with the famous Maloja wind being an almost daily occurrence in summer, it's extremely popular with windsurfing and kiteboarding enthusiasts. Like all the main lakes of the valley, shoreline paths provide gentle but scenic walks, and this particular suggestion is a reminder of pleasures to be had without leaving the valley floor.

There are several paths which lead from Sils Maria to the southern end of the lake, so take whichever is most convenient, then wander along the right-hand shoreline

127

where woods of larch and pine come down to the water's edge for much of the way. At the northern end of the lake the path forks. Take the left branch to cut across meadows to the distinctive building of **Crap da Sass** where you come onto a road linking Surlej with Silvaplana. Bear left and cross between the Silvaplanasee on the left and Champfersee (Lej da Champfer) on the right. Walk up into the heart of **Silvaplana** from where you can catch a bus back to Sils.

ROUTE 35

Sils Maria (Furtschellas: 2313m) – Lej da la Fuorcla (2489m) – Hahnensee (Lej dals Chöds: 2153m) – St Moritz-Bad (1772m)

Start	Sils Maria (Furtschellas: 2313m)
Distance	12km (7.5 miles)
Height gain	176m (577ft)
Height loss	717m (2352ft)
Grade	2
Time	4hr
Location	Northeast of Sils Maria

Making a high-level traverse of hillsides below Piz Corvatsch, this route has plenty of variety and a panoramic view of the Engadine lake region that arranges and rearranges itself as the walk progresses. There are pools and small mountain tarns, and refreshments available at Hahnensee, otherwise known as Lej dals Chöds. At the end of the walk there are buses by which to return to Sils.

Leave the Furtschellas cablecar station and take the upper path signed to Murtèl and Fuorcla Surlej heading northeast along the hillside, soon twisting up to the pools of Ils Lejins. Beyond the pools, and shortly after crossing a stream, the path slopes downhill to a junction where you bear right. Without going up to the middle station of the Corvatsch cableway (Murtèl), cross into the rather desolate hanging valley below Fuorcla Surlej to reach the little **Lej da la Fuorcla**.

Beyond the tarn take the left-hand path seen cutting across the hillside ahead. This brings you to a more extravagantly vegetated hillside, with shrubs and trees and direct views to the sprawl of St Moritz in the valley ahead. Losing height on a good path, shortly before reaching Hahnensee pause to enjoy the view back towards Sils; it's a very fine prospect of lakes and mountains framed by rich shrubbery. Eventually come to the secluded lake of **Hahnensee** (Lej dals Chöds) with its restaurant offering welcome refreshment.

There's a choice of onward routes. One cuts down to the left to Surlej and Silvaplana; one descends directly to Champfer; while another angles northeastward across the wooded hillside and before long offers several routes down to **St Moritz-Bad**. This is the one to take.

ROUTE 36
Surlej (Murtèl: 2699m) – Fuorcla Surlej
(2755m) – Pontresina (1805m)

Start	Surlej (Murtèl: 2699m)
Distance	13km (8.1 miles)
Height gain	56m (184ft)
Height loss	950m (3117ft)
Grade	2
Time	3½–4hr
Location	Southeast of Silvaplana

One of the classic views of the Upper Engadine region is that which is gained from the vantage point of Fuorcla Surlej, where the magnificent ice-coated peaks of Piz Bernina, Piz Scerscen and Piz Roseg rise abruptly from

Fuorcla Surlej is one of the great Alpine viewpoints, with Piz Bernina (left) and Piz Roseg dominating

the depths of Val Roseg directly opposite. It's a view that adorns many a Swiss calendar, but no amount of familiarity can detract from the grandeur of the scene, and it forms one of the highlights of this walk.

You are recommended to begin by riding the Corvatsch cablecar from Surlej to the middle station at Murtèl, although fit walkers could, of course, add another 2½hr to their day by walking all the way (the route is signed from Surlej). Please note that at the time of writing it was possible to buy an all-in-one ticket (the Rundreise) which covers the cablecar ascent to Murtèl, and the return bus journey from Pontresina *bahnhof* (railway station) to Surlej, thereby making a considerable saving.

Out of the cablecar middle station turn left onto a marked path which descends a little into a stony, barren landscape, then curves right as a broad and easy trail swinging southeastward round a rocky basin below Piz Murtèl. The way passes below a small remnant glacier, and a few minutes before reaching the Fuorcla Surlej saddle, joins another path rising from Hahnensee and Surlej. A few twists then bring the path onto the obvious pass of **Fuorcla Surlej**, about 40–50min from Murtèl. A small tarn, or pool, lies just below, giving reflected views of Piz Bernina and its neighbours across the valley. A few paces to the right stands Berghaus Fuorcla Surlej, where you can obtain refreshment and/or accommodation (Tel 079 791 48 84).

Pass in front of the *berghaus* and descend for 5min to where the path forks. Here you take the left branch (the right fork goes to the Coaz Hut) where the sign suggests a rather generous 1¼hr to Val Roseg, and 3hr to Pontresina. The descent to Val Roseg enjoys consistently fine views. The path is clear and well trodden; it visits two alps on the way (Margun Surovel at 2461m, and the lower Alp Surovel at 2250m), and reaches the valley floor at 1999m by **Hotel Roseggletscher** (Tel 081 842 64 45 www.rosegg-letscher.ch) about 1hr from Fuorcla Surlej.

A track now heads down-valley to Pontresina, soon crossing the glacial stream of **Ova da Roseg** on a bridge, where it then turns left. Here you have a choice of either following the track/dirt road all the way (there are footpath short cuts), or keeping to the right bank of the stream where an alternative path weaves a course through larch woods. Both routes emerge from Val Roseg near **Pontresina** railway station, where you can catch a bus back to Surlej or one of the Engadine villages that lie between Pontresina and Silvaplana.

ROUTE 37

Surlej (Murtèl: 2699m) – Fuorcla Surlej (2755m) – Coaz Hut (2610m)

Start	Surlej (Murtèl: 2699m)
Distance	8km (5 miles)
Height gain	56m (184ft)
Height loss	145m (476ft)
Grade	2
Time	3hr
Location	Southeast of Silvaplana

Set at the head of Val Roseg, the Coaz Hut (Chamanna Coaz) makes a splendid destination for a walk. This is one of the very best approach routes, for it has exquisite high mountain views to enjoy all the way from Fuorcla Surlej, and a path that makes no great demands. As with the previous walk, the recommendation is to take the Corvatsch cable car from Surlej to the Murtèl middle station, and begin the walk there. Note there's a bus which links Pontresina station with Surlej, should it be your intention to descend from the hut through Val Roseg.

Follow directions given under Route 36 as far as the **Fuorcla Surlej** saddle (40–50min), and descend to where the path forks about 5min below Berghaus Fuorcla Surlej. Here you take the right branch, which continues to descend, and about 30min below the saddle the way forks again at a marked junction at 2560m. Ignore the left-hand option and continue ahead, and 15min later reach the junction with a trail that goes to Alp Ota and then descends into the **Val Roseg**. Once again keep ahead.

The way now rises a little with the Sella peaks and glaciers that enclose the head of the valley looking magnificent ahead. The Italian border runs along the ridge crest, which is punctuated by a series of small peaks down whose north flank cascade icefalls that spawn the Vadrets da Roseg and la Sella. The Coaz Hut will be found on the left bank of the former.

Come to another path junction, about 1hr 15min from Fuorcla Surlej. This offers the most logical way down into Val Roseg from the Coaz Hut and is recommended for the return. From this point on, the hut may be seen perched on a great slab of rock on the moraine wall southeast of here. The path contours towards the head of the valley, picks a way among rocks and boulders, and reaches the 16-sided **Coaz Hut** about 3hr from the Murtèl cablecar station. ▶

See Route 54 for a descent to Pontresina. For approach routes to the Coaz Hut from Pontresina, see Routes 52 and 53.

At the beginning of the season the Coaz Hut may be half-buried in snow

Approaching the Coaz Hut from Fuorcla Surlej the glacier-clad headwall of Val Roseg is on show for much of the way

COAZ HUT

Chamanna Coaz (2610m) is a curiously shaped building, but its situation could scarcely be more dramatic, with a glacial backdrop and a long view north along the extent of Val Roseg to a hint of Pontresina in the distance. Icefalls hang nearby, while almost 500m below lies the post-glacial Lej da Vadret (the Glacier Lake). Owned by the Rätia section of the SAC, the hut has 80 places and is staffed at Easter, Whitsun, and from end June to October. For reservations Tel 081 842 62 78 www.coaz.ch.

ROUTE 38

Silvaplana (1815m) – Lej da la Tscheppa (2616m) – Silvaplana

Start	Silvaplana (1815m)
Distance	9km (5.6 miles)
Height gain	801m (2628ft)
Height loss	801m (2628ft)
Grade	2–3
Time	5hr
Location	West of Silvaplanc

Lying in a stony basin high above the Engadine's left bank, Lej da la Tscheppa is the largest of several tarns that adorn the southern slopes of Piz Polaschin (another lies on the northern side of the Crasta Tscheppa ridge). This circular walk is fairly strenuous, but with plenty of interest and some fine viewpoints that take in Piz de la Margna and Piz Corvatsch. It goes through marmot country, and you're bound to see plenty of these creatures on the walk.

It begins in the main street near Hotel Engiadina where a sign directs the path out of the village and heading left to a junction where you then turn right. Now angling along the hillside above the Ova dal Vallun towards the Julier Pass, the path is part of the long-distance Via Engiadina, but after a while you leave this before it crosses the stream, and break left on a steeply climbing path which uses zigzags to gain height.

In a little over 2hr from Silvaplana you pass the little pools of **Muttaun** (the Lejets da Muttaun) where the gradient is less challenging, and continuing southwestward come to the **Lej da la Tscheppa** in another 30min or so. Another smaller tarn lies a short distance beyond it. This is a semi-barren basin, in direct contrast to the view out across the Engadine, but there's a possibility of sighting ibex on the upper slopes.

The descent path follows the tarn's outflow stream, and zigzags down the steepening hillside until it rejoins the Via Engiadina trail at a four-way junction. Turn left and wander along the wooded hillside back to **Silvaplana**.

ROUTE 39

Silvaplana (1815m) – Lej Marsch (1818m)
– Lej Nair (1864m) – Silvaplana

Start	Silvaplana (1815m)
Distance	5km (3.1 miles)
Height gain	49m (161ft)
Height loss	49m (161ft)
Grade	1
Time	1½hr
Location	Northeast of Silvaplana

This gentle, easy walk is best tackled in the early morning – the earlier the better. With the sun just up on a summer's morning there's a stillness in the air, and as the first part of the walk leads alongside the lake of Champfer (Lej da Champfer) there may well be the flash of trout to disturb the peace. Then into woods where, if you tread quietly, there's every possibility of catching sight of deer or chamois grazing in the clearings. Both tarns of Lej Marsch and Nair are good places to observe animals coming down to drink in the freshness of early morning, and on several occasions I've sat among the shrubbery as both red and roe deer have grazed just a few metres from me.

Cross the bridge leading from Silvaplana to Surlej, and immediately take the path heading left which takes you alongside **Lej da Champfer.** When the lake ends continue ahead beside the River Inn, but then fork right to **Lej Marsch**, a small tarn surrounded by woodland. Ignore the first path on the right, but take the second, which climbs among trees and brings you to the clearing in which you'll find **Lej Nair** with a path on either side. Take the path which goes to the right, and follow this back to the Surlej to **Silvaplana** road.

ROUTE 40

St Moritz (Signal: 2130m) – Alp Suvretta (2211m) – Julier Pass road – Crevasalvas (1941m) – Maloja (1815m)

Start	St Moritz (Signal: 2130m)
Distance	19km (11.8 miles)
Height gain	292m (958ft)
Height loss	613m (2011ft)
Grade	2
Time	5–5½hr
Location	Southwest of St Moritz

Created largely by linking existing footpaths, the Via Engiadina, of which this is but one section, stretches the length of the valley and runs along its left flank throughout. By concentrating on the 19km stretch between St Moritz and Maloja, the best of the Upper Engadine's lake-and-mountain scenery can be fully appreciated. It's a moderately easy ramble on well-graded paths, and with several opportunities to descend to the valley should the weather change during the walk. Please note that once you leave the Signal cablecar station there are no refreshment facilities until you reach Maloja, so take food and drink with you.

The route begins at the midway station of the Signal cableway (*Signalbahn*) which rises from St Moritz-Bad to an altitude of 2130m.

On leaving the cablecar station the signed path heads west and rises steadily round the hillside to enter the valley of Suvretta da San Murezzan, in which you come to **Alp Suvretta** (2211m) about 45min from Signal. Just beyond the alp come to a path junction and turn left, descending first alongside, then crossing the Suvretta

137

stream. The way then angles across the slopes of Piz Albana, keeping to the upper path where it forks, and sloping down to the **Julier Pass road** in 1¾hr.

South of the road the Via Engiadina path cuts round the wooded slopes above Silvaplana with views between the trees of the Lej da Silvaplana below; the lake in summer bright with yachts and sailboards skimming to and fro. The way comes down almost to road level near Sils Baselgia, before rising again through sparse larchwoods. Emerging from the trees cross a patch of marshy pasture to a junction at 1895m. The upper path is signed to Grevasalvas, and this rises under crags to mount a high-point at 2011m from which you look directly down on the lovely alp hamlet.

About 4hr from the start of the walk you come into **Grevasalvas**. Here you turn right on a track that winds uphill between pastures leading to **Blaunca**, a huddle of stone-built chalets and barns at 2037m, reached about 20min from Grevasalvas. From here the way continues

On the Via Engiadina near Grevasalvas (Photo: Jonathan Williams)

as a footpath between more pastureland, with views ahead that show peaks walling the Val Bregaglia. But before long the path begins its descent to **Maloja**, which it reaches in a little over 30min, depending on which of the path options you choose. Once you come onto the road, you will find several halts on the postbus route that leads back down-valley to St Moritz.

ROUTE 41

St Moritz (Signal: 2130m) – Alp Suvretta (2211m) – Pass Suvretta (2615m) – Val Bever – Bever (1708m)

Start	St Moritz (Signal: 2130m)
Distance	21km (13 miles)
Height gain	485m (1591ft)
Height loss	907m (2976ft)
Grade	2–3
Time	5½–6hr
Location	West and north of St Moritz

This long but interesting walk makes a loop round the mountain mass formed by a ridge of minor peaks running from Piz Nair to Piz Ot above both St Moritz and Samedan. North of Piz Nair the country has a remote feel to it, and although the way is not difficult, you'll need settled weather to tackle this particular route. There's a distinct possibility of sighting ibex and/ or chamois in the high country above Val Bever, and in autumn the hillside colours can be spectacular.

Take the cableway from St Moritz-Bad to Signal, and follow directions for Route 40 as far as **Alp Suvretta** (45min). At the path junction turn right to continue heading up through the valley of Suvretta da San Murezzan to reach the little tarn of **Lej Suvretta** just 35m below Pass Suvretta (2615m/2hr).

On the north side of the pass the way descends through the narrow valley of Suvretta da Samedan, which spills into Val Bever at another **Alp Suvretta**, this one lying at an altitude of 2145m, and gained about 1½hr from the pass. The way now curves to the right and soon crosses the Beverin stream, which flows through the valley. A long ridge crest walls the left-hand side of Val Bever, while Piz Ot is the main peak above the right (south) bank. Refreshments are available at Berggasthaus Suvretta at **Alp Spinas** near the Bever-Bergün railway tunnel, from which point you have a choice of either continuing down-valley to Bever on a footpath on the left of the stream, or on a minor road which parallels the railway. In either case you should arrive in **Bever** about 2hr from Alp Suvretta in Val Bever.

For a return to St Moritz take either a train or postbus.

PIZ NAIR CIRCUIT

To the east of Pass Suvretta stands the 3057m **Piz Nair**, which has cable access from Corviglia above St Moritz. A 3½hr circuit of this mountain, crossing both Pass Suvretta and Fuorcla Schlattain north of the summit, can be made from **Corviglia**, while the **Jenatsch Hut** (Chamanna Jenatsch) can be reached in about 3hr from Pass Suvretta by crossing the 2968m **Fuorcla Suvretta** to the west.

ROUTE 42

St Moritz-Bad (1779m) – Piz da l'Ova-Cotschna (2716m)

Start	St Moritz-Bad (1779m)
Distance	4km (2.5 miles) to the summit
Height gain	937m (3074ft)
Grade	2–3
Time	2½–3hr
Location	South of St Moritz-Bad

Looking across the valley from St Moritz the mountain which forms the valley's southeastern wall, and which catches the glow of evening, is Piz Rosatsch (3123m). In effect, Rosatsch is made up of several peaklets that form individual features on the crest of a broad massif. This massif dips at its southern end below Munt Arlas to the saddle of Fuorcla Surlej, and at its northern extremity falls to Val Bernina opposite Pontresina. While the massif has little to interest climbers, it does possess a number of easily accessible points that give entertaining views. From Piz Mezdi (2992m), for example, the Bernina massif is on show; Rosatsch has similar views – albeit a little more extensive than those of Piz Mezdi. But the lesser point of Piz da l'Ova-Cotschna (hardly a peaklet, but a lump below the glacial coombe of Piz Rosatsch) provides a short ascent with features all its own. It's also a splendid belvedere from which to study the area immediately below, and the Engadine stretching away in the distance. Go early in the day and stay alert for a sighting of chamois, deer or marmots.

The path begins behind the French Protestant church near the *Heilbad* in St Moritz-Bad. This is the start of several routes, as the signpost testifies, but the path to take climbs ahead in larch and pine forest, with tight zigzags leading up steeply to gain a main traversing path. Bear left here, and follow this a short distance to another signed junction where you take the upper right-hand option;

the same route as that for Piz Mezdi. On reaching a rib that forms the east wall of the steep little valley through which you've been climbing, continue up until you see a small tarn on the right. The path forks and you cut right to reach the little **Lej da l'Ova-Cotschna**, set in a rocky bowl, then continue up to the viewpoint of **Piz da l'Ova-Cotschna** on the west side to enjoy a splendid overview of the Upper Engadine.

PIZ MEZDI

If you branch left at the trail junction near the tarn, the continuing path climbs to the 2992m summit of Piz Mezdi (4hr from St Moritz-Bad). Across Val Roseg to the south the snowy Bernina massif holds your attention. Allow 3hr for the descent by the same route.

Other walks from St Moritz

Numerous walks are possible from St Moritz (Dorf and Bad), either through the valley or along its walling hillsides accessed by a variety of mechanical means. The following is just a small sample.

A gentle circuit of the **Lej da San Murezzan** (St Moritzersee) makes a popular after-dinner stroll which can be extended by straying along any number of woodland paths.

A short (1¼hr) walk via **Lej da Staz** crosses an area of woodland and meadow to the east of the St Moritz lake, and leads to **Pontresina**. Taken in the early morning or on a summer's evening, there's a distinct possibility of sighting deer. Either return by the same path or take the train or bus.

Above Lej da Staz to the south, **Alp da Staz** makes a worthwhile visit (path from St Moritz-Bad), and there's a continuing path which leads to the viewpoint of **Muottas da Schlarigna** (2306m) on the spur between the Engadine and Val Roseg, but which also overlooks Val Bernina.

On the left bank of the valley above St Moritz-Dorf, the non-technical ascent of **Piz Julier**, an attractive armchair-shaped mountain of 3380m, can be made in 4hr from the Signal cablecar station (3hr for the descent).

UPPER ENGADINE – VAL BERNINA

The unmistakable shape of Piz Palü is seen to best effect from Diavolezza (Photo: Jonathan Williams)

The River Inn's most important tributary in the early stages of its journey through the Upper Engadine is the Flaz, the name given to the river that collects the Bernina massif's glacial drainage. This river, and the valley that carries it, spills into the Engadine at a broad, open flood plain between Celerina and Samedan. Val Bernina cuts back to the southeast, stretching for 18km to the Bernina Pass below Piz Palü. This leads to the highest and most spectacular mountains of the whole Engadine region.

Considerably shorter, and much narrower than the Engadine, Val Bernina nonetheless has tremendous appeal. From the main valley two side glens carve into the southern wall of mountains: the Vals Roseg and Morteratsch. These are glaciated valleys with snowpeaks soaring above them and trails that reward with some of the most exciting views of the area.

At the head of Val Roseg, the glacial Lej Vadret (Glacier Lake) reflects the Sella peaks (Routes 51, 52 and 54)

On the north side of Val Bernina rises a wall of green and grey mountains. There are side glens here too, but they've lost their glaciers. Instead, they boast pastures rich in alpine flowers, with chamois and herds of ibex roaming the upper slopes.

Towards the head of the valley, approaching the Bernina Pass, the landscape takes on sombre colours; there are no trees, and the grass looks tired and almost khaki throughout spring and summer. Winter is heavy and spring arrives late. The pass is at 2328m, while the railway reaches 2253m before spiralling down into Val Poschiavo. You can stand here in May, knee-deep in snow, and gaze down to Poschiavo 1300m below where spring is in the meadows and a peardrop of a lake dazzles Mediterranean blue. Beside you Lago Bianco remains hidden beneath layers of ice.

But turn to the Bernina massif – to Piz Palü, Bellavista, Piz Zupò, Bernina, Roseg and Piz Morteratsch – and there are scenes to compete with any in the Alpine chain. It is these that provide a focus for so many local walks.

MUOTTAS MURAGL WALKS

Overlooking the confluence of the Upper Engadine and Val Bernina midway between Celerina and Pontresina, Muottas Muragl (2453m) is a much-loved vantage point from which to view the Engadine's lake region framed by the Rosatsch and Piz Julier massifs.

Reached from Punt Muragl by a steep funicular inaugurated in 1907, Muottas Muragl has a *berghotel* and restaurant perched 700m above the Samedan basin (Berghotel Muottas Muragl Tel 081 842 82 32 www.muottasmuragl.ch). Behind it stretches Val Muragl, a shallow hanging valley walled by a grassy ridge on the north and a higher crest on the south side, which extends beyond Piz Muragl (3157m) to Piz Languard southeast of the valley's boundary. At the head of the valley, above a small tarn, the Fuorcla Muragl carries a walker's route into the seemingly remote Val Prüna. But it's the incomparable Engadine view that gives Muottas Muragl its fame and appeal. That, and its footpaths. No visit to the Engadine would be complete without sampling at least one of the walks from this classic balcony.

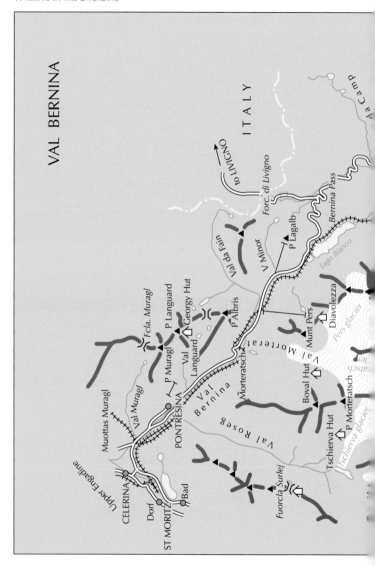

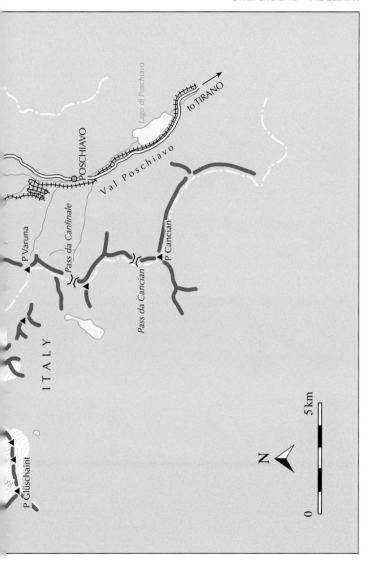

ROUTE 43

Muottas Muragl (2453m) – Lej Muragl
(2715m) – Punt Muragl (1738m)

Start	Muottas Muragl (2453m)
Distance	9km (5.6 miles)
Height gain	262m (869ft)
Height loss	977m (3206ft)
Grade	1–2
Time	3–3½hr
Location	Southeast of Muottas Muragl

Concentrating on the wild attraction of Val Muragl, this route is best made into a full day's outing with, say, a lakeside picnic before descending to Punt Muragl.

Muottas Muragl is a classic vantage point from which to study the Upper Engadine (Photo: Jonathan Williams)

Behind the *berghotel* and funicular station you have a choice of three paths. Take the central trail, signed to Lej Muragl in 1¼hr. This rises a little, then contours along the north flank of Val Muragl heading southeast, before rising again at an easy gradient below the Tschimas ridge. The little Lej Muragl is seen tucked in a stony hollow at the head of the valley, and a little over 1hr after setting out, just above the tarn, the path forks. Ignore the left branch and descend to the western shoreline of **Lej Muragl** (2715m) where there's another junction.

For the descent to Punt Muragl it's necessary to take the right-hand option, but time should first be spent at the lake, so you're recommended to continue to the far end – there are several idyllic picnic sites with fine views down-valley.

To descend, go round the western end of the lake curving south, then southwest, and you'll soon join the tarn's outflow stream which you accompany down-valley. About 25min from the lake the path forks. Continue along a little spur of raised ground, and in another 5min the path forks again. (The left branch crosses the stream and goes to Chamanna Segantini, Alp Languard and Pontresina.) Keep heading down-valley, and you'll shortly come to the solitary building of **Alp Muragl**, or Margun, where the path divides once more. ▸

Should you decide to return to Muottas Muragl from Alp Muragl, take the upper trail where the path divides.

For Punt Muragl go past the alp building and descend steadily through pastureland honeycombed with marmot burrows. Soon after coming to the first trees you reach the three buildings of **Tegia Muragl** (2092m/2hr) which face a superb view. Here the path veers left and crosses the stream to yet another junction. Take the right branch and descend along the left bank of the stream, soon twisting among larchwoods and eventually coming onto a track. After a while a path breaks away from the track on the left, continues to twist among trees, then returns to the track once more. This feeds into a narrow tarmac lane among a few chalets at **Punt Muragl**, and at a signed junction you turn right and wander down to the valley station of the funicular.

ROUTE 44
Muottas Muragl (2453m) – Fuorcla Val Champagna (2806m) – Samedan (1721m)

Start	Muottas Muragl (2453m)
Distance	12km (7.5 miles)
Height gain	353m (1158ft)
Height loss	1085m (3560ft)
Grade	2–3
Time	3½–4hr
Location	Southeast and north of Muottas Muragl

Val Champagna is one of those little-known valleys tucked away from the popular resorts with no particular feature to entice the visitor into their recesses. Thus we have one of the best of all reasons for tackling this route! It begins among the crowds at Muottas Muragl, follows the previous route as far as Lej Muragl, then turns away from well-trodden ways to cross Val Muragl's walling ridge and descends into the narrow, uninhabited glen that eventually spills into the Engadine near the Samedan airfield. Once you leave Muottas Muragl there are no opportunitites for refreshment, so take supplies with you.

Follow directions for Route 43 as far as the path junction just above **Lej Muragl** (1hr), and take the left branch. The way mounts the hillside, swings to the right and crosses **Fuorcla Val Champagna** (2806m) about 15–20min later. Piz Vadret looms above the pass on the right. Now the path slopes down into the head of this tight 'V'-shaped wedge of a valley, and makes a steady descent along the right (north) bank of the stream, reaching the hutments of **Chamanna Val Champagna** (2371m) in a little over 1hr from the pass. Continuing briefly on the right bank, the path soon crosses to the left side of the stream, and the gradient then steepens where the valley is squeezed towards the northwest. Entering woodland you come to a

From a high path above Val Muragl you gain long views of the Engadine lakes

spur and a path junction at **Chantaluf** (1958m) where you join a more direct path descending from Muottas Muragl. Continue to descend, in tight zigzags now, to **Acla Chuoz** (1712m/3¼–3½hr) and another path junction at the foot of the slope. ▶

For Samedan keep to the path which cuts round the northern end of the airfield runway, then returns along its western side before branching across the valley to **Samedan** village. There are bus routes from here which serve Punt Muragl and Pontresina.

To return to Punt Muragl from the path junction at Acla Chuoz, turn left and follow the path through woodland virtually all the way, reaching the valley station of the Muottas Muragl funicular in 1hr.

ROUTE 45

*Muottas Muragl (2453m) – Fuorcla Muragl (2891m)
– Val Prüna – Val Chamuera – La Punt (1697m)*

Start	Muottas Muragl (2453m)
Distance	18km (11 miles)
Height gain	438m (1437ft)
Height loss	1194m (3918ft)
Grade	3
Time	5½–6hr
Location	Southeast of Muottas Muragl

This long cross-country trek makes an exploration of hidden valleys that lie close to the Italian border. Val Prüna is seen from the summit of Piz Languard (see Route 55), and it feeds into the longer Val Chamuera, a valley used as a link between the Engadine and Livigno on the Italian side of the mountains. Although not a difficult route, the walk goes through some remote country with just a handful of alp farms, and is one that requires settled weather to attempt.

Take the path to **Lej Muragl** described in Route 43, continue along the lake's north bank, and at the far end begin the short ascent to the obvious saddle of **Fuorcla Muragl** (2891m), which is reached in about 1½hr. On the eastern side of the pass Val Prüna flows northward from its headwall tucked under Piz Languard, and our descent path is led by waymarks down the slope to meet the valley stream about a third of the way to its confluence with Val Chamuera. Heading down-valley the path crosses the stream and comes to **Alp Prüna** (2270m), about 1½hr from the pass.

North of the alp recross the stream to its left bank and continue down to a second alp, **Serlas** (2017m), at a multi-path junction now in the Val Chamuera. Here you cross to the right bank of the Ova Chamuera and walk

down-valley alongside it, soon crossing the mouth of Val Lavirun and continuing without diversion all the way to Chamues-ch and La Punt. Take the train from **La Punt** back through the Engadine to your base.

After a late spring, little Lej Muragl remains partially frozen (Photo: Jonathan Williams)

A lovely belvedere of a path takes walkers high above Pontresina (Photo: Jonathan Williams)

ROUTE 46

Muottas Muragl (2453m) – Unterer Schafberg (2231m) – Pontresina (1805m)

Start	Muottas Muragl (2453m)
Distance	8km (5 miles)
Height loss	648m (2126ft)
Grade	1
Time	2hr
Location	South of Muotta Muragl

One of the shortest walks from Muottas Muragl, this route is nonetheless highly recommended for its splendid views and the ease of the trail as far as Unterer Schafberg, where there's a mountain restaurant. From there the descent to Pontresina is steep in places, but nowhere is it difficult.

From the path junction above Muottas Muragl take the right-hand option sloping southeastward down the hillside to **Alp Muragl** (Margun), a solitary building in the little Val Muragl. At the path junction ignore the right-hand option, and keep ahead to the stream where you'll find another trail junction at 2368m. Cross the stream by footbridge and branch right onto what becomes a delightful belvedere of a path. Paved in places, it soon rewards with spectacular views, first to the Engadine's west flank, then the string of lakes spread out below.

About 20min from the stream crossing another path breaks away to descend to Tegia Muragl and Punt Muragl, but we continue along the high path, which now looks directly along the Val Roseg. Then, turning a spur, Piz Palü dominates the scene, often framed by pine or larch trees. It's a classic view, and one that is often replicated on local postcards and calendars.

The path junction marked as **Unterer Schafberg** (2231m) is reached about 1hr or so from Muottas Muragl. Turn right here and in a few paces come to the Restaurant Munt de la Bes-cha (refreshments).

ALTERNATIVE ROUTE

The high path which continues from Unterer Schafberg leads to **Alp Languard** in 1hr and is a recommended alternative route which provides more splendid views. From Alp Languard you can either ride the chairlift down to **Pontresina**, or take a much-trodden path which takes almost 1hr to reach the village.

Below the restaurant the path descends the wooded slope in zigzags, and eventually brings you to a junction immediately below a major avalanche defence system. The left-hand path leads to Giarsun (Pontresina's upper end), while the right branch will take you down to **Pontresina Laret** and the lower part of town.

ROUTE 47

*Muottas Muragl (2453m) – Chamanna
Segantini (2731m) – Alp Languard
(2325m) – Pontresina (1805m)*

Start	Muottas Muragl (2453m)
Distance	9km (5.6 miles)
Height gain	278m (912ft)
Height loss	926m (3038ft)
Grade	2
Time	3½hr
Location	Southeast of Muottas Muragl

This is one of the most popular, and more demanding, walks from Muottas Muragl, for the path to Chamanna Segantini (Segantini Hut) – where the painter died in 1899 at the age of 41 – is very steep in places. But the extensive panorama gained from the hut is magnificent, as it is from the continuing trail on the way to Alp Languard.

Follow directions given under Route 46 as far as the stream crossing in **Val Muragl**. Over the footbridge take the left-hand option which climbs the steep hillside with a series of zigzags to turn the ridge-spur of Munt de la Bes-cha (2647m), and continue gaining height to reach the **Chamanna Segantini** (refreshments only Tel 079 681 35 37 www.segantinihuette.ch) about 1½hr from Muottas Muragl. The panorama takes in the Bernina massif, Piz Palü and snowpeaks blocking the head of Val Roseg, and is tremendous, but the view also includes the Upper Engadine lake region and peaks of the Albula Alps.

The way continues across the steep hillside, heading southeast, then forks. One option makes the ascent of the ridge leading to Piz Muragl; another path shortly after descends steeply to Unterer Schafberg (see Route 46) and Pontresina. We continue to the next junction (**Las Sours**)

One of many scenic paths that lead from Muottas
Muragl above Val Bernina (Photo: Jonathan Williams)

Easily reached from Pontresina, Val Roseg is one of the finest in the Engadine region

at 2664m, then descend steeply to a major path junction in **Val Languard**. Turn right and in a few minutes come to Alp Languard and a chairlift link with Pontresina. Refreshments are available at the chairlift station. A clearly signed footpath takes you down to **Pontresina**, which you reach via the church of Ste Maria in the old (upper) part of the village.

EXTENDED VERSION

A longer version of this walk visits **Chamanna Paradis** (Paradishütte) which sits on the ridge-crest on the south side of Val Languard, at 2540m. Once again, like Chamanna Segantini, this has a wonderful outlook and a closer view of the Bernina mountains to the south. To include this hut in the walk, do not descend to Val Languard from the Las Sours junction, but continue across the flank of Piz Muragl before descending below Piz Languard – paths are well signed. Crossing Val Languard a good path angles across the hillside to gain the ridge at the Paradishütte, then continues along the crest before making a steep descent to **Pontresina** – a 6hr walk from Muottas Muragl.

VAL ROSEG WALKS

South of Pontresina, near the mouth of Val Bernina, Val Roseg stretches deep into the mountains to define the western limit of the Bernina massif. It's a beautiful car-free valley with larchwoods in its lower levels, a glacial plain around the midway point, and a wilderness of moraine banks, milky torrents, a lake and fast-receding glaciers towards its head. Its western wall is steep, but with a mid-height terrace of rough pasture; its summits are mostly snow-free, and a walker's route crosses the ridge to the Engadine at Fuorcla Surlej (2755m). The east wall of the valley is very different, for it rises south of Piz Morteratsch to the majestic Piz Bernina (4049m) which, with its consorts Piz Scerscen and Roseg, dominates the valley. But blocking Val Roseg at its southern end, a graceful wall of hanging glaciers sparkles in the sunlight.

The valley boasts two SAC huts (the Tschierva and Coaz), and the Hotel Roseggletscher (22 beds and 100 dormitory places; open year-round except May and November Tel 081 842 64 45 www.roseggletscher.ch). All walks in the valley are rewarding, while horse-drawn carriages convey those disinclined to walk from Pontresina station as far as the hotel.

ROUTE 48
Pontresina (1805m) – Hotel Roseggletscher (1999m)

Start	Pontresina (1805m)
Distance	7km (4.3 miles) one way
Height gain	194m (637ft)
Grade	1
Time	2hr
Location	Southwest of Pontresina

The walk to Hotel Roseggletscher is arguably the most popular outing for visitors to Pontresina, and it will rarely be walked in solitude. But the valley is a delight in every season, and it doesn't matter whether you stroll along it in full summer, or swish through it on langlauf skis in winter; whether you explore it for the first time or the twentieth, there's always something new to see and enjoy. In June the meadows are bright with flowers, in October the larches form a golden avenue; there are squirrels in the woods, chamois on the slopes above, and marmots in the glacial plain near the hotel. And as you emerge at the central part of the valley near the hotel, views are enticing. There are, in fact, two routes through the lower valley; one follows a track/dirt road all the way, the other is a woodland path, which remains on the east side of the river until 5min before reaching the hotel. Both are worth tackling (the track is used by horse-drawn carriages but is forbidden to motorised traffic other than delivery vehicles), so why not make the outward journey by footpath, and return along the track – there are footpath options.

Make your way from Pontresina down the road towards the railway station, but on coming to a car park just before the Bernina garage, take a clearly marked footpath on the left signed to Hotel Roseg. It's a clear path with a number of signed junctions within the first 20min or so, the Roseg path being obvious each time. The way leads through larch and pinewoods with the Ova da Roseg flowing below to your right. Shortly after the track crosses to the east bank, the footpath joins it. The valley suddenly opens out with a stony glacial plain ahead. The track now bears round to the right, crossing a bridge, and a few minutes later reaches **Hotel Rosegggletscher** (accommodation, refreshments). ▸

For a clearer view of Piz Bernina and Piz Roseg, which rise above the left-hand side of the valley, continue a short distance beyond the hotel on the path in Route 51.

ROUTE 49
Pontresina (1805m) – Hotel Roseggletscher (1999m) – Fuorcla Surlej (2755m)

Start	Pontresina (1805m)
Distance	11km (6.8 miles) one way
Height gain	950m (3117ft)
Grade	2
Time	4–4½hr
Location	Southwest of Pontresina

Fuorcla Surlej is an obvious saddle in Val Roseg's west-walling ridge, and a popular crossing point between the valley and the Upper Engadine (see Route 36 for a walk coming from the Engadine). The route is not difficult, although it's moderately strenuous, while a *berghaus* at the pass exploits one of the truly great Alpine views, and makes a suitable destination.

Guided by directions for Route 48, start the day by walking to **Hotel Roseggletscher**. The path to Fuorcla Surlej begins nearby and is clearly signed. Tacking back and forth it climbs out of the valley, then makes a long leftward slant to **Alp Surovel** (2250m). Views grow in extent as you gain height, and are spectacular looking towards the head of the valley. With a few more twists the path angles more steeply across the hillside to the upper alp of **Margun Sarovel**, then slants to the right before cutting back across the upper slope to a junction just 30m below the pass. Take the right branch and a few mins later come to the *berghaus* and a small tarn at the **Fuorcla Surlej**.

Allow 3hr for a return to Pontresina by the same route.

OPTIONAL DESCENTS

Alternatively you could descend on the north side to the middle station of the Corvatsch cablecar (40min) and ride down to **Surlej** in the Upper Engadine; walk all the way to Surlej by clear path in 2½hr, or to **St Moritz** via Hahnensee in 3–3½hr.

BERGHAUS AT FUORCLA SURLEJ

The *berghaus* has accommodation for 55, and is open from July to end September. For reservations Tel 081 842 63 03.

ROUTE 50

*Pontresina (1805m) – Tschierva Hut
(Chamanna da Tschierva: 2583m)*

Start	Pontresina (1805m)
Distance	11km (6.8 miles) one way
Height gain	778m (2553ft)
Grade	2–3
Time	3½hr
Location	South of Pontresina

Some of the finest climbs in the Bernina range (including the famed Biancograt on Piz Bernina) are begun from the Tschierva Hut. As a consequence, and also because it's accessible to non-climbers, it is very popular and often crowded during the high summer season and at weekends. Built on the right-hand lateral moraine of the Tschierva Glacier immediately below Piz Morteratsch, the hut has a magnificent panorama of high peaks and tumbling icefalls. Well-fed marmots can be seen close to the hut, and chamois often stray nearby in the early morning and evening.

Take the much-trodden path or track through the lower Val Roseg from Pontresina (Route 48), but leave it when the track swings right to cross the bridge about 5min from Hotel Roseggletscher. At this point a signed path continues ahead on the east bank of the stream. It crosses the pastures of **Alp Misaun** and soon begins to climb away from sparse slopes of pine and larch towards the moraine wall. The path zigzags away from the alp of Margun-Misaun, and rises through the ablation valley alongside the moraine, before going up onto its crest (gaining dramatic views of a turmoil of ice) which it follows to the hut.

TSCHIERVA HUT

With 100 dormitory places, full meals service and a guardian in residence from end March to mid-May, and from mid-June to mid-October, Chamanna da Tschierva belongs to the Bernina section of the SAC. For reservations Tel 081 842 63 91 www.tschierva.ch

ROUTE 51

Pontresina (1805) – Lej da Vadret (2160m)

Start	Pontresina (1805m)
Distance	11km (6.8 miles) one way
Height gain	355m (1165ft)
Grade	2
Time	3½hr
Location	Southwest of Pontresina

Almost at the head of Val Roseg, beyond the big moraine wall of the Tschierva Glacier which threatens to divide the valley in two, lies the milky glacial lake of Lej da Vadret below the confluence of the Sella and Roseg glaciers. A short distance along the lake's west bank a small freshwater pool lies among low-growing shrubs, with a bench seat placed beside it. It's a charming site with a fabulous view beyond the lake's flotilla of icefloes to the glaciers that coat the valley's headwall. The scene is

sublime, and the walk to it both visually rewarding and educational, in that it unfolds the story of the glaciers that moulded the valley. Although it forms a large part of an approach to the Coaz Hut, it is treated to a route of its own in order to entice walkers who might otherwise be deterred from going as far as the hut.

Follow Route 48 from Pontresina to **Hotel Roseggletscher**, then take the continuing path (signed to Chamanna Coaz) which leaves the hotel along its left-hand side. It hugs the right flank of the valley and before long comes to a small hut at 2022m – **Alp Ota Suot**. Views from here are very fine of Piz Bernina and Roseg across the valley. Ignore the path which branches right here and continue up-valley across scant grassland sliced with streams; the views becoming better and more dramatic with almost every step.

With a big lateral moraine appearing to block progress, the path rises and crosses just to the right of where the glacial torrent from the upper valley has cut a way through. Now you enter the upper valley and wander across a little glacial plain, beyond which you reach the northern end of **Lej da Vadret**. Keep to the western (right-hand) side, and about 10min later you will come to the freshwater pool and bench seat mentioned above. Unless you intend visiting the Coaz Hut, there's no point walking beyond this point, as views don't get any better than this.

Allow at least 2½hr to return to Pontresina.

ROUTE 52

Pontresina (1805m) – Coaz Hut
(Chamanna Coaz: 2610m)

Start	Pontresina (1805m)
Distance	14km (8.7 miles) one way
Height gain	805m (2641ft)
Grade	3
Time	4½hr
Location	Southwest of Pontresina

Perhaps the least-used of the three approach routes to the Coaz Hut (described as Routes 37, 52 and 53), this is perhaps the most scenically varied. It is, in fact, a continuation of Route 51, from which the way becomes much steeper and more strenuous. The Coaz Hut itself enjoys a dramatic location in full view of magnificent glaciers and icefalls.

Follow Route 51 to **Lej da Vadret** and continue along the west bank of the lake until the path starts to climb the steep, rough slope of old moraine. The angle eases above the moraine crest, then steepens once more to gain a broad high shelf of hillside where you join another path coming from Fuorcla Surlej and Alp Ota.

The hut can be seen quite clearly against the valley's headwall, about 30min from here. Bear left on an easy contour, then curving left come to **Chamanna Coaz** on its promontory of rock.

Lej Vadret and Val Roseg; the view from the Coaz Hut (Photo: Jonathan Williams)

COAZ HUT

Chamanna Coaz is owned by the SAC's Rätia section, and is staffed from March to mid-May, and from mid-June to the beginning of October. It has 80 places and a full meals service. Behind the hut there's a cascade of ice, while the view down-valley looks beyond the Lej da Vadret all the way to Pontresina. For reservations Tel 081 842 62 78 www.coaz.ch.

ROUTE 53

Pontresina (1805m) – Alp Ota
(2257m) – Coaz Hut (2610m)

Start	Pontresina (1805m)
Distance	14km (8.7 miles) one way
Height gain	805m (2641ft)
Grade	3
Time	4½hr
Location	Southwest of Pontresina

Rather less strenuous than Route 52, this walk is the more popular approach to the Coaz Hut from Pontresina.

Take Route 48 from Pontresina to **Hotel Roseggletscher**, and continue from there along the path described in Route 51 as far as the little hut of **Alp Ota Suot** (2022m). A few paces beyond the hut slant right when the path forks, and head gently up the hillside to the building shown on the map as **Margun da l'Alp Ota** (2257m). The way continues across the Alp Ota pastures, and after about 3hr comes to a junction at 2569m, meeting the path from Fuorcla Surlej (Route 37). Heading south the way rises a little across the pastures with the head of the valley dazzling, its snowfields and glaciers in contrast to a foreground of rock-pocked grassland. About 30min after joining the Fuorcla Surlej trail, there's another junction – the left branch descends to Lej da Vadret. Keep ahead and the path soon curves leftward on the final approach to the hut.

The Sella peaks block the head of Val Roseg (Photo: Jonathan Williams)

ROUTE 54

*Coaz Hut (2610m) – Lej da Vadret
(2160m) – Pontresina (1805m)*

Start	Coaz Hut (2610m)
Distance	14km (8.7 miles)
Height loss	805m (2641ft)
Grade	2–3
Time	3¾–4hr
Location	Northeast of the Coaz Hut

This is the most direct and varied route of descent to Pontresina. It's a splendid walk, wild in its early stages, romantic in the lower valley. It was described in ascent as Route 52.

From the hut retrace the approach route for 20–25min where you come to the first path junction. Here you take the right branch, which descends steeply at first, twisting among rocks, then easing across a more gentle grassy area. The angle then steepens again as you descend a rocky hillside with marmot burrows everywhere. Briefly the path eases once more across a natural terrace, then descends among rocks and small boulders – views are magnificent almost every step of the way.

At the foot of the slope the path brings you alongside the milky, silt-laden **Lej da Vadret** (ice-flows adrift in the water) at the snout-end of the Roseg Glacier. Shortly before you reach the northern end of the lake there's a charming spot with a small freshwater pool with a seat beside it, and low-growing shrubs nearby.

Beyond the lake you gain impressive views up to Piz Bernina, Scerscen and Roseg, then cross a small grassy plain and come to the left-hand lateral moraine of the **Tschierva Glacier** (Vadret da Tschierva). The glacial stream from the Roseg and Sella glaciers has cut its way through this moraine wall, while the path crosses and descends the moraine to the next level of valley left of the stream.

About 2hr from the Coaz Hut come to **Hotel Roseggletscher** (1999m, accommodation, refreshments) at the head of the track/dirt road which leads to Pontresina. Follow this down-valley. Shortly after crossing a bridge over the Roseg stream you have a choice of either remaining on the track all the way to Pontresina railway station, or of taking a footpath which remains on the right bank of the stream and weaves a way among larchwoods to the mouth of the valley. In either case you will reach **Pontresina** station in another 1½–1¾hr.

Other Val Roseg walks

All the main walks in Val Roseg have been described, although there are plenty of opportunities for making shorter there-and-back walks and loop trips within the lower valley, and more challenging walks in the upper valley by linking routes already described.

From **Hotel Roseggletscher**, for example, one could take Route 49 to the **Fuorcla Surlej**, then return to the valley by following Route 37 as far as the path junction at 2569m, where you then descend to the hotel by way of **Alp Ota**.

Another route links the **Coaz Hut** path with the **Tschierva Hut** by going up the ablation valley alongside the left-bank lateral moraine of the Tschierva Glacier to about 2500m, then crossing a fairly level part of the glacier to the hut. This is not for general tourists, however, and normal precautions should be taken.

And finally, the 2499m spur of **Muottas da Puntraschigna** forms the eastern gateway to Val Roseg, and this can be reached by a walk of about 2½hr.

ROUTE 55
Pontresina (1805m) – Piz Languard (3262m)

Start	Pontresina (1805m)
Distance	5km (3.1 miles) one way
Height gain	1457m (4780ft)
Grade	2–3
Time	3½–4hr
Location	East of Pontresina

A justifiably famous vantage point, for generations the ascent of Piz Languard has been a favourite with visitors to Pontresina. It's one of the easiest ascents of a 3000m mountain in this corner of the Alps, and the summit view is so extensive as to have been afforded a pull-out panorama in the early Baedeker guides. That view (according to Baedeker) extends southwest to Monte Rosa, southeast to the Adamello, northwest to the Tödi, and northeast to the Zugspitze. However, it is the nearer view of the Bernina group across the valley to the south that focuses one's attention; that, and the Engadine lake region to the southwest. A short distance below the summit the Georgy Hut provides refreshment and limited overnight accommodation (reservation essential), and for those who want the experience, is perfectly placed to capture the magic of sunset and sunrise over the Alps. A herd of ibex roams the neighbourhood, including the upper slopes of the mountain, and may be seen on the ascent.

The church of Santa Maria is one of Pontresina's oldest buildings; original 12th-century tower and, inside, 13th- and 15th-century wall paintings. Next door is an old tower, La Spaniola.

From the main street in Pontresina, make your way to the Alp Languard chairlift station. (Use of the chairlift will reduce the ascent time by about 1hr.) To walk all the way, leave the chairlift station on your left and continue along the street (Cruscheda) as far as Pension Hauser where you turn left. Walking uphill you soon reach the little church of Santa Maria and take the path rising along its left-hand side. ◄

At first a broad stony path, it becomes a narrower trail as it twists up steep grass slopes, and in about 45min comes to the building of **Alp Languard** set on a shelf of grassland with fine views of Piz Palü and Bellavista. Just above the building there's a junction of paths where you veer left, and 5min later take the right branch at another junction. Shortly after you will arrive at the Alp Languard chairlift station and restaurant (2326m/1hr refreshments).

Riding the chairlift to Alp Languard reduces the climb to Piz Languard by about an hour (Photo: Jonathan Williams)

Piz Languard rises to the east, and you may be able to detect a flag flying a short way below the summit to mark the position of the Georgy Hut. The signed path now goes along the upper left-hand side of the rather bleak little hanging valley of Val Languard (a lower path leads to Chamanna Paradis and Lej Languard). Keeping above the valley the trail twists uphill, then veers right to cross a stony basin on the way towards Piz Languard's southern arête, and comes to a junction with the so-called *Steinbockweg* which branches left to the Segantini Hut. Continuing, in another 10min (at 2805m) yet another path breaks to the right for Lej Languard and Chamanna Paradis.

The path now begins to ascend the ridge, and a few minutes later (for the last time) another trail cuts off to the right, while ours twists more steeply up the ridge, and in about 3–3¼hr reaches the **Georgy Hut** (3186m accommodation, refreshments).

GEORGY HUT

Privately owned, Chamanna Georgy (or Berghaus Languard) stands just 76m below Piz Languard's summit. It has 20 dormitory places, and is manned from about mid-June to mid-October. For reservations Tel 081 833 65 65. There's been a hut here for more than 100 years.

Above the hut the path steepens over rocks, but with excellent waymarking to guide you, and in another 15min you reach the summit with its large metal trig point. Given favourable conditions, the view is tremendous. While such distant summits as Monte Rosa are not exactly prominent, they belong to a great sea of peaks which fill a 360° panorama. More notable local mountains are Piz Palü, Piz Zupò, Bellavista, Piz Bernina, Morteratsch, Roseg and Piz Tschierva giving prominence to the southerly view, while Piz Kesch (NNW) and sharply pointed Piz Linard (NNE) stand out elsewhere.

Allow about 2½hr for the descent to Pontresina by the same path.

ROUTE 56

*Pontresina (1805m) – Crasta Languard
– Fuorcla Pischa (2837m) – Val da
Fain – Bernina Suot (2046m)*

Start	Pontresina (1805m)
Distance	12.5km (7.8 miles)
Height gain	1032m (3386ft)
Height loss	791m (2595ft)
Grade	3
Time	6hr
Location	Southeast of Pontresina

Crossing Piz Languard's southeast ridge, this fairly long tour could be adopted as an alternative route of descent from Languard's summit. Crossing the ridge at the Fuorcla Pischa, the way descends into the wild Val da Fain and returns to Val Bernina with a glorious direct view of Piz Palü. There's the strong possibility of sighting chamois, ibex and marmots, while Val da Fain is noted for its abundant alpine flora.

Follow directions for Route 55 to a point on Piz Languard's southern arête where the signed path forks for the last time. The continuing ascent route which leads to the Georgy Hut climbs steeply left, but we branch right on an airy path that cuts across the head of Val Languard just below the **Crasta Languard**. It forks again above Lej Languard, but we continue ahead to reach the col of **Fuorcla Pischa** about 3½hr from Pontresina.

The eastern side of the col is wild and somewhat desolate, with bare rocks and pools, and the Lej da la Pischa lying below. One path descends to that tarn, but we take the right branch and angle round the hillside along the east flank of Piz Albris, inhabited by a large herd of ibex. In another 30min or so from Fuorcla Pischa cross a point known as Fuorcla S-chüdella (2790m – unmarked on the map), then descend steeply to the left of the outflow stream from the Pischa tarn, with the distinctive Piz Alv rising directly ahead.

Reaching a track in **Val da Fain**, turn right and follow this down-valley with Piz Palü seen in all its glory across Val Bernina to the south. Emerge into Val Bernina a short distance from the Diavolezza cablecar station and turn right to reach Berggasthaus Berninahaus (30 beds, 34 dormitory places; Tel 081 842 64 05 e-mail: berggasthaus@berninahaus.ch website: www.bern-inahaus.ch) and the railway station of **Bernina Suot** for a return to Pontresina.

VAL DA FAIN

Val da Fain (the Heutal, or Val Torta) is not only known for its colony of marmots, but is one of the finest in the whole Engadine region for alpine flowers. It is noted among botanists, many of whom come here specifically to study this valley and the neighbouring Val Minor on the other side of Piz Alv. The list of special plants includes: the lovely pale yellow *Sempervivum wulfenii*, the beaked lousewort (*Pedicularis rostratospicata*), the delicate Triglav gentian (*Gentiana terglouensis*), and the hybrid *Primula x berninae* (*hirsuta x latifolia*).

Other walks in Val da Fain
The following walks may be of particular interest to alpine flower enthusiasts.

A walk through the length of Val da Fain, from **Bernina Suot** to **Alp la Stretta** (2427m/1hr 10min) and up to the 2476m **Pass la Stretta** (2hr) on the Swiss/Italian border. Allow 1½hr for the return to Bernina Suot.

A more strenuous route branches left at **Alp la Stretta** to climb the northerly hillside to **Fuorcla Chamuera** (2790m), and from there descends to **Alp Prünella** at the confluence of Val Chamuera and Val Prünella. Either descend through Val Chamuera to **Chamues-ch** and **La Punt**, or go up-valley through Val Prünella to cross the 2834m **Fuorcla Tschüffer** to Lej da la Pischa, above which you join the path used by Route 56 to return to **Val da Fain**.

ROUTE 57
Pontresina (Alp Languard: 2326m)
– Chamanna Paradis (2540m)

Start	Pontresina (Alp Languard: 2326m)
Distance	2km (1.2 miles) one way
Height gain	214m (702ft)
Grade	1–2
Time	1hr
Location	Southeast of Pontresina

Given just half a day to spend in relaxing surroundings with a wonderful view, this short trip is worth considering. Chamanna Paradis (the Paradis Hut) is set on a green ridge with a direct view along Val Morteratsch to the snow giants of the Bernina massif.

Take the chairlift to **Alp Languard** and from there choose one of two paths. The first descends into Val Languard, then climbs the opposite flank directly to the ridge, then wanders along the crest heading southeast to reach the **Chamanna Paradis**. The other descends into Val Languard further upstream towards Piz Languard, crosses the stream and continues a short way up-valley to meet a crossing path. Here you turn right to angle up the slope directly to **Chamanna Paradis**. Refreshments are available there on the most idyllic of vantage points. Val Bernina lies 700m below, but all eyes are on the great wall of ice-clad mountains opposite.

ROUTE 58

Pontresina (1805m) – Morteratsch – Boval
Hut (Chamanna da Boval: 2495m)

Start	Pontresina (1805m)
Distance	10.5km (6.5 miles) one way
Height gain	690m (2264ft)
Grade	2
Time	3½hr
Location	Southeast of Pontresina

After wandering in Val Roseg, this must be the next most popular excursion from Pontresina – or at least, the walk from Morteratsch (railway station and large car park) which is 1½hr shorter. The Boval Hut has an outlook of impressive beauty, while the route to it along Val Morteratsch is one of increasing visual drama. One of the dominant features is the Morteratsch Glacier. Formed among the headwall of lofty peaks that almost reach 4000m, great billows and ice cliffs are plastered across the face of the mountains. Near the Boval Hut the main glacier is joined by the Pers Glacier whose birthplace is on the uppermost slopes of Piz Palü. Where the two icefields join forces, there stands the rocky island of Isla Persa, below which the glacier noses down the long Morteratsch Valley. However, the Morteratsch Glacier has been receding for decades, and from its snout down to the valley's entrance a series of marker posts indicates the rate of this recession. If you have time, it would be worth walking along the lower track from Morteratsch station as far as the glacial snout, to see what this recession is about.

The path to Morteratsch begins on the Val Roseg side of the valley opposite Pontresina, where a signed route takes you through light woodland to the Surovas station. From here the path keeps company with the railway line for a while, edging larch- and pinewoods. But as you make progress, so the way branches to the right and gains height to avoid an unnecessary detour to Hotel

Val Morteratsch, with Piz Palü left, and Piz Bernina on the right

Morteratsch and the railway station at the mouth of Val Morteratsch. Rising through woods, about 2hr from the start, come to a junction of paths, where the left branch is the direct route from Morteratsch.

SHORTER ROUTE FROM MORTERATSCH

Saving about 1½hr, the walk could begin by taking the train to **Morteratsch station**. There's a hotel next to it, the 2-star Hotel Morteratsch (beds and dormitory accommodation; open all-year except May and November; (Tel 081 842 63 13 e-mail: mail@morteratsch.ch website: www.morteratsch.ch). Take the broad track which strikes south from the station on the right-hand side of a glacial torrent, and in 1min branch right on a path which soon twists uphill among larch, pine and alpenrose. After about 10min come to an open viewpoint which shows the great snowy range to the south. In another 10min join the trail from Pontresina.

Shortly after the Chünetta turning (see sidebar) another path breaks left this time, and descends to the broad track which runs between Morteratsch station and the glacier. Should you be interested in plotting the course of glacial recession, it would be worth taking this path on return from the Boval Hut. ▸

Continuing up-valley views grow in extent to include (from left to right) Piz Cambrena, all three peaks of Piz Palü, the lofty Bellavista crest, Crast'Agüzza, Piz Bernina and Piz Morteratsch. Some of the route traces a crest of lateral moraine; in other places the way deserts the moraine for the ablation trough – note that the route is not permanent, but depends on the stability of the moraine wall. Watch for painted arrows that indicate the current route.

Just 2min after the junction an alternative path breaks away right to reach a fine vantage point: Chünetta (2083m). This 5min detour is worthwhile (although there are similar views en route to the hut).

The path to the Boval Hut makes a very fine walk

Climbing steadily, the way eventually turns a rocky corner and twists up a final slope to reach the **Boval Hut** which enjoys a splendid location with the famed Biancograt on Piz Bernina showing its icy arête above to the south. Thereafter wave upon wave of snowpeaks curve eastward to Piz Cambrena.

Allow 1¼hr for the return to Morteratsch; 2¼hr to Pontresina.

BOVAL HUT

Chamanna da Boval is one of the busiest of Swiss Alpine Club huts. It has 90 places, and a full meals service when manned. This is from late March to mid-May, and from mid-June to mid-October. For reservations Tel 081 842 64 03. The first Boval Hut was built in 1877, but destroyed by avalanche in 1906. The present hut – which replaced it – was built by the Bernina section of the SAC in 1913.

ROUTE 59

Bernina Suot (2046m) – Berghaus Diavolezza (2973m)

Start	Bernina Suot (2046m)
Distance	6km (3.7 miles) one way
Height gain	927m (3041ft)
Grade	2
Time	3hr
Location	Southeast of Pontresina

Known to tens of thousands of skiers and summer visitors, thanks to easy access by cablecar, the panorama from Berghaus Diavolezza is one of the finest, not just in the Engadine region, but in all the Alps. It's a view initially dominated by the great triple-buttressed gem of Piz Palü, seen full on. But it also spreads along the Bellavista ridge to incorporate Piz Bernina and Piz Morteratsch above glaciers that cascade in waves of ice and snow. Be there in the early morning to capture the dye of sunrise melting the snows to a rose-tinted wash; or in the evening as shadows distort the icefalls; or perhaps during the night with stars overhead and a moon dusting the summits with its cold lunar beams. (It's not bad in the middle of the day, either!)

Few walk the track and trail to Diavolezza out of choice; the cablecar option is too tempting for that. But for those who would shun mechanical aid, and prefer to earn their views through a bit of effort, the following route is offered. It's not one of the best in the book, but it has its pleasures, and you will certainly enjoy the views when you arrive.

From the Bernina Suot station walk up the road a short distance towards the Diavolezza cablecar station and car park, until a sign on the right sends a path snaking up the hillside to join a broad track which is the main route from the cablecar station.

The track rises beneath the cableway, enters a hanging valley, and after a while approaches **Lej Diavolezza**, a cold green tarn in a stony basin. Leave the track here and take a narrower path on the left which goes up onto the shoulder of Sass Queder, and gaining height with zigzags gives views down to the Bernina Pass with the hint of Val Poschiavo below. The way now turns into a high coombe packed with *névé*, and climbs to the left of this towards a ski-tow installation. On gaining the head of the slope turn right, climb a short ladder, then follow waymarks along the curving ridge to reach **Berghaus Diavolezza**.

DIRECT ROUTE FROM DIAVOLEZZA CABLECAR STATION

Take the broad track which leaves the car park immediately west of the cablecar station, and heads up the slope a little to the right of the cableway. This is soon joined by the route from Bernina Suot.

A view onto the upper reaches of Val Bernina is to be had from the Diavolezza path (Photo: Jonathan Williams)

BERGHAUS DIAVOLEZZA

This is privately owned with a large restaurant whose windows face directly out at Piz Palü. It has hotel-standard rooms and dormitory accommodation; open throughout the year except mid-October to end November. For reservations Tel 081 842 62 05 (e-mail: berghausdiavolezza@bluewin.ch website: www.diavolezza.ch).

ALTERNATIVE ROUTE TO THE BERNINA PASS

The path which goes onto the shoulder of **Sass Queder** above Lej Diavolezza offers an alternative route by cutting southeast into the Val d'Arlas, and continues from there by descending to Lej Pitschen, Lej Nair and Lago Bianco at the **Bernina Pass** – about 1hr from Lej Diavolezza. (Return by train from the pass.)

ROUTE 60
Berghaus Diavolezza (2973m) – Munt Pers (3207m)

Start	Berghaus Diavolezza (2973m)
Distance	2km (1.2 miles) one way
Height gain	234m (768ft)
Grade	1–2
Time	1¼hr
Location	Northwest of Diavolezza

Munt Pers is the insignificant summit that rises northwest of Berghaus Diavolezza, whose panoramic view is truly spectacular. It provides a 360° vista of snowpeak and deep green valley, looks out to far-off mountains of Switzerland, Italy and Austria, and has become a popular short excursion from Diavolezza.

A visit to Berghaus Diavolezza is a 'must' for all visitors to the Engadine region, whether by path or by cablecar. Close views of the Bernina massif are stunning (Photo: Jonathan Williams)

An equally impressive viewpoint is Piz Trovat (3146m), about 1hr southeast of Berghaus Diavolezza. Follow the ridge round towards the Sass Queder ski tow, then fork right.

The path is easy and well defined, leading from the *berghaus* along the left-hand side of the crest, before veering south (left) to avoid the crags of Pt 3141m, then ascending a few zigzags to gain the summit of Munt Pers. ◄

ROUTE 61

Berghaus Diavolezza (2973m) –
Boval Hut (Chamanna da Boval:
2495m) – Morteratsch (1896m)

Start	Berghaus Diavolezza (2973m)
Distance	10km (6.2 miles)
Height loss	1077m (3534ft)
Grade	3 (involves glacier crossing; guides available)
Time	3½–4hr
Location	West and northwest of Diavolezza

Throughout the summer, weather permitting, this classic route – which crosses the Pers and Morteratsch glaciers – is led by professional guides as a way of safely introducing walkers to the beauty and intricacies of the glacier world. For those already experienced in glacier crossing, and with the necessary equipment, the route is not at all difficult. The route described here descends from Berghaus Diavolezza to the Pers Glacier, crosses to the rocks of Isla Persa, then makes a traverse of the Morteratsch Glacier to the Boval Hut. From there it's a straightforward walk along a good path to the Morteratsch station. The guided route usually avoids the Boval Hut and continues down the length of the glacier.

GUIDE INFORMATION

At the time of writing, this route was guided on Sunday, Tuesday, Wednesday and Friday from mid-June to early July, and from September to mid-October; and daily from early July to the first week of September. For more information contact the Schweizer Bergsteigerschule at the tourist office in Pontresina (Tel 081 838 83 33 e-mail: info@bergsteiger-pontresina.ch).

The **Pers Glacier** lies about 250m below Berghaus Diavolezza, and the path to take descends steeply to it, coming onto the ice where the glacier is reasonably level and with few crevasses. In a normal summer there will be ample tracks to show the way across to the rocky mound of **Ilsa Persa** (1hr), where a narrow path leads across grassy ledges and down slabs and rocks heading west, before descending to an ablation valley containing a small tarn (**Lej da l'Isla**). Guided by cairns the route skirts this to the south and comes to the edge of the **Morteratsch Glacier**. Crossing this (usually dry) section of glacier should not be unduly troublesome, for there will invariably be sufficient marks from previous climbers and trekkers making a reasonable trail. If not, swing south of west, keeping alert for crevasses near the centre of the glacier, then veer northwestwards to gain the moraine bank. A path climbs along this to reach the **Boval Hut** (2495m) in about 2½–3hr.

BOVAL HUT

Chamanna da Boval is owned by the Bernina section of the SAC, and is manned from late March to mid-May, and from mid-June to mid-October. It has 90 dormitory places and full meals service. For reservations Tel 081 842 64 03 – see Route 58.

Take the descending path from the hut, which curves along the moraine slope above the Morteratsch Glacier, and follow this heading north; sometimes on the moraine crest, sometimes in the ablation valley, and after about 1¼hr from Chamanna da Boval it brings you to **Morteratsch** station.

With Piz Palü dominating the scene, the view from Diavolezza encompasses the full expanse of the Bernina massif (Photo: Jonathan Williams)

Other walks in Val Bernina
There will be no shortage of ideas for additional outings in Val Bernina and the surrounding area, for a glance at the map will reveal numerous possibilities. A few examples are given below.

A short distance from the Bernina Pass there's the Piz Lagalb cablecar station at Curtinatsch. Piz Lagalb itself is partly moated by the **Val Minger** (another botanical paradise), and an easy walk leads through this past a few pools as far as **Lej Minor** (2361m). It's also perfectly feasible to make a complete circuit of the mountain by continuing beyond the lake.

By riding the cablecar to within a 15min walk of the 2959m summit of **Piz Lagalb**, several routes may be tackled – see the map for options. The summit makes another splendid vantage point, for not only is the nearby Bernina massif on show, but beyond Switzerland's borders you can see Austria's Ötztal Alps, and Italy's Ortler range, while Val Poschiavo lies below to the southeast.

From the **Bernina Pass** a trail leads down to **Alp Grüm** and **Lagh da Palü** (both good places to find alpine flowers), with options for continuing down to **Val Poschiavo** (train back to the Bernina Pass).

On the eastern side of the Bernina Pass road, **Val da Camp** is worth exploring. It's a luxuriously green valley, with woods and meadows, alpine flowers, and lakes near its head. From either **Pozzulasc** (in 2hr) or **Restaurant Sfazù** (1½hr) on the pass road, signed paths lead to Lungacqua and **Rifugio Saoseo** at 1985m (80 dormitory places, manned from mid-February to end April, and from mid-June to mid-October; Tel 081 844 07 66 www.sac-bernina.ch). Nearby, at Alp Camp in the mouth of the tributary Val Mera, dormitory beds are also available at **Ostello Crameri** (Tel 081 844 04 82 e-mail: riservazione@valdicampo.ch). Two lakes to visit here are **Lagh da Saoseo** and the larger **Lagh da Val Viola** in the upper Val Viola. Almost 300m above this last-named lake you could cross into Italy by way of the 2432m **Pass da Val Viola**. A shorter loop trip visits **Plan da Genzana** on the north flank of Val Viola, with a possibility of extending it to Pass da Val Viola. Alternatively, there's a route through **Val Mera** which crosses **Pass da Val Mera** (2671m) into Italy's Valle di Livigno. All are worth exploring.

UPPER ENGADINE –
NORTHERN REGION

Below the wooded sill of St Moritz-Dorf the Engadine suddenly loses height, but then settles in the broad flood plain at its confluence with Val Bernina. Here the valley takes on a very different appearance to that of the upper lake region, running in a straight shaft between mountains that fold away on either side to allow lateral valleys to feed into the parent valley. These mountains conform to a general rule of orderliness. They're wooded almost to mid-height, then grassy slopes lead up to bare crowns. With few exceptions they have little permanent snow, no lengthy glaciers, no wild coombes, bristling ridges or abrupt walls to lure climbers; both mountain and valley alike reveal a gentle face that is not without its charms.

The valley floor is mostly flat, and the Inn has been contained within its bed by concrete walls to hold back the threat of flooding. It's a fertile land whose tributary glens are lush and rich with greenery. In these valleys

The Es-cha Hut, with Piz Kesch and a huge moraine wall towering over it

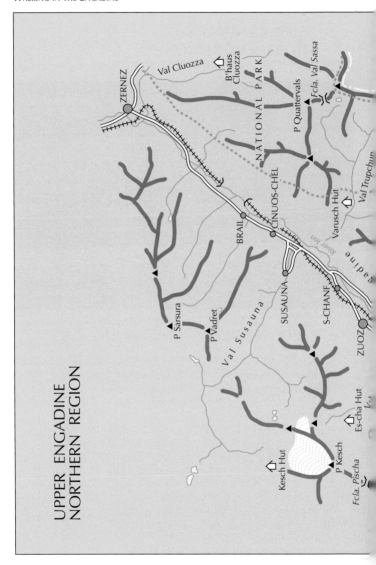

UPPER ENGADINE
NORTHERN REGION

ZERNEZ

Val Cluozza

B'haus Cluozza

Fcla. Val Sassa

P Quattervals

NATIONAL PARK

CINUOS-CHEL

Varusch Hut

Val Trupchun

River Inn

Engadine

BRAIL

SUSAUNA

S-CHANF

ZUOZ

P Sarsura

P Vadret

Val Susauna

Es-cha Hut

Kesch Hut

P Kesch

Fcla. Pischa

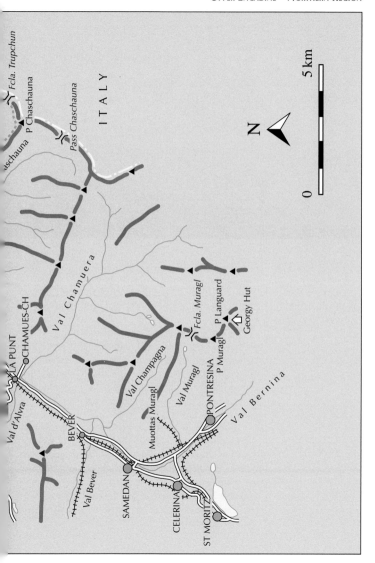

ITALY

N

5 km

0

Fcla. Trupchun

P Chaschauna

Pass Chaschauna

aschauna

Val Chamuera

Fcla. Muragl

P Languard

Georgy Hut

CHAMUES-CH

LA PUNT

Val d'Alvra

Val Champagna

Val Muragl

P Muragl

PONTRESINA

Val Bernina

Muottas Muragl

BEVER

Val Bever

SAMEDAN

CELERINA

ST MORITZ

you can experience a greater sense of solitude and isolation than may be found in the Engadine itself for, caught between Upper Engadine extravagance and Lower Engadine tradition, this is a region largely neglected by mass tourism.

Bypassed by the main road, villages of this northern region have their own brand of charm, especially Madulain, Zuoz and Susauna – tucked away in a pastoral valley 2km from passing traffic. Each one, it seems, has managed to develop at its own pace, and an unhurried appreciation of each will surely reward the discerning visitor.

For mountain interest, the prime focus of attention will be on Piz Kesch, the 3418m undisputed 'king' of the Albula Alps which rises above Madulain and Zuoz. With its classic proportions, shrinking glaciers and massive moraines, a visit to either of its flanks will repay the walker with brisk exercise and rewarding views. But then, much the same could be said of the whole region.

ROUTE 62

Bever (1708m) – Val Bever – Jenatsch
Hut (Chamanna Jenatsch: 2652m)

Start	Bever (1708m)
Distance	16km (9.9 miles) one way
Height gain	944m (3097ft)
Grade	2
Time	5hr
Location	West of Bever

Tucked away in a seemingly remote location between Piz d'Err and Piz Suvretta at the head of Val Bever, Chamanna Jenatsch is used by ski-touring enthusiasts in winter and springtime, and by trekkers embarked upon long mountain tours in summer. Although it can be reached by shorter routes (by taking the cablecar from St Moritz to Piz Nair, then via Fuorcla Suvretta, for example; or from the Julier Pass road at La Veduta and over Col d'Agnel), the long walk through Val Bever, from its wood-guarded discharge into the Engadine to its stony head, makes a very pleasant and uncomplicated approach on a good path for most of the way.

Choose one of the three routes that lead out of Bever into the valley striking west of the village. The central one of these is a minor road that accompanies the railway as far as the station at the entrance to the Bever-Bergün Tunnel at **Spinas** (1hr). The way continues up-valley on the right-hand side of the stream among larchwoods for a while. About 1hr from Spinas the path forks at **Palüd Marscha** (2052m), where the right branch leaves the main trail for a crossing of Fuorcla Crap Alv on the way to the Albula Pass (see Route 63). Our route continues alongside the stream, and crosses to the south side shortly before reaching **Alp Suvretta** (2145m/2½–3hr) where the valley – and the path – forks.

Recross to the north bank of the Beverin stream, and continue to gain height towards the amphitheatre that closes the valley in the southwest. The arc of 3000m mountains that create the cirque wear small remnant glaciers and tiny snowfields which give an impression of greater height than the map would suggest. At last the path deserts the stream to climb northwest towards Piz d'Err, and with a couple of twists brings you to the **Jenatsch Hut**.

Above the hut a curving rim of crags supports the summits of Piz Jenatsch, Piz d'Err, Piz Calderas and Tschima da Flix, with the little glaciers of Calderas and Err clinging to their upper slopes. To the south the crater-like cirque continues with Piz d'Agnel and Piz Surgonda; these too hang on to their last glacial remnants and add a wild appeal to this remote corner.

Allow 3½hr for the return to Bever by the same path.

JENATSCH HUT

Chamanna Jenatsch is owned by the Bernina section of the SAC, and has 60 dormitory places. It's usually manned over the Christmas/New year period, from the end of January to mid-May, and from July to end October. For reservations Tel 081 833 29 29 (e-mail: allegra@chamannajenatsch.ch website: www.chamannajenatsch.ch).

ROUTE 63

*Bever (1708m) – Val Bever – Fuorcla Crap Alv
(2466m) – Albula Pass (2312m) – La Punt (1697m)*

Start	Bever (1708m)
Distance	19km (11.8 miles)
Height gain	758m (2487ft)
Height loss	769m (2523ft)
Grade	3
Time	5½hr
Location	West and north of Bever

Val Bever is walled on its northern side by a long ridge of mountains extending westward from Crasta Mora above Bever. On the northern side of this ridge the Albula road pass links the Engadine with central Graubunden via the splendid village of Bergün. The long loop walk described here crosses the ridge at the Fuorcla Crap Alv, catches a glimpse of Bergün's pasture-lands, and returns to the Engadine roughly by following the course of the Albula road.

Follow directions for Route 62 as far as **Palüd Marscha** (2052m/2hr) where the path forks. Take the right branch and angle up the steep 400m slope to find the breach of **Fuorcla Crap Alv** among the ridge crags. This is gained about 1hr from the path junction. On the northern side of the pass the way curves to the right round the crags, and shortly comes to a group of tarns and tiny pools. The path forks here, with the left branch descending to Crap Alv, while we take the right branch ahead to make an easy descending traverse of grass slopes towards the **Albula Pass**. Cross the road and contour to the pass (refreshments) which is reached in 1hr from the ridge crossing. The continuing path is on the right-hand side of the road, and after passing alongside a lake on the pass itself, it leads without difficulty all the way down to the Engadine at **La Punt**. From there you can take a train back to Bever.

ROUTE 64
La Punt (1697m) – Albula Pass
(2312m) – Bergün (1367m)

Start	La Punt (1697m)
Distance	18km (11.2 miles)
Height gain	615m (2018ft)
Height loss	945m (3101ft)
Grade	2
Time	6hr
Location	West of La Punt

This long but relatively undemanding walk takes you away from the Engadine and down to the charming village of Bergün on the other side of the Albula road pass. Although it follows the course of the road from start to finish, traffic is light and there's some very pleasant scenery to enjoy.

From La Punt a path keeps close company with the Ova d'Alvra stream which drains from the Albula Pass. Gaining height quite steeply in places, it brings you to **Alp Nova (2114m)** in about 1½hr, after which the gradient eases as the valley opens out on the way to the pass. This is reached in 3hr from La Punt. Also known as Pass d'Alvra, the **Albula Pass** has the inevitable hospice where you can obtain refreshments.

The path now crosses to the north side of the road, heading west and descending almost 300m before coming to **Crap Alv** (refreshments). The way recrosses to the left-hand side of the road to visit the tree-rimmed Lai da Palpuogna tarn with paths on both banks, and continues to **Preda** where the railway emerges from its long tunnel (entered at Spinas near Bever) at 1789m. Again refreshments are available here.

TOBOGGAN RUN

In winter Preda is at the head of a famous 5km toboggan run which ends at Bergün. Wooden sleds can be rented at the station, and on reaching Bergün you can return to Preda on the train to repeat the experience *ad nauseam*. Special day tickets are available to encourage several rides, and as the route is lit after dark and trains run late you can get your money's worth! In summer scooters (*trottinettes*) are rented out for a similar downhill run to Bergün.

From Preda to Bergün the path crosses and recrosses the railway several times, until the two part company by the Rugnux Tunnel where the path stays on the left bank of the Alvra Albula stream, while the Rhätische Bahn strikes across the opposite hillside. **Bergün** is reached about 1¼hr after leaving Preda.

Take the train back to La Punt via Bever.

BERGÜN

Bergün makes an attractive base for a few days of a walking holiday, with a variety of routes splaying from it. It's a mostly Romansch-speaking village with sturdy stone houses similar in style and decoration to those of the Lower Engadine. There are several hotels, and a campsite. For details contact the tourist information office: Bergün Ferein, CH-7482 Bergün. Tel 081 407 11 52 e-mail: info@berguen.ch website: www.berguen.ch.

ROUTE 65

La Punt (1697m) – Val Chamuera – Serlas (2017m)

Start	La Punt (1697m)
Distance	7.5km (4.7 miles) one way
Height gain	320m (1050ft)
Grade	2
Time	2hr
Location	Southeast of La Punt

This gentle valley walk leads to an alp at a junction of several paths that climb to high passes. Much of the walk is among woods with meadows rising from them, and rocky crests that build to bigger peaks on the Swiss/Italian border.

Cross the Engadine from La Punt to its twin, **Chamues-ch**, with which it is linked by a road. **Val Chamuera** cuts into the mountains behind Chamues-ch, and a track pushes into the narrow mouth of the valley alongside the Ova Chamuera stream. When this ends continue on a path that remains on the left of the stream all the way. Although both flanks of the valley are wooded at its entrance, as you make progress, the north bank reveals its hillsides and allows open views ahead. Shortly before reaching the Serlas alp, cross the Ova Lavirun below the alp building of Acla Veglia which guards the entrance to Val Lavirun. **Serlas** is at a four-way junction, so given time, energy and inclination, you could extend the walk in various directions (see below).

To return to La Punt, allow about 1½hr.

WALK OPTIONS FROM SERLAS

Take the path which leads into Val Lavirun and follow this up to **Fuorcla Lavirun** (2816m) on the Italian border, reached about 2¾hr from Serlas. The upper valley is noted for its wildlife and alpine flora.

A second route into Val Lavirun branches north just below Fuorcla Lavirun, and crosses **Fuorcla Chaschauna** (2804m). The way then descends through Val Chaschauna before spilling into the Engadine near **S-chanf** – 4hr from Serlas.

By continuing up the Val Chamuera it's possible to reach **Fuorcla Federia** (2801m), then descend into the Italian Valle di Federia, which leads to **Livigno**. (More route options for returning to the Engadine by several passes – see the map for ideas).

Also in the upper Val Chamuera, **Alp Prünella** sits at a confluence of streams at 2213m. The valley forks here, with the eastern branch carrying a trail over **Fuorcla Chamuera** to **Val da Fain**, while the western branch (Val Prünella) gives a route over **Fuorcla Tschüffer** and **Fuorcla Pischa**, and down to Alp Languard and **Pontresina** (see Route 56).

Finally, the right-hand path from Serlas goes into **Val Prüna**, crosses **Fuorcla Muragl** (2891m) and continues through Val Muragl to **Muottas Muragl**, described in the reverse direction as Route 45.

ROUTE 66
*La Punt (1697m) – Zuoz (1716m) – Chapella
(1646m) – Cinuos-chel (1628m)*

Start	La Punt (1697m)
Distance	14km (8.7 miles)
Height gain	263m (863ft)
Height loss	332m (1056ft)
Grade	1–2
Time	4½–5hr
Location	Northeast of La Punt

A number of footpaths and farm tracks contour the hillsides on the left bank of the Engadine between La Punt and Cinuos-chel; some of which have been linked to form a section of the long-distance Via Engiadina (see Route 40 for another section of this route). This walk outline adopts part of that route, although you are urged to take any path or track that takes your fancy to vary the route at will – there's no shortage of signposts giving destinations and times.

Start by taking the trail that rises out of La Punt along-side the stream issuing from the Albula Pass. After about 40min, at an altitude of 1960m, cross the road onto a track which contours along the partly wooded hillside. This takes you above Madulain, after which Zuoz can be seen in the valley ahead. The way slopes down to visit this most attractive of villages in 2½hr or so. **Zuoz** is well worth a lingering examination, so allow ample time for this. To continue the walk, a sign in the centre of the village sends the Via Engiadina up a side street and out across open hillsides once more. On making a sharp twist in the trail, a junction offers the option of descending to S-chanf, otherwise remain high to visit the alp of **Acla Laret** before sloping down through forest at the entrance to Val Susauna, to visit the hamlet of **Chapella** (4–4½hr).

Cross the main valley road and take the signed footpath, which swings round the lower hillside and brings you to the railway station at **Cinuos-chel**.

ROUTE 67

Madulain (1684m) – Es-cha Hut (Chamanna d'Es-cha: 2594m) – Madulain

Start	Madulain (1684m)
Distance	14km (8.7 miles)
Height gain	910m (2986ft)
Height loss	910m (2986ft)
Grade	2–3
Time	4½–5hr
Location	Northwest of Madulain

Standing below the Southeast Face of Piz Kesch, the Es-cha Hut not only enjoys a direct view of the mountain, but also has a surprising distant view of the Bernina massif across an intervening ridge to the south. It's a fine, atmospheric hut, and the aproach from Madulain, although more arduous than the more direct route from the Albula Pass road, is both varied and rewarding. Rather than return to Madulain by the same path, this route offers an interesting alternative.

Take the cobbled street rising between houses on the west side of Madulain's onion-spired church. Crossing the railway line it becomes a tarmac lane, then a farm track, then a footpath climbing towards a gorge. Over a crossing track continue uphill, then loop to the right to reach a narrow lane which you follow uphill between pastures and larchwoods. The lane becomes a stony track, and about 50min from Madulain you emerge from woodland to an open slope of pasture, then pass the building of **Alp Es-cha Dadour** (2063m).

Continue up the track to a junction a short distance above the alp, where you gain a first view of Piz Kesch. Ignoring alternatives, keep ahead to maintain direction into the little valley which lies directly below Piz Kesch. With Alp Es-cha Dadains seen ahead, fork right on a signed path angling across the hillside. After crossing a stream the gradient increases as the path zigzags steeply up a cone of vegetated moraine. At the top of the zigzags walk along the moraine crest to reach the hut at 2594m (about 2½–3hr from Madulain).

ES-CHA HUT

Chamanna d'Es-cha belongs to the Bernina section of the SAC. It has 60 dormitory places and a full meals service when manned – from mid-March to mid-April, and from late-June to mid-October. For reservations Tel 081 854 17 55 www.sac-bernina.ch.

To return to Madulain by the same path would take about 1½hr, but the variation given here makes a very fine alternative outing. Pass to the left of the hut

Madulain, an attractive village on the left bank of the Inn

on a well-signed path that cuts round the hillside heading southwest below Piz Kesch. It descends a little into a basin beneath a great slope of scree, then rises easily among rocks with splendid views ahead of the snowy Bernina Alps.

Rounding a spur cross steep grass slopes on an easy contour that takes you into the mouth of the hanging Pischa Valley (the uppermost part of Val d'Es-cha), crosses a stream on a footbridge, then resumes its contour round to **Fuorcla Gualdauna** (2490m) about 45min from the hut. This grassy saddle offers a way down to the Albula Pass road, from where the shortest and easiest route to the Escha Hut takes only 1½hr or so. Our route, however, does not cross the saddle, although a few paces beyond it rewards with an uninterrupted view of the Bernina mountains.

ALTERNATIVE DESCENT TO MADULAIN

By continuing on the path down the south side of Fuorcla Gualdauna, then taking the left branch when it forks, an alternative return to Madulain can be achieved. The path leads to and across the Albula Pass road, and comes to Alp Nova. Continue down to **Alp Proliebas**, then follow the road as far as its first hairpin bend. At this point break away left onto the Via Engiadina/Via Segantini which leads to **Madulain**, reached about 2½hr from Chamanna d'Es-cha.

Without crossing the saddle turn left at the signpost where waymarks direct the route, for there is no evident path at first. Before long, however, the way becomes a narrow trail that loops down the hillside passing numerous marmot burrows, then slants down to the Ova Pischa stream near the buildings of **Alp Es-cha Dadains**. Cross on a footbridge, come onto a track and follow it down-valley, soon reaching the junction of tracks above Alp Es-cha Dadour. Now on familiar ground, return to **Madulain** by following the same track and footpaths used on the upward route.

Alp Es-cha Dadaint below Piz Kesch, reached by a delightful walk from Madulain

Routes from the Es-cha Hut

Several outings could be achieved from the Es-cha Hut, apart from climbing routes. The following offers a selection:

- The 3008m **Porta d'Es-cha** is a pass in the ridge linking Piz Kesch and Piz Val Müra. The northern side of this pass is glaciated, but the southern approach is ice-free, and takes about 1½hr to reach from the Es-cha Hut.
- A crossing of the **Porta d'Es-cha** to the **Kesch Hut** on the northern side of Piz Kesch involves descent of the Porchabella Glacier, so is restricted to experienced trekkers with the necessary equipment and expertise to deal with crevassed glaciers. But for those with this experience, a fine 2-day circuit of the mountain could be achieved.
- On the south side of Piz Kesch, **Fuorcla Pischa** (2871m) provides an opportunity for trekkers to make a crossing of the Albula Alps down to **Chants** in Val Tuors, followed by a walk down that valley to **Bergün**, from where trains travel back to the Engadine.

ROUTE 68

*Zuoz (1716m) – Chamues-ch (1708m)
– Punt Muragl (1738m)*

Start	Zuoz (1716m)
Distance	14km (8.7 miles)
Height gain	22m (72.2ft)
Grade	1
Time	4hr
Location	Southwest of Zuoz

A valley walk from start to finish, this route accompanies the River Inn upstream through flat meadowlands away from villages that are all reasonably accessible should you decide at any stage to foreshorten it. Paths and tracks are easy, making a leisurely stroll through a gentle landscape, lured on by the unmistakable Piz de la Margna beckoning at the head of the valley. Note that the route described stays close to the river for much of the way, although there is a parallel route which skirts the forested slopes nearby, and it would be easy to vary the walk if required by adopting sections of that route too.

From Zuoz station take the road leading down to the river, pass beneath the main valley road and turn right at the Resgia farm onto a track. This takes you below Madulain, and between meadows towards the bridge that carries a road from La Punt to Chamues-ch. La Punt is on the far side of the river, while **Chamues-ch** lines the road at the mouth of Val Chamuera on the left. ▸

For the riverside walk, go between some houses near the bridge, cross the Chamuera stream, and continue ahead on the riverbank path.

Opposite **Bever** there's another option to either take the forest-edge path, or continue alongside the river. This latter choice goes between the river and some large pools

Access to the forest-edge path can be had by straying towards the church in Chamues-ch, then branching right shortly before you reach it.

(nice reflected views), then along the perimeter of the Samedan airfield before drawing close to the railway, and following this round to **Punt Muragl** at the entrance to Val Bernina.

Take the train to return to Zuoz.

ROUTE 69

S-chanf (1669m) – Varusch Hut
(Chamanna dal Parc Varusch: 1771m)

Start	S-chanf (1669m)
Distance	5km (3.1 miles) one way
Height gain	102m (335ft)
Grade	1
Time	1¼hr
Location	East of S-chanf

Set in a small meadow close to the national park entrance in Val Trupchun, the Varusch Hut is a charming building in a tranquil location, and the walk to it, mostly through woodland, makes a very pleasant outing – even without delving into the park beyond. If you're looking for an undemanding but rewarding stroll, this could be the answer.

There are two walking options from S-chanf. One follows a narrow lane to the Prasüras car park at 1690m, then takes a woodland path. The other crosses meadowland, then climbs into woodland for a higher approach, before joining the main path about 15min below the hut. If you have your own vehicle, you can drive to the Prasüras car park (fee payable), from where the hut is just 40min away; alternatively, you can take a bus from either S-chanf or Zernez to the 'Val Trupchun' bus stop about 500m west of Prasüras, and walk from there.

From S-chanf railway station walk along a minor road parallel with the river, then over the river to an underpass beneath the main valley road. The footpath route now breaks away from the road, crosses low valley meadows to the wooded slopes and comes to a junction of paths. Bear left. Rising through the woods of larch and fir, the way curves round the spur marking the entrance to Val Trupchun. There are other path options, but the Varusch route is clearly signed, and the path continues among trees before sloping downhill to meet the route from Prasüras by a bridge spanning the **Ova da Chaschauna**.

The Varusch Hut stands just outside the national park boundary in Val Trupchun

ALTERNATIVE ROUTE FROM PRASÜRAS

Coming from S-chanf, follow the lane from the railway station. When it forks take the right branch and shortly arrive at the **Prasüras roadhead** car park at 1690m. There are refreshments here, and a large information board. The path to the Varusch Hut breaks away to the right and very soon enters woodland. In just 2min the path forks; take the left branch. About 25–30min from Prasüras come to the bridge across the **Ova da Chaschauna**, to be joined by the alternative route from S-chanf.

Across the bridge come onto a dirt road. Turn left over the main valley stream, the Ova da Varusch, then right on an unsealed road which eventually leads to the hut. However, leave this after just 1min, and take a footpath slanting among trees above the road. Before long it brings you out to the little meadowland with the **Chamanna dal Parc Varusch** just ahead, and Piz Fier and Piz Saliente for a backdrop.

For a return to S-chanf, allow 1¼hr; to Prasüras, 30min. For walks in the national park, see Routes 74–85.

THE VARUSCH HUT

This hut is privately owned, and open from June to October. It has 35 places and restaurant service. (Tel 081 851 54 54 www.varusch.ch)

ROUTE 70

S-chanf (Prasüras: 1690m) – Alp Chaschauna (2210m) – Pass Chaschauna (2694m)

Start	S-chanf (Prasüras: 1690m)
Distance	10km (6.2 miles) one way
Height gain	1004m (3294ft)
Grade	2–3
Time	4hr
Location	Southeast of S-chanf

On the headwall of Val Chauschauna, Pass Chaschauna is an old trading route across the mountains to Livigno. The Swiss/Italian border runs along the crest of this headwall, while the national park boundary traces the valley's right-hand walling ridge. The walk up to the pass is not unduly taxing, although snow may still be lying on the upper slopes in midsummer, and it makes a good, if long, day out. (The return to Prasüras will take about 3hr – so allow a total of 7hr for the round trip.) Refreshments may be had on the Italian flank, a little under 100m below the pass at Rifugio di Cassana, so if you plan to take advantage of this, don't forget to take your passport and some Euros with you.

From the Prasüras car park take the path for the Varusch Hut (Route 69), but at the first junction (2min) take the right fork – signed Pass Chaschauna. This rises through woods and joins a path coming from S-chanf. Bear left and follow this to the next junction where again you take the right branch curving south into the narrow Val da Scrigns. On coming to a bridge at 1857m, cross the **Ova da Chaschauna** and follow the river upstream to a second bridge at 1892m, where you return to the west bank. Soon come to a third bridge where the path forks. Ignore the right-hand path here, which goes to Alp Vaüglia in a side valley, and cross for a last time to the east bank.

At a crossing path continue up-valley, now curving into **Val Chaschauna**. Across the valley to the south another tributary glen can be seen (Val Chaschanella), and there's a route into that too, but we ignore this and continue ahead, coming at last to **Alp Chaschauna** (2210m) about 2½hr from the Prasüras car park. From here continue up-valley, rising gently to another junction where the path forks. The right branch goes to Fuorcla Chaschauna for a crossing into Val Lavirun and Val Chamuera (see Route 65). We, however, take the left-hand option, climbing to the alp of **Margun** (2362m), then more steeply in zigzags to gain **Pass Chaschauna** (2694m), about 1½hr from Alp Chaschauna.

Allow about 3hr for the return to Prasüras.

ON THE ITALIAN FLANK

Rifugio di Cassana lies just below the pass on the Italian flank at 2601m overlooking the steep Valle di Fedaria. It has 15 places and full meals service (Tel +39 0342 997205 www.rifugi.lombardia.it/rifugio-cassana.html). Below the hut the valley flows into Valle di Livigno, while a mass of peaks and ridges fills every horizon. A path descends below the hut on the way to **Pian dei Morti**, then on to Livigno.

ROUTE 71
Cinuos-chel (1628m) – Susauna
(1682m) – Alp Funtauna (2192m)

Start	Cinuos-chel (1628m)
Distance	10km (6.2 miles) one way
Height gain	564m (1850ft)
Grade	1
Time	3–3½hr
Location	WNW of Cinuos-chel

Briefly seen from the main Engadine valley road, Val Susauna makes little immediate impact. From here it's an unremarkable valley, with nothing at its entrance to indicate that it would repay a visit. But this walk should change that impression, for it's a truly delightful valley, and the deeper you delve into it, the more it reveals, and in the open pastureland of Alp Funtauna near its head there's much to enjoy. On the way to it, there's a good chance of sighting deer and chamois, while the upper pastures are busy with marmots. The route is straightforward and undemanding, on a farm track for most of the way.

Susauna consists of an attractive group of old Romansch stone buildings and a small chapel. Refreshments are available at the Usteria da Susauna near the chapel.

Begin at the Cinuos-chel/Brail railway station which has a marked stony track running south (up-valley) alongside the railway line. This soon ducks beneath the main road to emerge on an access road at the mouth of Val Susauna near the entrance to Camping Chapella. A short way into the valley the road forks among the houses of Chapella (La Resgia on the map). Take the right branch, and at a crossroads continue ahead to the small farming hamlet of **Susauna** (1682m), reached about 1hr from the start. ◄

The road now becomes a stony track rising between pastures, and crosses to the left side of the Vallember stream. For a while the valley is more wooded than at its entrance, although the woodland thins out as you gain height. Recrossing the stream at **Punt da Splu** (1776m),

about 1hr from Susauna the valley opens with the tributary Val Viluoch spreading left. Across the Vallember can be seen the solitary building of Alp Pignaint, with the conical Piz Viroula rising at the head of the glen behind it. An alternative track crosses to the alp, but we remain on the right-hand side of the stream and continue up-valley through more pastures with views ahead to the Kuhalphorn, which stands behind Alp Funtauna.

Once more the track crosses to the left side of the stream, then climbs more steeply and recrosses yet again to the right-hand side. Now the valley is changing character; it's more rocky and narrow, although there are still small patches of pastureland. The upper valley is separated from the lower levels by a minor gorge up which the track climbs, crosses a side stream from the Vallorgia, rises a little further to cross a second stream, then swings left to **Alp Funtauna** after about 3½hr.

Allow about 2½hr for a return to Cinuos-chel.

The charming little farming hamlet of Susauna

ALP FUNTAUNA

This is a splendid sunny alp in open pastures at a confluence of streams. Across its pastoral basin the Vallorgia is headed by a good-looking cirque of mountains formed by ridges linking the Scalettahorn, Piz Grialetsch and Piz Vadret. Behind the alp building stretches Val Funtauna, which carries a route to the **Ravais-ch lakes** (Route 72) and the **Kesch Hut** (Route 73), while other worthwhile destinations accessed from here include the hamlet of **Dürrboden** (linked with Davos by infrequent postbus in summer) across the 2606m Scaletta Pass.

ROUTE 72

Cinuous-chel (1628m) – Alp Funtauna
(2192m) – Lai da Ravais-ch-Suot (2505m)

Start	Cinuous-chel (1628m)
Distance	17km (10.6 miles) one way
Height gain	934m (3064ft)
Height loss	57m (187ft)
Grade	2–3
Time	5–5½hr
Location	Northwest of Cinuos-chel

Tucked among ancient moraines in a small hanging valley below the Sertig Pass, about 2hr from Alp Funtauna, the two Ravais-ch lakes are glistening gems overlooked by towering rock peaks.

Follow directions for Route 71 as far as **Alp Funtauna** (3–3½hr). Pass along the left-hand side of the alp building, cross a stream by a footbridge and wander up into the gentle **Val Funtauna**, an open, treeless grassy valley, with numerous marmots, and a few sprays of juniper and low-growing bilberries. As you make progress through this valley, make a point of looking back to enjoy the view of craggy Piz Grialetsch at the head of the Vallorgia.

Remain on the left-hand side of the Ova Funtauna, and in 30min or so from the alp building, the way curves left into what is known as **Val dal Tschüvel** – in effect the upper reaches of Val Funtauna. Gaining height, Piz Kesch begins to rear up at the head of the valley, and shortly before the path takes you across the stream on a footbridge (at 2395m), the Kesch Hut comes into view. Shortly after this you will reach a junction of paths where you turn right. (The path left goes to the Kesch Hut – see Route 73.) Our path contours along the hillside heading roughly north, and crossing a few streams enters the little Val Sertiv, a scoop between Piz Murtelet and a spur of the Kuhalphorn. Looking back, Piz Kesch is suitably impressive to the south.

Rising steadily through this little valley, come to the first of the lakes, **Lai da Ravais-ch-Sur** at 2562m, which drains into Val Funtauna, and eventually the Inn which, of course, feeds the Danube. This is a lovely spot, but the second lake is even better. To reach this entails a descent of almost 60m across the watershed. There's a path junction beyond the first lake (the right-hand path climbs to the Sertig Pass – a way to reach Davos), and from this

The pastoral Val Susauna has a number of rewarding walks

Piz Grialetsch is seen to good effect from Alp Funtauna

you descend northwest with the 3063m Hoch Ducan dominating the view with its grey rock walls plunging to the lake. The deep **Lai da Ravais-ch-Suot** lies at 2505m, and is worth the effort to reach. Unlike its neighbour, this drains down to the Val Tuors and, eventually, into the Rhine.

To return to Cinuous-chel from here will take about 3½hr.

ALTERNATIVE DESCENTS

You could descend southwest through the Val da Ravais-ch to **Chants** (refreshments) at the confluence with Val Tuors, and take the bus from there to Bergün, then train to Cinuos-chel via Bever. Or return to the path junction in Val dal Tschüvel and follow Route 73 to the **Kesch Hut** for overnight accommodation.

ROUTE 73

Cinuos-chel (1628m) – Alp Funtauna (2192m)
– Kesch Hut (Chamanna digl Kesch: 2632m)

Start	Cinuos-chel (1628m)
Distance	15km (9.3 miles) one way
Height gain	1004m (3294ft)
Grade	2
Time	5–5½hr
Location	West of Cinuos-chel

With a direct view of the heavily glaciated North Face of Piz Kesch, the Kesch Hut makes a very fine destination. It's a long walk, but apart from the 2½hr approach from Chants above Bergün, all non-glacier routes to the Kesch Hut are at least 4½hr long. The approach described here is an extension of Routes 71 and 72, but it makes a very fine walk in its own right.

From Alp Funtauna (see Route 71) pass along the left-hand side of the building and wander up into **Val Funtauna**. Route 72 describes the continuing walk through this valley and into its upper reaches known as Val dal Tschüvel. On coming to the path junction shortly after the stream crossing, ignore the right-hand path which goes to the Ravais-ch

The Kesch Hut, reached by a long walk from Cinuos-chel

lakes, and keep ahead, rising easily up-valley. The path only becomes steep shortly before reaching the hut, which it does about 1½–2hr after leaving Alp Funtauna.

Allow at least 3½hr for a return to Cinuos-chel by the same route.

KESCH HUT

Chamanna digl Kesch belongs to the Davos section of the SAC. A modern timber and glass-walled hut on a prominent site below the Porchabella Glacier and North Face of Piz Kesch, with a view west down Val Tuors. It has 92 dormitory places and a full meals service when manned. This is at Christmas/New Year, in March and April, and from late June to mid-October. For reservations Tel 081 407 11 34 (www.kesch.ch). From the hut it's a 1½hr descent to Chants, on the way to Bergün, while a 2½hr crossing of Porta d'Es-cha leads to the Es-cha Hut on the southeast side of Piz Kesch – see see Route 67.

Routes from the Kesch hut

Options for cross-country treks and circuits from a base at the Kesch Hut are either signed from the hut itself, or devised by study of the map. The following is a small selection:

- A visit to the **Lej da Ravais-ch** is an obvious walk (see Route 72). Reached in about 1–1½hr, simply return down the approach path through Val dal Tschüvel as far as the path junction above the stream, and continue on the upper path leading into the little Val Sertiv where the two lakes are found.

- Apart from the direct descent to **Chants** and **Bergün** west of the hut, a longer and more interesting route goes via the **Ravais lakes** (as above), from where a continuing path curves west and south to descend through **Val da Ravais-ch** to Chants at the confluence with Val Tuors. From Chants there's a summer postbus link with Bergün; otherwise a 2½hr walk.

- The 2739m **Sertig Pass** carries a route north to **Sertig Dörfli** in the pastoral Sertigtal (3½hr from the hut), from where there's an hourly bus service to **Davos**.

LOWER ENGADINE

The path to Blockhaus Cluozza

LOWER ENGADINE

Val Tasna, with its view across the Lower Engadine

By contrast with the Upper Engadine's snow and ice peaks, its extensive lakes and side valleys blocked by glaciers, the Lower Engadine (Engiadina Bassa, or Unterengadin) is a more tranquil region. Its lakes are no more than small mountain tarns, and there's very little ice or permanent snow. Instead the valley and its tributaries are noted for their meadows, their deep green forests and upper grass slopes from which bare grey peaks protrude. Tucked away from the rest of Switzerland the Engadine here is a deep, river-cut swathe tended with care and attention to detail. Seductively appealing, its unfussed landscape wins many admirers among first-time visitors.

Some 55km separate Punt Ota from the Inn's exit into Austria, and in that distance the valley establishes and confirms its own unique identity. Opposite Val Susauna on the Engadine's east flank lies Switzerland's only national park, and between Val Trupchun and Zernez, where the Spöl's valley cuts back towards the Ofenpass and Val Müstair, all the eastern mountains up to the Italian border are under the park's protection.

From the little flood plain where Zernez guards a junction of roads, the Inn veers a little to the north before resuming the northeasterly course it then maintains as far as the Austrian border. Among its east-walling mountains here, the

218

so-called Engiadina Dolomites astride the enchanting Val S-charl are among its most attractive features. On the left bank the Albula Alps extend only as far as the Flüela Pass, before the Silvretta Alps take over. Shared with Austria, these mostly 3000m peaks block a succession of tributary glens and form a dramatic backdrop to a number of walks.

But it will be the villages as much as the mountains that win admiration for the Lower Engadine, for this is a valley that holds dear to its traditions. The Romansch language is spoken everywhere, while the vernacular architecture of its houses is a heritage of great beauty handed down through the generations. Amid sunny pastures, on hillside ledges or in the bed of the valley set a little above the Inn, ancient communities cluster round a cobblestoned square whose centrepiece is invariably a fountain that pours non-stop into a trough. Romantic houses with misshapen stone walls bowed by the weight of centuries look on. Their huge arched doors are deeply set, and in some cases reached by a ramp off the street or alleyway. Their windows are tiny, and similarly deep-set behind ornate wrought-iron grilles, surrounded by patterns of *sgraffito* etched in the plaster. Some of the walls are pink-washed; most are plastered white with grey-toned scrolls or geometric shapes that form an edging to doorways and windows, and even to the corner walls and under the eaves. Now and then you'll discover a house whose frontage is given over to a pictorial image, sometimes hundreds of

Wild country at the head of Val Sagliains, en route from Lavin to the Vereinapass

years old (the Adam and Eve house in Ardez is a prime example); others will be a more recent expression by a plasterer or architect intent on maintaining a valued local tradition.

Every village has its architectural gems. But the best are to be found in Guarda, Ardez and the old heart of Scuol. These are villages to match the mountains, set in a valley that is one of the most unspoilt in the country.

ACCESS AND INFORMATION	
Location:	Draining roughly northeast from Punt Ota near Brail, to where the Inn flows into Austria
Maps:	LS 259T Ofenpass, 258T Bergün & 249T Tarasp at 1:50,000
	Kümmerly + Frey Unterengadin at 1:60,000
Bases:	Zernez (1471m), Susch (1426m), Guarda (1653m), Scuol (1243m), Sent (1430m)
Information:	Tourist information Zernez; (Tel 081 856 13 00 www.zernez.ch and www.myswitzerland.com/en/zernez. html)
	National Park Visitor Centre, Zernez (Tel 081 851 41 41 www.Nationalpark.ch)
	Tourist information Susch, (Tel 081 860 02 40 www.zernez.ch)
	Tourist information Guarda, (Tel 081 861 88 27 www.scuol.ch.guarda)
	Tourist Information Scuol (Tel 081 861 88 00 https://scuol-zernez.engadin.com)
	Tourist information Sent (Tel 081 861 88 29 www.sent-online.ch).
Access:	By train via Bever or St Moritz as far as Scuol. A drive-on/drive-off car-carrying train uses the 19km-long Vereina Tunnel from Klosters to Lavin (Sagliains). By road across the Flüela Pass (closed in winter), or via the Julier Pass and Upper Engadine. The Lower Engadine is also served by postbus from Landeck in Austria. Postbuses run from Scuol to villages not served by railway, and from Zernez across the Ofenpass to Val Müstair.

MAIN BASES

ZERNEZ (1471m) stands at the junction of the main Engadine road with that of the Ofenpass (Pass dal Fuorn), beyond which lies the gentle, Italian-flavoured Val Müstair. With regular postbus and train services, almost every part of the valley can be reached with some ease. It's a small, unpretentious township with several hotels graded up to 3-star, and a campsite (Camping Cul) beside the River Inn, open May to mid-October (Tel 081 856 14 62 https://.camping-cul.com). Zernez has a selection of shops, bank, PTT, restaurants, railway station, and the national park headquarters in the National Park House; a visit is recommended.

SUSCH (1426m) is a small village at the foot of the Flüela Pass road. With little in the way of tourist infrastructure, it nonetheless has four hotels, several holiday apartments, and a campsite open mid-May to mid-October, Camping Muglinas (Tel 081 856 19 27).

Scuol, a popular tourist base in the Lower Engadine

GUARDA (1653m) is arguably the most attractive and romantic village in the whole Engadine region, and must rank as one of the finest in all Switzerland. Standing on a natural terrace 200m and more above the Inn's left bank below Val Tuoi, Guarda has five hotels and several holiday apartments to let.

SCUOL (1243m) is the district's largest community, and has by far the most facilities for the visitor of any village in the Lower Engadine. With neighbouring Tarasp-Vulpera it's a spa resort as well as catering for the skier in winter and walker in summer. Scuol is the terminus of the railway. It has more than 20 hotels of all grades, numerous holiday apartments, and a campsite on the south side of the river that is open all-year except mid-April to mid-May, and from mid-October to mid-December; Camping Gurlaina (Tel 081 864 15 01 www.tcs.ch). There's a good selection of shops, restaurants and banks in the 'new' village that spreads just below the main road. The attractive old village stands a little lower than the shopping area, and consists of delightful traditional buildings gathered round a square.

SENT (1430m) is reached by a side road that cuts across the hillside northeast of Scuol. Enjoying an open sunny position, it's popular throughout the year with Swiss visitors. The village has several shops, restaurants, bank and PTT. There are four hotels, and a very wide range of apartments for holiday let.

OTHER BASES

Other Lower Engadine villages offer accommodation too, and the brief outline below also includes outlying hotels, pensions and dormitory facilities where known.

Between Zernez and the Ofenpass, several opportunities exist for spending a night or two on the edge of the national park. At **OVA SPIN** the Naturfreundehaus Ova Spin has 30 dormitory places (Tel 079 419 07 76 www.engadin.stmoritz. ch/gruppen/naturfreundehaus-ova-spin), and Wegerhaus Ova Spin has 20 dormitory places (Tel 081 856 10 52 www.strimer.ch). At **IL FUORN**, about 8km from the Ofenpass, the renamed Hotel Parc Naziunal has standard rooms, but there's dormitory accommodation for 20 in the Lager Il Fuorn (Tel 081 856 12 26 www. ilfuorn.ch) – contact details are for both buildings.

The next village down-valley from Susch is **LAVIN** which lies directly below Piz Linard, highest of the Silvretta Alps. Lavin has two hotels, the Crusch Alba, and 3-star Hotel Piz Linard, as well as several holiday apartments (www. scuol.engadin.com/lavin).

ARDEZ competes with Guarda for handsome buildings. Lying on the same hillside terrace as Guarda, but a little further east, it's a lovely village that has just two hotels, the 2-star Alvetern Ardez, and

S-charl window (Routes 97–100)

3-star Hotel Aurora, and a large number of holiday apartments. For details Tel 081 861 88 00 www.scuol.engadin.com/ardez.

With direct road access from Scuol, **FTAN** is another hillside village several hundred metres above the valley floor. It has four hotels: the modestly priced Garni Chesa Allegra, the tiny Sömmiin with just 2 double rooms, 3-star Hotel Engiadina, and upmarket Hotel Haus Paradies. Ftan also has a large number of apartments for holiday let. (Tel 081 861 88 00 www.scuol.engadin.com/ftan).

The hamlet of **S-CHARL**, 13km along the valley of the same name south of Scuol, is a very fine 'back-of-beyond' base for a walking holiday. It has three hotels: the Landsgasthof Mayor, Garni Chasa Sesvenna, and Landgasthof Crusch Alba – details from Scuol tourist information (Tel 081 861 88 00 www.scuol.engadin.com/s-charl).

At the entrance to Val Sinestra, northeast of Sent, **RAMOSCH** has accommodation at Pensiun Bellavista, Pensiun Ustaria Heinrich, and Hotel Posta, while tiny **VNÀ**, up a steeply twisting road above Ramosch, has the 30-bed Pensiun Arina (Tel 081 861 88 00 www.scuol.engadin.com/ramosch).

There are campsites at **SUR EN** in the valley below Sent, and at **STRADA** below Tschlin – Strada also has 3 double rooms at Café Sper l'En San Niclá. At **TSCHLIN** on the left flank of the valley where it narrows towards Martina, Pension Macun has 4 double rooms and a 6-bed dormitory. while **MARTINA** has the modestly priced Pension/Restaurant Rezia, and Hotel/Restaurant Chasa Engiadina.

MOUNTAIN HUTS

Several mountain huts are accessible from the Lower Engadine; some belong to the SAC, others are either privately owned.

BLOCKHAUS CLUOZZA (Chamanna Cluozza: 1882m) A rustic building set deep within the Val Cluozza about 3hr from Zernez. Apart from Hotel Il Fuorn on the Ofenpass road, this is the only overnight accommodation available within the national park. Owned by the park authority, it has 70 places and a full meals service, and is open from late June to mid-October. For reservations Tel 081 856 12 35.

CHAMANNA GRIALETSCH (2542m) Built by the St Gallen section of the SAC, the Grialetsch Hut stands below Piz Grialetsch and Piz Vadret in the Albula Alps, and is reached by a walk of about 2½hr from Roven on the Flüela Pass road, or 4½hr from Susch. With 61 dormitory places, and a full meals service when manned, the hut is fully open in March and April, and from July to mid-October. For reservations Tel 081 416 34 36 www.grialetsch.ch.

BERGHAUS VEREINA (1943m) Reached by a 4½hr walk from Roven on the Flüela Pass road, Berghaus Vereina stands at a junction of paths at the mouth of the Vernela Valley in a remote corner of the Silvretta Alps. Open from end June to mid-October, it has 40 places, and full meals provision (Tel 081 422 12 16 www.berghausvereina.ch).

LINARD HUT (Chamanna dal Linard: 2327m) Standing on the slopes of Piz Linard, about 2½hr from Lavin, this SAC-owned hut has 46 dormitory places and meals provision during the short summer season when manned: from July to mid-September. For reservations Tel 079 629 61 91 www.linardhuette.ch.

CHAMANNA MARANGUN (2025m) Owned by the Lavin *gemeinde*, the Marangun hut lies near the head of Val Lavinuoz, about 2–2½hr walk from Lavin. The hut has 12 places, but is unmanned. Self-catering facilities are provided, but all food must be carried in. Contact 081 862 26 51 www.vs-wallis.ch/graubunden/huetverz/marangun.html.

TUOI HUT(Chamanna Tuoi: 2250m) Built at the head of Val Tuoi below Piz Buin, this fine hut belongs to the Engiadina Bassa section of the SAC, and is reached by an easy, very pleasant walk of 2½hr from Guarda. There are 74 places and a full meals service when manned: at New Year, then permanently from mid-June to mid-October. For reservations Tel 081 862 23 22 www.tuoi.ch.

CHAMANNA CLER (2476m) Owned by the Ardez Ski Club, this unmanned hut stands 1000m above – and a 2½hr walk from – Ardez village. There are places for 22, solar-powered lighting, a wood-burning stove and self-catering facilities, but all food supplies must be carried in. The hut is permanently locked. For bookings and the key Tel 081 860 38 83 www.ski-ardez.ch.

LISCHANA HUT (Chamanna Lischana: 2500m) With 42 dormitory places and full meals provision when guarded, the Lischana Hut stands in the Val Lischana below the west flank of Piz Lischana, about 4hr from Scuol. It is manned from July to mid-October. For reservations Tel 081 864 95 44 www.lischanahuette.ch.

HEIDELBERGER HUT (2264m) This very large hut (156 places) belongs to the Heidelberger section of the DAV (German Alpine Club), and sits in the Val Fenga (Fimbertal) which drains north into Austria. Reached by a walk of about 5½–6hr from Sent, it's manned with full meals service throughout the year except mid-May to mid-June,and mid September to Christmas. For reservations Tel (0043) 664 42 53 070 www.heidelbergerhuette.at.

LOWER ENGADINE –
THE NATIONAL PARK

From Val Trupchun in the south, to the west bank of Val S-charl in the north, the Swiss National Park is contained within the boundaries of the Engadine Valley, the only road intrusion being that which crosses the Ofenpass into Val Müstair. It's a unique park, not only from a Swiss perspective, but within a European context, for nature here is given absolute priority, and allowed to develop unhindered by human intervention.

Established in 1914, the only national park in Switzerland covers an area of 172km² with an altitude range from 1400m to 3173m. Of the 13 national parks in the Alps, it's the second smallest and the oldest, but within it nature is afforded the very highest degree of protection. Here, Man is very much subordinate to the demands of Nature, and strict rules govern all who stray within the park's boundary. As a result it remains a pristine wilderness.

On the way to Alp Grimmels from Ova Spin (Route 80)

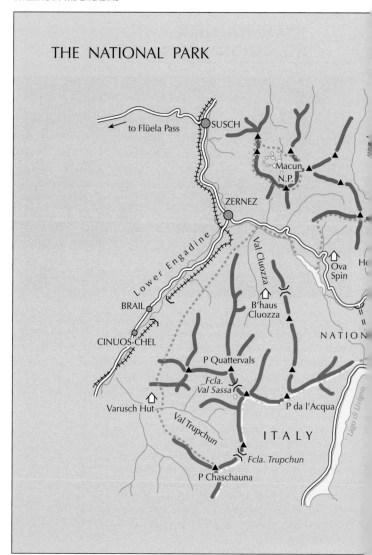

THE NATIONAL PARK

to Flüela Pass

SUSCH

Macun
N.P.

ZERNEZ

Lower Engadine

Val Cluozza

Ova
Spin

B'haus
Cluozza

BRAIL

CINUOS-CHEL

NATION

P Quattervals

Fcla.
Val Sassa

Varusch Hut

P da l'Acqua

Val Trupchun

ITALY

Lago di Livigno

Fcla. Trupchun

P Chaschauna

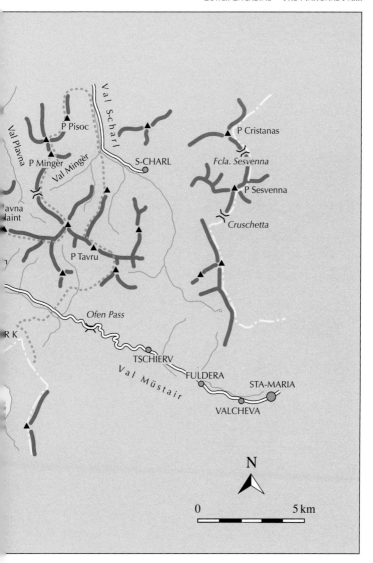

Val Cluozza in the national park (Route 76)

From the outset, the prime objective of the park was to enable nature to run its natural course without interference, so everything in it is protected: plants, animals, stones, timber. If a tree falls, for example, it's left to rot where it lies, and while forest fires are monitored, they're allowed to burn. Visitors are free to explore its valleys, but are restricted to 80km of marked paths and may only enter on foot – cycling, riding and skiing are forbidden. Camping and bivouacking are not allowed; neither is it permissible to spend a night in a motor vehicle on the Ofenpass road which runs through it.

Such restrictions (and there are many more) may seem unnecessarily authoritarian, but there are few enough places left in this world which man has not moulded to his own use, and it's no bad thing to allow nature the freedom to go unchecked in one small corner of the Alps. If you're observant you will recognise the benefits when walking quietly through some of the park's valleys.

Since domestic cattle, sheep and goats have been banned from most of the park since its inception, many of its valleys are now densely wooded, with pine and larchwoods growing as high as 2300m. Above them alpine meadows are carpeted with flowers in spring and early summer. Not surprisingly wildlife is abundant; the red squirrel, marmot, fox, hare, chamois, ibex, red and roe deer all roam freely. There are various woodpeckers and owls. The nutcracker is at home among the cembra pine trees, while the nuthatch favours glades in the larchwoods; there are golden eagles, bearded vultures, ravens and kestrels and alpine choughs and dozens of other species.

NATIONAL PARK INFORMATION

Information on the internet: www.nationalpark.ch

Guided walks: Between the end of June and mid-October, guided walks are arranged within the national park. Reservations in advance at the National Park Centre in Zernez is essential (Tel 081 851 41 41).

Walking in the Swiss National Park can be an education, but if you want to make the most of the experience, you're strongly advised first to visit the National Park Centre in Zernez where many fascinating exhibits, informative leaflets and a film show will give a clue as to what you might expect to see. Then wander the paths with eyes and ears tuned, and you'll be enriched.

ROUTE 74
Varusch Hut (Chamanna dal Parc Varusch: 1771m) – Alp Trupchun (2040m)

Start	Varusch Hut (Chamanna dal Parc Varusch: 1771m)
Distance	4km (2.5 miles) one way
Height gain	269m (883ft)
Grade	1
Time	1½hr
Location	East of S-chanf

In the weeks of early summer the pastures of Alp Trupchun are heavily grazed by deer, chamois and even ibex; although ibex more often roam the upper hillsides. In the cool of morning, and in the evening, it's possible to see large herds of red deer on this walk. Watch for ibex near Alp Purcher (salt leaks from nearby rocks attract the animals); there may well be chamois on the slopes of Piz d'Esan above the entrance to Val Müschauns, and marmots near Val Mela. Later, as summer develops, it may be necessary to go as far as Fuorcla Trupchun in order to see wildlife, but this gentle, easy walk is worth tackling whether there's wildlife on show or not.

Route 69 gave a description of the approach to the Varusch Hut from S-chanf. Leaving the hut take the path heading up-valley on the north bank of the Ova da Trupchun, and in a little under 10min you will reach the national park boundary. Continue up-valley, then cross to the south side of the stream to reach the one-time pig farm of **Alp Purcher**

Val Trupchun, southernmost valley in the national park

(1858m) where there's a junction of paths. Shortly afterwards recross to the north bank where the path forks. The left branch enters **Val Müschauns** for a crossing of Fuorcla Val Sassa (see Route 75), but we continue ahead, rising steadily and passing another bridge over the stream near the entrance to the wild little Val Mela. ▶

Just beyond Val Mela you reach **Alp Trupchun** at the base of the cirque which encloses the upper valley. This is one of the best places for watching marmot, deer and ibex.

The bridge (near Val Mela) connects with a path on the south side of the valley, which could be used for an alternative route back to the Varusch Hut.

ROUTE EXTENSION TO FUORCLA TRUPCHUN (2782M)

To continue as far as Fuorcla Trupchun, a good if narrow path is followed all the way. Leading from Alp Trupchun the slope is undemanding at first, but the gradient increases as you gain height, and for much of the upper 300m the way climbs steeply over scree. **Fuorcla Trupchun** is reached in a little under 2hr from the alp, with a splendid view on the Italian side looking down onto the dammed Lago di Livigno. Ibex can often be seen on the ridge either side of the pass. Allow 1hr for the descent to **Alp Trupchun**.

ROUTE 75

Varusch Hut (1771m) – Fuorcla Val Sassa
(2857m) – Blockhaus Cluozza (1882m)

Start	Varusch Hut (1771m)
Distance	13km (8.1 miles)
Height gain	1086m (3563ft)
Height loss	975m (3199ft)
Grade	3
Time	5½hr
Location	East and northeast of the Varusch Hut

This walk is used as one of the stages on a traverse of the national park (see Route 79). It's a walk with several highlights, splendid views, the possibility of sighting wildlife and a very pleasant hut at the end of it. Should it be your intention to stay overnight at Blockhaus Cluozza, you are advised to reserve a bed in advance as it is extremely busy in summer. (Hut details are given at the end of the route description.)

From the Varusch Hut follow directions for Route 74 as far as the junction of paths at the entrance to **Val Müschauns**. A wooden bridge takes the path across the Ova da Müschauns and works a way up-valley along the west bank of the stream, at first through larch and pine-woods, then above the timberline on the southeast flank of Piz d'Esan. The path recrosses the stream at 2081m, after which it starts to climb more steeply. It is up here that chamois and ibex can often be seen on the opposite flank. Then, working round to the east, the trail becomes steeper and a little exposed. Crossing the stream again, which flows from the glacial Lai da Müschauns (this will be seen from the pass), head up to a grassy bluff, beyond which the way zigzags up screes to gain the **Fuorcla Val Sassa** (2857m) in 3hr or so from the Varusch Hut.

Looking back, the Lai da Müschauns tarn can be seen 120m below (apparently it disappears through evaporation in hot summers), while the snowy Bernina Alps hold your attention to the south. Above the pass to the north stands Piz Quattervals, the highest mountain in the national park at 3165m.

On the eastern side of the pass the path descends over screes and, invariably, slips of old snow, into the glacial basin of **Val Sassa**, the 'Valley of Stones'. This is a steep chute of a valley littered with limestone debris, the so-called 'rock glacier' funnelled between ridges extending on the left from Piz Quattervals, and on the right from Piz Serra. At the foot of a long 900m descent through Val Sassa you come to **Plaun Sassa** at the junction with Val Dal Diavel, the upper reaches of Val Cluozza.

The path now follows the Ova da Cluozza downvalley on the left bank of the stream. On coming to the wooded **Plan Valletta** a bridge takes you across the stream at 1835m (where there's a junction with a path from Val Valletta). There follows a brief climb among pine trees, to find **Blockhaus Cluozza** (1882m).

BLOCKHAUS CLUOZZA

Owned by the national park authority, the rustic Blockhaus Cluozza was built in 1910, but modernised in 1993 without compromising its former atmosphere. It can sleep 63, and is invariably very busy during the peak season and at weekends. Meals and light refreshments are available. The hut is open from late-June to mid-October. Reservations essential: Tel 081 856 12 35 www.nationalpark.ch.

ROUTE 76
Zernez (1471m) – Blockhaus Cluozza
(Chamanna Cluozza: 1882m)

Start	Zernez (1471m)
Distance	6km (3.7 miles) one way
Height gain	729m (2392ft)
Height loss	318m (1043ft)
Grade	2
Time	3hr
Location	Southeast of Zernez

Val Cluozza is densely forested. As you climb steeply up a hillside an hour or so from Zernez, there's a brief 'window' in the tree cover, through which a sudden panorama is revealed to show the deep 'V' cut of the valley stretching southward; a seemingly impenetrable blanket of pine and larch covering its lower-to-middle reaches, and bare mountains rising from it with scratch marks of streams carved in their flanks. It's a view that displays better than most the great scenic differences between valleys of the national park and those, for example, of the Bregaglia or upper reaches of the Engadine or Val Bernina. This could almost be taken for Canada. In 1909 Val Cluozza was the first valley acquired by the newly formed Swiss Society for the Protection of Nature, who created around it the reserve that became the national park five years later.

This approach to Blockhaus Cluozza is along a fairly steep switchback of a trail, zigzagging through forest to gain access to Val Cluozza over a shoulder of mountain, before levelling on a brief traverse, then dropping to the valley floor. Crossing the Ova da Cluozza stream, the way then climbs steeply to the hut, set on a clifftop among pine and larch trees from where red deer may be seen feeding in the early morning and evening. Should you plan to stay overnight at the hut, it is essential to reserve a space before setting out (Tel 081 956 12 35).

The path begins about 1km from the centre of Zernez, on the road leading to the Ofenpass. On the right-hand side of the road a covered wooden bridge spanning the River Spöl marks the start of the route. Over the bridge take the farm track on the left that takes you through terraced meadowland, then into forest. Gaining height in long sweeps, the track becomes a path that zigzags steeply up the rounded spur forming the western gateway to **Val Cluozza**. It's a fragrant walk among sun-warmed pines, with red squirrels in the branches overhead, and prospects of sighting deer through the trees.

About 1hr after leaving the road, the path enters the national park, although it has been following its boundary for some time. Now and then you'll catch a brief glimpse of the Val Cluozza stretching ahead, then you top a bluff and gain a lovely view of forest, valley and mountain. The way now contours along the valley's west flank, then rises to a high point of 2126m before sloping downhill, crossing minor streams, or bare-earth scars where springtime avalanches have swept through the trees. Then the path

Val Cluozza was the first valley leased to the national park

descends more steeply, passes what once must have been an alp, then crosses the Ova da Cluozza on a wooden bridge for a final climb up the east bank slope to gain the hut. (For hut details, please see Route 75.)

To return to Zernez by the same route, allow 2½hr.

ROUTE 77

Vallun Chafuol (1766m) – Murter (2545m) – Blockhaus Cluozza (Chamanna Cluozza: 1882m)

Start	Vallun Chafuol (1766m)
Distance	7km (4.3 miles)
Height gain	897m (2943ft)
Height loss	781m (2562ft)
Grade	3
Time	3½–4hr
Location	Southeast of Zernez

This third approach route to Blockhaus Cluozza is from the east, beginning on the Ofenpass road about 3km beyond Ova Spin at Parkplatz no:3 (there's a postbus stop here – ask for Vallun Chafod). This walk forms a link between Val dal Spöl and Val Cluozza, and crosses a high ridge northwest of Piz Murter. On both sides of the ridge the path is a steep one, making the route quite strenuous, despite its modest length. Once again, should you have plans on staying overnight at Blockhaus Cluozza, you are urged to telephone in advance to book a space (Tel 081 856 12 35).

Where the rivers Spöl and Fuorn meet they reveal different colours; the dark waters of the Spöl contrasting with the lighter, almost white, Fuorn stream.

The signed path begins at the northern end of the Vallun Chafuol parking place, where it descends through forest for about 10min before crossing the Spöl a short distance from its confluence with the Ova dal Fuorn.

The way now climbs to the small clearing of **Plan Praspöl** where the path forks; the left branch heading up-valley to Punt Periv, while ours begins the long 850m climb to the Murter ridge.

A seemingly unending series of zigzags mounts the steep hillside among stately Engadine pine and spruce, then as you gain height, so these give way to larch and dwarf pine. At 2338m come onto a small grassy plateau shown on the map as **Plan dals Poms**, from where you gain a fine bird's-eye view of the narrow Spöl reservoir 700m below. The worst of the climb is now behind you, and the final 200m to the Murter saddle is less demanding as you wander up former alp pastures where marmots, chamois and ibex may be seen.

The near-level saddle of **Murter** (2545m) is reached after about 2½hr. It's worth spending time here (weather permitting) to enjoy a fine vista that stretches east to the Ortler Alps in Italy, the nearer Engiadina Dolomites on the north side of the Ofenpass road, as well as Piz Quattervals and its neighbours across Val Cluozza in the southwest, and the Albula Alps to the west and northwest. Deer and chamois can often be seen grazing the slopes of Piz Terza nearby.

On the west side of the ridge the path descends across grassy meadows rich with alpine flowers in early summer. A few ruined alp huts lie near the path as you come down to the first of the mountain pines, and the way then zigzags down to wooded slopes of Scots pine and larch to emerge near Blockhaus Cluozza, which is reached about 1hr from the saddle. (Hut details will be found under Route 75.)

ROUTE 78

Blockhaus Cluozza (Chamanna Cluozza: 1882m) – Piz Quattervals (3165m)

Start	Blockhaus Cluozza (Chamanna Cluozza: 1882m)
Distance	5km (3.1 miles) one way
Height gain	1330m (4364ft)
Grade	3
Time	5–5½hr
Location	Southwest of Blockhaus Cluozza

As the highest summit in the national park, Piz Quattervals naturally attracts the attention of experienced mountain walkers. Only one route to the summit is permitted, and that is from the north by way of Val Valletta. It's not a technical climb, but the ascent should only be tackled by fit walkers with scrambling experience. It makes a demanding day out, and you'll need settled weather. Better to start early, for the full there-and-back outing will take 8–8½hr, plus rests.

Take the path heading up-valley (south) from the Cluozza hut, descending to a bridge over the stream at 1835m. Across this the path forks in Plan Valletta. Take the right branch to enter the **Val Valletta**, which rises southwest-ward. The path is waymarked with the white-blue-white stripes of an Alpine route, at first on the right of the Valletta stream, but gradually fading until there is no actual path to be seen. Above about 2100m there are no more waymarks, and you must choose your own route.

Work up through the valley, crossing two rock bands (at around 2200m and 2400m). In summer snow patches are likely to be met from about 2700m, and if these are firm and extensive (as in the early part of the season), it's preferable to use these as a ramp to mount the north side directly to the summit. If, however, the snow is either soft or having melted completely to reveal loose rock, climb the northwest ridge and reach the summit from there.

The summit makes a magnificent vantage point, providing a 360° panorama that includes a vast array of peaks spilling far off across both the Eastern and the Central Alps.

Allow 3hr for the descent to Blockhaus Cluozza by the same route.

ROUTE 79

Blockhaus Cluozza (Chamanna Cluozza: 1882m) – Murter (2545m) – Punt Periv (1659m) – Il Fuorn (1794m)

Start	Blockhaus Cluozza (Chamanna Cluozza: 1882m)
Distance	14km (8.7 miles)
Height gain	798m (2618ft)
Height loss	886m (2907ft)
Grade	3
Time	6½–7hr
Location	East of Blockhaus Cluozza

This long route can be taken as the second stage of a traverse of the national park. (Stage 1 was described as Route 75.) For the majority of the way it reverses Route 77 by crossing the Murter saddle and descending steeply into the Val dal Spöl, but it then veers right to cross the Spöl upstream near the Italian border before cutting back to the Ofenpass road and Il Fuorn. As with most walks in the national park, there's a good chance of sighting a variety of wildlife.

Leaving Blockhaus Cluozza turn left on the path which heads south, and at the junction shortly after, take the left branch to climb among larch and Scots pine, then in zigzags among more pine trees before coming out to open meadows and the ruins of former alp huts. The

239

climb continues up steep slopes to gain the flat saddle of **Murter** (1545m) after about 2½hr. Given good conditions, the views from this high point are far-reaching and memorable.

Descending the east side of the ridge the path leads over open slopes to the flat grassy shoulder of **Plan dals Poms** (2338m), then more steeply in countless zigzags among dwarf pine on the northern side of the little Vallun Praspöl. From dwarf pine to forested slopes of massive Engadine pine and spruce, emerge in a small clearing, **Plan Prospöl**, where the path forks. Take the right branch and contour for almost 4km along the wooded hillside of the Spöl's gorge. Chamois may be seen as you cross the mouth of the Vallun Verd, and there's a chance of sighting deer in the meadow of **Plan de l'Acqua Suot** after crossing the stream issuing from Val da la Föglia. There are plenty of twists, dips and climbs on this section before you cross the Spöl on the sturdy **Punt Periv**.

A brief climb brings the path to a junction with a trail that breaks away to the right and follows the river to the dammed Lago di Livigno on the Swiss/Italian border. Our route, however, keeps ahead (the left branch), an easy woodland walk that eventually brings you round to **Punt la Drossa** and a bus stop on the Ofenpass road at 1771m.

PUNT LA DROSSA

This is the entrance to a tunnel which carries traffic beneath the slopes of Munt la Schera to the duty-free Valle di Livigno in Italy. The southern end of the tunnel emerges beside Lagi di Livigno on the border, and completes the journey to the long straggling town of Livigno alongside the lake. The road then continues through the valley and eventually crosses back into Switzerland to link with the Bernina Pass.

Cross the road to a continuing path that goes between the road and the Ova dal Fuorn, and shortly before reaching **Il Fuorn** recross the road for the final approach to the hotel.

HOTEL PARC NAZIUNAL

This is a large traditional lodge, open from May to October with standard bedrooms, and with dormitory accommodation available nearby. Despite the proximity of the road, red deer and chamois can be seen grazing close by during the evening and early morning. To reserve beds at either the hotel or Lager Il Fuorn, Tel 081 856 12 26 www.ilfuorn.ch).

Walks from Il Fuorn

The continuation of a traverse of the national park, leading from Il Fuorn to S-charl, is described in full as Route 82. However, a few local walks from a base here are worth giving in outline, as below.

- A 3hr circular walk begins by heading east alongside the road as far as Parkplatz no:9 (it's possible to take a postbus for this section), then going north into **Val da Stabelchod**. At Alp Stabelchod (1958m) roe deer, red deer and chamois can sometimes be seen grazing. Towards the head of the valley there are huge screes and dolomitic towers of rock in view as you climb to the high point of the walk at **Margunet**, a saddle at 2328m, then descend into **Val dal Botsch** to the west of the Stabelchod Valley. The path follows the stream most of the way down to the Ofenpass road, where you then return to Il Fuorn.

- A short (1½hr) walk can be had by following a nature trail to Buffalora. This begins on a path on the south side of the road heading east (the same path that began the above walk to Stabelchod), among woodland just above the Ova dal Fuorn stream. Immediately after leaving the national park boundary at Gasthaus Stradin, break off to the right on a path that crosses the stream and wander across open country to **Alp Buffalora** (2038m). Either return to Il Fuorn by the same route, catch a postbus, or take the longer route outlined below.

- From **Alp Buffalora** (see above), a route goes south then west to pass the entrance to an old mine used in the Middle Ages. Over a saddle at **Fop da Buffalora** re-enter the national park, then contour round a shoulder of **Munt la Schera** (very fine views) before sloping down to the meadows of **Alp la Schera** and a path junction. Take the right fork and curve north through mixed woods to arrive at the Ofenpass road a short distance from Il Fuorn (4½hr from Alp Buffalora).

ROUTE 80

Ova Spin (Parkplatz no:1: 1842m) –
Alp Grimmels (2055m) – Ova Spin

Start	Ova Spin (Parkplatz no:1: 1842m)
Distance	6km (3.7 miles)
Height gain	280m (919ft)
Height loss	280m (919ft)
Grade	1
Time	2–2½hr
Location	Southeast of Ova Spin (on the Ofenpass road)

On the northern side of the Ofenpass road, Alp Grimmels is noted for its marmot colony, and this short and easy circular walk provides an opportunity to study the animals at fairly close quarters.

If you're staying at Ova Spin, take the roadside footpath to reach the start of the route.

Take the postbus (or drive, if you have your own vehicle) to **Parkplatz no:1** on the Ofenpass road. This is found about 600m beyond Ova Spin on a hairpin bend. ◄

On the south side of the parking place a narrow footpath climbs behind some barriers, and keeping to the edge of the forested slope it takes you above the road, and about 15min later brings you to a junction. On the road below is **Parkplatz no:2**. Our path now rises steadily through forest, and about 10min from the previous junction, the way forks. (The right branch goes to Vallun Chafuol, Parkplatz 3.) Keep ahead on what is a

very pleasant path with a gentle gradient, and you'll go through a series of open glades to gain views of the heavily forested valley leading to the Ofenpass. After contouring for a while the path rises once more to gain a wooded saddle at about 2085m, over which you descend into the sloping meadows of **Alp Grimmels** (2055m/1¼hr).

Alp Grimmels, a national park meadow noted for its colony of marmots

Yellow-topped marker posts designate the areas in which you can rest to watch whatever animals may be grazing nearby. Marmots are almost guaranteed, but you may see chamois and/or deer too. Views are splendid: to the east the slope descends to Il Fuorn, set among meadows beside the Ofenpass road, while far beyond it glacier-clad peaks signal the Ortler Alps in Italy; to the north we look into the Val Ftur headed by Piz Sampuoir and flanked by Piz Laschadurella and Piz Murters; and to the south across the Spöl valley to mountains of the Stelvio National Park.

Wander across the meadows on the footpath, which then slopes downhill among pines to another junction. The right-hand path here goes to Il Fuorn (see Route 81), while we veer left through a narrow meadowland to the one-time alp of Champlönch, passing a small marshy area where a stream sidles through the meadows. Leaving the meadows behind the path now slopes down through a wooded gully, at the foot of which lies **Parkplatz no:1**.

243

ROUTE 81
Ova Spin (Parkplatz no:1: 1842m) –
Champlönch (2015m) – Il Fuorn (1794m)

Start	Ova Spin (Parkplatz no:1: 1842m)
Distance	5km (3.1 miles) one way
Height gain	173m (568ft)
Height loss	221m (725ft)
Grade	1
Time	2hr
Location	Southeast of Ova Spin (on the Ofenpass road)

This second walk from Ova Spin (or the parking area just beyond it) reverses a section of Route 80 as it makes an easy yet enjoyable crossing to Il Fuorn. Surprising as it may seem, the path follows what was the original route to the Ofenpass before the road was built in the 19th century. Both start and finishing points are accessible by postbus, so there should be no difficulty in returning to Ova Spin at the end of the walk.

From Parkplatz no:1 take the path that climbs eastward through a wooded gully, at the top of which you are soon drawn into the long meadows of **Champlönch**, a one-time alp whose far end is a little marshy but rich in flowers in late spring and early summer. Beyond the meadows you come to a narrow funnel of trees where the path forks at 2015m. The right-hand option goes to Alp Grimmels (see Route 80), but we continue ahead to descend the wooded **Badachül coombe** in long loops that provide enticing views into Val Ftur which is, sadly, off-limits. The best of these views is to be had from the footbridge over the Ftur stream, which is as close as we can get to exploring that fine-looking glen. Over the bridge the path rises gradually, then contours round the hillside before crossing an avalanche chute and descending to **Hotel Parc Naziunal**. (For hotel or dormitory accommodation, please see details at the end of Route 79.)

To return to Ova Spin, there's a postbus stop near the hotel.

ROUTE 82

Il Fuorn (1794m) – Fuorcla Val dal Botsch (2677m) – Sur il Foss (2317m) – S-charl (1810m)

Start	Il Fuorn (1794m)
Distance	14km (8.7 miles)
Height gain	930m (3051ft)
Height loss	914m (2999ft)
Grade	3
Time	7hr
Location	Northeast of Il Fuorn

This long and fairly strenuous day's walking effectively completes a traverse of the national park, previous sections of which were described between S-chanf and Hotel Il Fuorn – but see Route 84 for the full itinerary. On this stage there are two passes to cross, but happily there's not too much height to lose between them.

From Hotel Il Fuorn start by taking the path on the south side of the road which follows the right bank of the Ova dal Fuorn upstream as far as Parkplatz no:7. Now head north into the wooded **Val dal Botsch** on a good path, which soon joins the valley's stream. At first narrow, the valley opens as you gain height through it, with an abrupt slope at its head. The path forks at 2176m, with the right branch heading for Margunet and the Val da Stabelchod (see Walks from Il Fuorn above). Our path continues towards the head of the valley, and soon begins to climb the steep grass slope with numerous zigzags. It's a 500m climb from the path junction, during which you may see herds of chamois or red deer.

Fuorcla Val dal Botsch is gained about 3hr from Il Fuorn. From it views back to the south show the Bernina Alps above intervening ridges and lesser peaks; to the north rise the so-called Engiadina Dolomites with Piz Plavna Dadaint dominating nearby, while the Ortler Alps gleam with snow and ice to the east.

Across the glacial cirque that forms the head of Val Plavna, the next pass, Sur il Foss, lies ENE on a curving ridge that carries the park boundary. Leaving the national park now, descend a long scree slope to a stream crossing almost 400m below the *fuorcla* where the path forks. Ignore the left branch and keep ahead to a second stream and contour along the right-hand hillside, ignoring a second path descending to the valley. Before long come onto the 2317m pass of **Sur il Foss**, about 1½hr from the Val dal Botsch pass (4½hr from Il Fuorn). Looking back, Piz Plavna Dadaint assumes a dramatic pose with its fingers of rock protruding from its south ridge.

The descent into **Val Mingèr** means a return to the national park. It's a fine valley, with dwarf pine, meadow and forest, and some bizarre sandstone rock formations. The path is clearly defined, and with Val S-charl seen below, it crosses the stream several times, and at last brings you in an easy 1½hr to a bridge over the Clemgia stream near its confluence with that from Val Mingèr. This is the Mingèrbrücke at 1664m. Across this you leave the national park and come onto an unpaved road where there's a bus stop for the (infrequent) postbus down-valley to Scuol.

For accommodation in the little village of **S-charl**, turn right. There's a path on the left of the road, and this last part of the walk will take about 45min to complete, on the way passing ruins, and on the right of the road a museum devoted to the region's mining history, which dates back to the 12th century.

S-CHARL

The village has accommodation in three hotels: the pine-clad Gasthaus Mayor with 26 beds (Tel 081 864 14 12 https://gasthaus-mayor.ch), Landgasthof Crusch Alba which has 40 beds (Tel 081 864 14 05 www.cruschalba.ch), and the much smaller Garni Chasa Sesvenna (Tel 081 864 06 18 www.sesvenna.ch). The first two hotels have restaurants, otherwise there are no tourist facilities in the village. But the walking potential is first class, as may be gauged by following Routes 96–100.

ROUTE 83
S-charl (Mingèrbrücke: 1664m) –
Val Mingèr – Sur il Foss (2317m)

Start	S-charl (Mingèrbrücke: 1664m)
Distance	5km (3.1 miles) one way
Height gain	653m (2142ft)
Grade	1–2
Time	3hr
Location	Northwest of S-charl

Val Mingèr is a delightful glen of flower meadows, cembra (or Arolla) pine, dashing streams and views of the dolomitic peak of Piz Plavna Dadaint (3166m) peering over the pass of Sur il Foss on the valley's headwall. A day spent wandering this outlying valley of the national park will be a day well spent, whether or not you decide to go as far as the pass. Chamois can often be seen on the slopes of Piz Mingèr, while red deer, at certain times of the day, may be seen grazing the open meadows.

Either walk or take the postbus from S-charl (or Scuol) to the flood control at **Mingèrbrücke**, a little over 3km northwest of S-charl village (add 30min if walking). A footpath sign here, in the area shown on the map as Pradatsch, directs the start of the walk on the left bank of the stream. At once the path plunges into a forest of pine

Between the two valleys a curious sandstone outcrop is known as the Witch's Head (Cheu de la stria in Romansch). Eroded by water, wind and frost, it can also be recognised as the outline of a raven's head.

and larch, and rises easily into **Val Mingèr**. Before long come out of the trees and cross a small, closely cropped meadow, only to re-enter woodland again on the far side. Soon the valley forks, with the Val Foraz (closed to the public) cutting south into the mountains. ◄

There's only one path through Val Mingèr, and it takes you in and out of forest, across more small meadows, passes the remains of old charcoal kilns, and crosses the stream several times. By the time you reach **Alp Mingèr** (2090m), Piz Plavna Dadaint can be seen above the obvious pass of **Sur il Foss** at the head of the valley. Continuing from here, keep alert for signs of wildlife, and on coming to a designated rest area at 2168m you're almost certain to see chamois and, quite possibly, red deer. The path now swings westward and makes an easy climb to the pass, from where the views are especially rewarding.

Return to S-charl by the same route in 2–2½hr.

LONGER ALTERNATIVE

A longer version of this walk could be created by descending from the pass into **Val Plavna**, and following a path roughly northward through the valley all the way to **Scuol** – allow 3–3½hr from Sur il Foss.

ROUTE 84
A traverse of the National Park

Start	S-chanf (1669m)
Finish	S-charl (1810m)
Distance	46km (28.6 miles)
Height gain	(accumulative) 2916m (9567ft)
Height loss	(accumulative) 2775m (9101ft)
Grade	3
Time	3–4 days (20–21hr total walking time)

By combining four routes previously described, a very rewarding traverse of the national park can be achieved. It's not only a fine multi-day trek, with wildly unspoilt scenery, but it gives lots of opportunities for observing wildlife along the way. To ensure accommodation is available at the end of each stage, you are strongly advised to telephone ahead to book room. Telephone numbers are given under individual sections described. Remember, camping and bivouacking are strictly prohibited within the national park.

Beginning in **S-chanf** in the Upper Engadine, make your way to the **Varusch Hut** (Chamanna Varusch) in **Val Trupchun** a short distance from the park boundary. This is described as Route 69; a short walk of just 1¼hr. Beyond the hut the way pushes deeper into the valley before turning northeast into **Val Müschauns** for the crossing of **Fuorcla Val Sassa** (2857m), and subsequent descent into the **Val Cluozza**, where a night is spent at the park-owned **Blockhaus** (Chamanna) **Cluozza**. Details for this 5½hr stage are found under Route 75.

The next stage crosses the east wall of Val Cluozza at the panoramic viewpoint saddle of **Murter** (1545m), a splendid place to watch chamois. This is followed by a steep descent into the **Val dal Spöl** whose stream is crossed close to the Swiss/Italian border, after which a woodland

Piz Plavna Dadaint, seen in the late springtime above Sur il Foss in the national park's Val Mingèr

path leads round to the Ofenpass road and **Hotel Il Fuorn** (1794m). Modestly priced dormitory accommodation as well as standard hotel rooms may be had here, at the end of a 6½–7hr day described as Route 79.

Having completed a crossing of the southern half of the national park, there follows a long (7hr) stage with two passes to tackle. These are **Fuorcla Val dal Botsch** (2677m), and **Sur il Foss** (2317m), with a 400m descent between them. After crossing the second of these, a path descends through the lovely **Val Mingèr** to **Val S-charl** and completion of the traverse (see Route 82).

ROUTE 85

Lavin (1412m) – Lai da la Mezza Glüna (2635m)
– Fuorcletta da Barcli (2850m) – Zernez (1471m)

Start	Lavin (1412m)
Distance	17km (10.6 miles)
Height gain	1524m (5000ft)
Height loss	1474m (4836ft)
Grade	3
Time	7½hr
Location	Southeast of Lavin

Lai da la Mezza Glüna is the highest among a collection of tarns nestling in a wild cirque of mountains at the head of Val Zeznina. In August 2000 this remote cirque was added to the national park; an impressive enclave amounting to 3.6km² rimmed by rugged peaks, several of which are more than 3000m high. This tough walk not only visits the Macun Lakes (as they are usually called), but makes a crossing of their south-containing ridge, followed by a steep descent to Zernez. Should the full route be too daunting, or snow is still lying on the upper slopes, a visit to the lakes will certainly be rewarding – allow 3½–4hr up, and 2½–3hr back down to Lavin.

Below Lavin cross the River Inn on a covered wooden bridge, and turn right along a gravel track for about 1200m, then take a narrower track on the left which leads through forest heading east to Plan Surücha. A path continues, steadily gaining height and turning a spur to enter **Val Zezvina** where the valley's draining stream is crossed on a footbridge. Over this the path forks and you take the right branch and shortly after reach **Alp Zeznina Dadaint** (1958m) in a little under 2hr.

Keeping to the left (east) side of the stream the path rises through the valley, then zigzags as the gradient steepens, at first up grass slopes, then among ancient moraine debris. A small tarn is passed below Piz Macun, and soon after you enter the national park enclave and the Macun basin. Here you come to the first of the **Macun lakes** (2616m), of which there are more than a dozen, including several pools dotted among the rumpled, vegetated moraines left behind by the glacier that scoured out the cirque long ago. The highest of the tarns, **Lai da la Mezza Glüna**, lies away from the trail to the west, at the foot of Piz d'Arpiglias. Well into summer, patches of old winter snow linger here, as well as elsewhere in this wild basin.

Continue south across the rough basin floor guided by waymarks, before the slope steepens for the final rocky scramble to gain the **Fuorcletta da Barcli**, a 2850m dip in the containing ridge, reached about 4–4½hr from Lavin. Views from here are very fine, but they are even better from the 2945m high point to the west. Traverse the exposed right-hand ridge with care to gain this, where – given clear conditions – you'll enjoy a tremendous vista of one mountain ridge after another spreading far off in all directions. The conical Piz Linard and unmistakable Piz Buin across the Engadine, the snowy Ortler to the southeast, and Bernina Alps in the southwest, are among the highlights. Zernez is intimidatingly far below, half-circled by the Spöl and the Inn, and the descent to it can be tough on tired legs and knees.

Go directly down the southwest spur to the crags of **Munt Baselgia**, losing about 250m, then twist to the right on a brief descending traverse before resuming more steeply downhill among a series of avalanche defences. Below **Plan Sech** come onto a track and follow this as it loops its way back and forth across the hillside, then through forest and across meadows to finally reach **Zernez**.

If you need to return to Lavin, the railway station is located off the Engadine road southwest of the church.

LOWER ENGADINE –
NORTHEASTERN REGION

While hillsides that form a natural terrace along the north wall of the valley offer some extremely pleasant, scenically delightful yet undemanding walks, the main attractions here will be found by exploring those tributary valleys that cut deep into the mountains. Each one has its own distinctive atmosphere and appeal, and a walking holiday concentrated on this end of the valley will have much to commend it.

In the bed of the valley the Inn rushes through gorges and low-lying meadows; a great challenge to white-water canoe enthusiasts. This is a serious stretch of river that should only be tackled by experts. Meadows that line it are mostly caught between river and forest; just a few haybarns dotted here and there until, about halfway along the valley, it broadens enough to enable communities like Tarasp, Fontana and Vulpera to exploit the sunniest locations. Tarasp Castle is perched on a steep hilltop

Tarasp Castle can be seen on its plug of rock in the valley below Ardez (Routes 94 and 95)

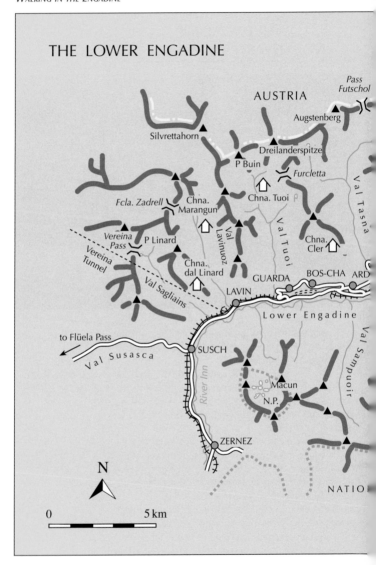

THE LOWER ENGADINE

AUSTRIA

Pass Futschol

Augstenberg

Silvrettahorn

Dreilanderspitze

P Buin

Furcletta

Chna. Tuoi

Fcla. Zadrell

Chna. Marangun

Val Lavinuoz

Val Tuoi

Val Tasna

Chna. Cler

Vereina Pass

P Linard

Chna. dal Linard

GUARDA

BOS-CHA

ARD

Vereina Tunnel

Val Sagliains

LAVIN

Lower Engadine

to Flüela Pass

Val Susasca

SUSCH

River Inn

Macun

N.P.

Val Sampuoir

ZERNEZ

NATIO

N

0   5 km

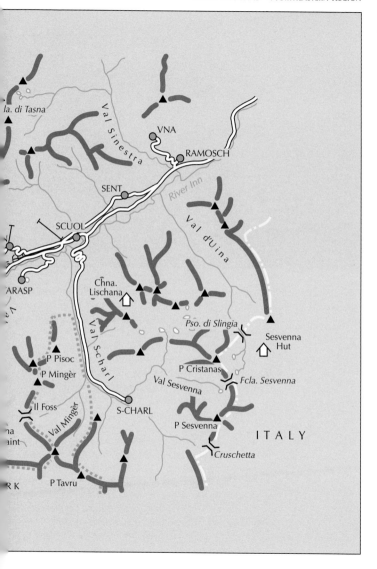

In early summer the meadows of Val Tuoi are full of wild flowers

plug overlooking lush pastures, a small tarn, and the attractive village to which it lends its name. From practically every corner of the village a view demands to be photographed.

The majority of Lower Engadine villages, however, are found not in the valley bed, but on the northern hillside, lining a natural terrace and standing astride the original narrow valley road that is still unpaved in places.

Of the Inn's feeder valleys that project into the high mountains of the Silvretta Alps above these terrace villages, some of the best are Val Tuoi, Val Tasna and Val Sinestra. There's much to be said for the others too, and time should be allowed, where possible, to explore each one. On the southern side, Val S-charl is a long, secretive valley nudging the national park's border. At S-charl village it opens out to a wonderland of streams, side valleys, meadows and mountains, and at the head of some of these side valleys walkers' passes lead into Italy, to the dreamy Val Müstair on the Italian side of the Ofenpass, or to the Ofenpass itself.

To the west of Val S-charl, Val Plavna offers enticing long treks with options at its head; next comes Val Sampuoir, and steep little hanging valleys that lead into mountains blocking Zernez, and from their high points views reveal snowpeaks on the border with Austria.

While offering an entirely different form of scenery to that of the Upper Engadine, or that of the Bregaglia, the Lower Engadine is by no means a poor substitute. No walker or mountain lover need be disappointed.

ROUTE 86
Zernez (1471m) – Carolina (1565m)
– Cinuos-chel (1628m)

Start	Zernez (1471m)
Distance	10km (6.2 miles)
Height gain	157m (515ft)
Grade	1
Time	2½hr
Location	Southwest of Zernez

A gentle valley stroll across meadows and through forests along the edge of the national park, this is an undemanding yet very pleasant half-day outing. It could be extended as far as S-chanf or Zuoz or, indeed, as part of a long-distance Engadine Valley traverse. On the other hand, it could be used as part of an approach to the Varusch Hut in Val Trupchun. As a walk in its own right it makes a satisfactory way of spending a morning or afternoon.

Walk south out of Zernez along the road in the direction of St Moritz. A short distance after crossing the Spöl, the road makes a right-hand curve. Take a footpath on the left, which crosses the railway and comes to a track where you turn right. Wandering among larch and pine-woods make your way towards the isolated station of

Carolina, ignoring other paths and tracks that branch away, most of which climb through the forest towards the national park boundary. Our route monitors the line of railway and river, until at last the railway line crosses the Inn to the station at **Cinuos-chel/Brail**. Shortly after a bridge takes us across to the station for a return to Zernez.

ROUTE 87
Zernez (1471m) – Susch (1426m) – Lavin (1412m)

Start	Zernez (1471m)
Distance	10km (6.2 miles)
Height loss	59m (194ft)
Grade	1
Time	2–2½hr
Location	North of Zernez

As with the previous route, this is another low-level valley walk, which follows the River Inn northward through the narrow cut it has made in the mountains just beyond Zernez. Adopted by both the Unterengadin Talweg and the Via Engiadina, like Route 86 it could be extended much further along the valley, to Guarda and Ardez (in another 3½hr), for example. There are also paths and trackways that continue through Tarasp and Scuol, and even beyond the Swiss border to Nauders in Austria. The undemanding walk described here catches the fragrance of forest and meadow with the sound of the Inn surging along to the left, while mountains rise steeply on both sides of the valley. As you round the bend just after Susch the valley opens out to capture the soft Engadine light that floods the hillsides.

The walk begins north of the prominent village church in Zernez on a track/lane that soon accompanies the River Inn that has been boosted by the Spöl – the river coming from the Ofenpass. After crossing a stream issuing from the little Val Gondas the way passes below the tree-owned knoll of Clus (1684m) and continues through meadow and forest to Susch, with its old ruins, and with the elegant cone of Piz Linard rising directly ahead.

Cross the river into Susch, then turn right and shortly after recross to the right bank of the Inn again at the next bridge. Immediately after passing between a row of buildings, fork left to rejoin the river, gaining a view across the valley to the rather ugly Sagliains station where vehicles are transported by rail through the Vereina tunnel. Once this is out of sight, you can continue to enjoy the natural beauty of the valley on the right bank of the river. When you reach a covered wooden bridge below Lavin, cross into the village to complete the walk.

For a return to Zernez, take the train from Lavin station.

ROUTE 88
Zernez (1471m) – Fuorcla Stragliavita (2687m) – Alp Sampuoir (1854m) – Ardez Station (1432m)

Start	Zernez (1471m)
Distance	16km (9.9 miles)
Height gain	1216m (3990ft)
Height loss	1255m (4118ft)
Grade	3
Time	7–7½hr
Location	East and northeast of Zernez

Zernez nestles below the western point of a large triangular wedge of mountains contained by the valleys of the Inn, the Spöl and Val Müstair (bridged by the Ofenpass), and the Italian Adige. The following route cuts across that wedge at almost its narrowest point. Even so, it's a long and fairly strenuous crossing with opportunities for some very fine views and a rich variety of alpine plants on both sides of the pass. Please note that the length of the walk could be reduced by about an hour by taking a postbus from Zernez to the mouth of Val Laschadura.

Walk out of Zernez along, or beside, the Ofenpass road for almost 3km to where a path angles above the road and cuts into and across the mouth of **Val da Barcli**. Across this the way forks. Take the upper route option which climbs into this valley a short distance, then angles round forested slopes to enter Val Laschadura where it is joined by a path from the right – this is the path which comes from the bus stop on the Ofenpass road.

Pushing deeper into the valley you emerge from the forest to more lightly wooded slopes and reach the buildings of **Alp Laschadura** (2000m) on the west bank of the valley's stream. Continue up-valley above the stream, but immediately after crossing a side stream at its confluence with the Ova da Laschadura, the path swings left and begins the steepening climb to the pass. Gained about 4hr after leaving Zernez, **Fuorcla Stragliavita** is a 2687m saddle on a ridge linking Piz Nuna (to the left) and the lesser summit of Ils Cuogns, and it marks the boundary between crystalline rock and dolomitic limestone. Looking back you have a direct view across the Spöl's valley to the densely wooded Val Cluozza in the national park.

Descend northeastward into a basin of rock and scree and, often, snow patches lying until early July. White-red-white paint flashes guide the way in the absence of a clear path, and losing height the angle of the slope steepens as you approach the chamois hunter's hut at **Plan Surröven** (2256m) where there's a choice of routes. Both eventually lead to the Lower Engadine below Ardez, but the recommendation here is to take the right-hand (lower) option which slopes down into the Val Sampuoir and, 1½–2hr from the pass, brings you to **Alp Sampuoir** (1854m).

North of the alp you come to forest as the valley is squeezed into gorge-like narrows. Do not cross the Sampuoir stream, but remain on the left bank, and eventually the path joins a track that curves left and angles down the hillside onto a minor road between Sur En (left) and the River Inn. Bear right along this road, which crosses the river and mounts the north slope to **Ardez railway station**.

Other walks from Zernez

The close proximity of the national park inevitably means that walkers based in Zernez will be drawn into the park, but there are other walks to consider too.

Mention must be made of the approach to **Blockhaus Cluozza** where you can spend a night in the heart of the national park. This is described elsewhere in this guide as Route 76.

Adopting the first part of the route to Blockhaus Cluozza, a variation to the 2579m **Murtaröl** viewpoint on the ridge marking the west wall of Val Cluozza has an excellent reputation. This suggestion diverts from the Blockhaus Cluozza route where Route 76 leaves the ridge to contour across the Cluozza's west flank. For Murtaröl a path continues along the ridge spur, and after reaching the high point, returns along the Engadine slope to make a 5hr circular walk from Zernez.

West of Zernez a 4hr circular walk, mainly through forest, can be achieved by taking a track-then-path up the hillside to **Alp Munt** (1987m). From there turn south on a rising traverse to **Charbuneras**, another alp hut at 2197m, after which you then loop back down the wooded slope to Zernez.

Walks from Susch

Located at the junction with the Flüela Pass road, Susch is a modest village, but one whose strategic importance may be imagined by the ruined keep of Chaschinas that stands on the Inn's right bank. The village could be useful as a short-term base for one or two local walks, or as the starting point for some longer routes, a selection of which are given below.

Forming a northern gatepost to Val Susasca, which carries the Flüela Pass road, Piz Murtera (3004m) has a secondary summit on its south-east spur, the 2850m **Piz Chastè**. A good day's exercise may be had by taking a clear farm track which loops back and forth up the hillside to the alp of **Suot Chastè** 500m below the summit, then by a waymarked path to the top (3½–4hr from Susch, plus 2½hr down).

The **Flüela Pass** (2383m) carries traffic between Susch and Davos. Closed by snow in winter, in summer it (and Val Susasca, which drains it to the east) is used as a means of reaching some otherwise remote corners of the mountains. A path links the pass with Susch, and you could either take the postbus to the Flüela Hospice and walk back down to Susch (2¾hr), or walk up through the valley from Susch to reach the pass in 3½hr.

From the **Röven** bus stop midway between Susch and the Flüela Pass, a path crosses the Susasca stream to **Alp Pra Dadoura**, and continues up-valley before curving south into Val Grialetsch on the way to the SAC's **Grialetsch Hut** (Chamanna da Grialetsch: 2542m) in 2½hr. If walking all the way from Susch, allow 4½hr.

On the northern side of the road from **Röven** a path takes walkers into Val Fless. At **Alp Fless Dadaint** (2119m) the path forks. The left branch climbs to the **Jörifless Pass** to visit the delightful **Jörisee** lakes in 2–2½hr from Röven.

The continuing path from **Alp Fless Dadaint** (see above) now curves through the Val Torta to cross the **Fless Pass** (2453m), then swings northwest through the Süsertal to reach **Berghaus Vereina** in 4hr from the Röven bus stop – or 5½hr from Susch.

Finally, a recommended long (6hr) trek begins by taking the postbus once more to the **Röven** stop, then walking through Vals Fless and Torta to cross the **Fless Pass** (as above), then curving northeast to traverse the 2585m **Vereinapass**, followed by a 3hr descending walk through Val Sagliains back to Susch.

ROUTE 89
Lavin (1412m) – Linard Hut
(Chamanna dal Linard: 2327m)

Start	Lavin (1412m)
Distance	5km (3.1 miles) one way
Height gain	915m (3002ft)
Grade	3
Time	2½hr
Location	Northwest of Lavin

Piz Linard is the highest summit in the Silvretta Alps. Unlike several of its neighbours, it has no glaciers, but its graceful conical outline, and its prominent position above the Engadine's northeasterly curve between Susch and Lavin, ensure that it is seen and admired by all who wander in and around Zernez. Quite simply, it dominates the skyline. Yet when viewed from villages further east along the main shaft of the valley it holds little significance, for it merely blends into the Engadine's long north wall.

The Linard Hut which serves the mountain stands in the mouth of the little Val Glims, a hanging valley flanked by Piz Linard's steeply plunging southwest and southeast ridges. It's a small hut, wardened during the peak season only, and is reached by a straightforward approach walk.

A sign in Lavin's main square directs the start of the walk along a track that ducks beneath the railway and adjacent bypass road, then crosses the Lavinuoz stream round a hairpin bend. There's no real chance of losing the way from here as it's well signed, but you have a choice of following the forest track for much of the way, making long sweeps at a steady gradient up the hillside above the Vereina rail tunnel, or of taking footpath short cuts which are inevitably steeper. Whichever route is chosen, you will eventually come to an isolated alp hut set in a clearing at 1957m near the head of the track. From here a path slants northwestward, rising above the treeline to grass slopes from which you gain fine views into the Engadine. Rounding a spur, continue on an easy-angled traverse before making a final steep uphill to the hut, with a foreshortened view of Piz Linard towering behind it.

LINARD HUT

Built in 1902 by the Unterengadin (Engiadina Bassa) section of the SAC, Chamanna dal Linard is a charming traditional hut with just 46 dormitory places. It is manned from July to mid-September, when meals are available, otherwise it remains unlocked and with self-catering facilities available. For reservations Tel 079 629 61 91 www.linardhuette.ch.

Routes from the Linard hut

Unless you intend to make a there-and-back walk to the hut, it's worth spending time in this peaceful, unspoilt location. Ibex can often be seen from the hut, and Chamois and marmots too may be seen nearby. The following are suggestions of walks either in the vicinity of the hut, or longer destinations from it.

- At the head of **Val Glims** below Piz Linard's South Face, **two small tarns** lie at 2563m and 2610m – a fine vantage point, reached by an obvious path in a little under 1hr.

- **Fuorcla da Glims**, 200m or so above and to the west of the tarns, is another excellent viewpoint worth visiting (1–1½hr from the hut).

- The ridge to the east of the hut is known as the **Sassautagrat**. It's possible to reach **point 2499m** on this ridge in little more than 30min. Overlooking Val Lavinuoz, views are splendid.

- Rather than descend directly to Lavin by the same route used on the ascent, an alternative is to wander up-valley to **Fuorcla da Glims** (2802m) and descend steeply from there into **Val Sagliains** which drains down to the Engadine just west of **Lavin** (about 4hr).

- A longer trek leads to **Röven** (postbus stop) on the Flüela Pass road in 5hr, by crossing **Fuorcla da Glims** into the head of Val Sagliains, then climbing west to

cross the **Vereinapass**, continuing southwest to the
Fless Pass, and down through the Vals Torta and Fless
to Röven where you can catch a bus to Susch, a short
walk from Lavin.

ROUTE 90
Lavin (1412m) – Chamanna Marangun (2025m)

Start	Lavin (1412m)
Distance	5km (3.1 miles) one way
Height gain	613m (2011ft)
Grade	2
Time	2–2½hr
Location	North of Lavin

Standing between streams near the head of Val Lavinuoz north of Lavin, the
unmanned (but generally unlocked) Marangun Hut is easily reached by this
valley walk which follows a track all the way.

From the *bahnhof* (station) in Lavin make your way to the
church where a minor road passes beneath both the railway line and the village bypass. Leave the road for a track
cutting left (west). This winds into the narrow wooded
entrance to Val Lavinuoz and remains on the east bank
of the stream as it climbs to Alp Dadoura (1779m) on the
forest edge. This is reached in about 1hr from Lavin. The
map shows a streamside path as an option from here, but
this is affected by flooding and may be incomplete, so it's
better to keep to the track which stays on the east bank
for another 30min as far as **Alp d'Immez** (1953m). Here
you cross a bridge and follow the west bank for about
1km before returning to the right-hand side of the stream
once more. Again, a path continues alongside the stream,

but it may be impassable in places. Instead, remain on the track all the way to the hut.

Return to Lavin will take about 1½hr.

MARANGUN HUT

Chamanna Marangun is a simple, self-catering hut owned by the Lavin *gemeinde*. Although unmanned it is fully equipped, and has places for 12. If you need to check that it is unlocked Tel 081 862 26 51.

TO BERGHAUS VEREINA

Northwest of the hut, on the high ridge connecting Piz Zadrell with the Schwarzkopf (otherwise known as the Chapütschin), the 2752m **Fuorcla Zadrell** provides an excellent means of crossing the mountains to Berghaus Vereina by way of the Val Vernela. Given reasonable conditions the route is straightforward: 3hr from the Marangun Hut to the pass; 2½hr from there to **Berghaus Vereina**. So, 5½hr hut to hut, or 7½hr from Lavin. The Berghaus itself makes a very fine base for a few days of a walking holiday; Tel 081 422 12 16 www.berghausvereina.ch.

Other walks from Lavin

The two hut routes described above are a mere sample of walks available from Lavin. A few other suggestions are given below.

The **Macun lakes**, trapped in a high glacial basin southeast of Lavin, make an obvious destination. As they are now protected as an enclave of the national park, the route to them – and beyond, on a long crossing to Zernez – is described in the national park section of this guide, as Route 85 (3½–4hr to the lakes; 2½–3hr back to Lavin).

An easy hillside walk along a track leads to the glorious village of **Guarda** in just 1½hr. This could be extended by footpath to **Bos-cha**, **Ardez**, **Ftan**, then down to **Scuol** (a total of 4½hr) where you can take the train back to Lavin.

The **Via Engiadina** offers an even better, if much longer and more devious, way of reaching Guarda. It first heads north into **Val Lavinuoz** (see Route 90), then breaks away from the Marangun Hut route at **Alp d'Immez**, climbs the eastern hillside, and makes a long southeasterly traverse. Turning out of Val Lavinuoz, the path works a way eastward before cutting into **Val Tuoi**. Crossing the Clozza stream at **Alp Suot**, Via Engiadina mounts the east flank of the valley to two more alps before descending to **Guarda**.

ROUTE 91

Guarda (1653m) – Tuoi Hut
(Chamanna Tuoi: 2250m)

Start	Guarda (1653m)
Distance	7km (4.3 miles) one way
Height gain	597m (1959ft)
Grade	2
Time	2½hr
Location	North of Guarda

Guarda is the loveliest of Engadine villages, Val Tuoi one of the nicest of its valleys. At the head of the valley, below Piz Buin and the Dreiländerspitze (which together carry the Swiss/Austrian border), Chamanna Tuoi is an attractive, well-appointed stone-built hut that makes an ideal destination for a day's walk, a base for climbs on neighbouring peaks, or a starting point for the crossing of high cols nearby. The approach walk from Guarda is undemanding, for it follows a track all the way. But that is not to suggest it is uninteresting, for the valley has much to offer.

Towards the upper end of Guarda's main street, a sign by a fountain and water trough indicates the start of the route, which goes between houses on a narrow tarmac lane. Out of the village it rises between pastures, then becomes a stony track. About 10min from the start cross a lane and continue ahead, and after 25min, at a junction, note the lower option signed to Chamanna del Bescher, for this is where the alternative return route rejoins this outward track.

The upper track now enters **Val Tuoi**, with Piz Buin seen at its head, while hillsides are dressed with small woodlands of larch and pine. Soon leaving trees behind the track pushes on along the east side of the valley, and about 1hr from Guarda, a short distance below the buildings of **Alp Suot**, the way forks again. Take the upper track once more. The gradient steepens to cross a bluff where you gain lovely views both up- and down-valley About 20min later the track forks yet again (the upper route goes to Lai Blau); this time choose the left branch which soon angles down to stream level, and before long enters the valley's upper pastures, where two small huts sit beside the track. Passing between these, the gradient steepens again, before easing for the final approach to **Chamanna Tuoi**.

The old Romansch village of Guarda is one of the most attractive in Switzerland

The Tuoi Hut, with Piz Buin (left) towering behind

Return to Guarda by the same route should take no more than 1½hr.

TUOI HUT

Owned by the Engiadina Bassa section of the SAC, the Tuoi Hut has 95 dormitory places and full meals service when manned. This is at New Year, weekends from February to mid-May, and permanently from July to mid-October. For reservations Tel 081 862 23 22 www.tuoi.ch.

ALTERNATIVE DESCENT

Descend by the track to the junction below Alp Suot, bear right towards the alp, then cross the stream on a wooden bridge and wander down-valley on a faint waymarked path (part of the Via Engiadina) which keeps close to the stream. After 20min or so ignore a second bridge and continue on the right bank as far as a third bridge and a track at **Salön**. Cross the bridge and walk up the track to a junction where you rejoin the outward route. Turn right and wander downhill to Guarda (about 2hr from Chamanna Tuoi).

Chamanna Tuoi has a clear view downvalley

Routes from the Tuoi hut

In addition to assorted climbs on neighbouring peaks such as Piz Buin, Dreiländerspitze, Piz Fliana, Silvrettahorn and so on, a number of mountain tours can be made starting from Chamanna Tuoi. A very brief outline only is given here.

- To **Chamanna Marangun** in Val Lavinuoz (see Route 90) by way of the 2848m **Fuorcla d'Anschatscha**, a col below Piz Fliana southwest of the Tuoi Hut, can be achieved in 5hr. This is supposedly easier in the opposite direction.
- To the **Silvretta Hut** across the wide snow saddle of the **Silvretta Pass** (3003m) in 6hr. Although quite straightforward for experienced and equipped parties, the pass has a crevass to contend with and normal precautions should be taken.
- To the **Wiesbaden Hut** on the Austrian side of the mountains. The most direct way is across the 2798m **Fuorcla Vermunt** just east of Piz Buin and north of the Tuoi Hut. This is a very old crossing point; there was even a mule track until it was destroyed in the 17th century. The lightly crevassed Vermunt Glacier

on the Austrian flank is shrinking fast, but still needs care to negotiate. In good conditions this is a 4–5hr crossing.

• To **Ardez** in 5hr via the glacier-free **Furcletta** (2735m) above and to the northeast of the hut. This popular walker's route is described below as Route 93.

ROUTE 92
Guarda (1653m) – Alp Sura (2118m)
– Lai Blau (2613m) – Guarda

Start	Guarda (1653m)
Distance	14km (8.7 miles)
Height gain	960m (3150ft)
Height loss	960m (3150ft)
Grade	2–3
Time	5½hr
Location	North of Guarda

Lai Blau is a small tarn set in a cattle-grazed plateau on the eastern slopes of Val Tuoi. From it you gain fine views into the head of the valley, and across to the Plan Rai Glacier leading to the Silvretta Pass. This circular walk is steep in places, both in ascent and descent, but otherwise not at all difficult.

Follow directions for Route 91 out of Guarda and across the lane (10min) shortly before you enter Val Tuoi proper. At the next track junction curve right and soon twist up the wooded hillside until a footpath short cut takes you more steeply uphill to cross and recross the track again. About 1½hr from Guarda you will arrive at **Alp Süra** (2118m). Now above the treeline bear left on the farm track, which makes a long traverse of the hillside. This is part of the Via Engiadina, and views are splendid.

Above Guarda, Val Tuoi leads walkers to the Tuoi Hut

Leave the Via Engiadina at **Marangun** (2176m) where the track begins to slope down to Alp Suot, and go ahead on a rising path which now angles across the hillside. Gaining another 450m of height, you finally come onto the little plateau to find **Lai Blau** about 3hr from Guarda.

Passing along the left-hand side of the tarn the path swings northwestward, losing height, then forks. One route continues ahead to Chamanna Tuoi, while we veer left and descend steeply to the main track in the valley which leads to the Tuoi Hut. On reaching the track turn left and either stay with the track all the way to **Guarda**, or use the alternative footpath option from **Alp Suot** outlined at the end of Route 90. In either case you will arrive back in Guarda in 2–2½hr after leaving Lai Blau.

ROUTE 93
*Guarda (1653m) – Tuoi Hut (2250m) –
Furcletta (2735m) – Ardez (1464m)*

Start	Guarda (1653m)
Distance	20km (12.4 miles)
Height gain	1082m (3550ft)
Height loss	1271m (4170ft)
Grade	3
Time	7–7½hr
Location	North and northeast of Guarda

A long and demanding excursion, this could (and perhaps should) be broken by spending a night at the Tuoi Hut, thereby making a two-day outing which allows more time to properly enjoy the surroundings. Although very different, both Vals Tuoi and Tasna are beautiful glens, and it is their linking via the Furcletta col that enables us to create this very fine trek.

Begin by taking Route 91 from Guarda to Chamanna Tuoi (hut details will be found at the end of the route text). The

273

On the way to the Furcletta, Piz Buin is reflected in a semi-frozen pool

Furcletta path begins behind the hut heading east, then northeast. Reaching a junction in 15min ignore the right-hand option (to Lai Blau – see Route 92) and continue up a zigzag path which rises steeply for a while before easing to a rock tip spilling from the ridge above. Cairns and waymarks aid route finding when the trail becomes scarce, but it improves just before you reach the Furcletta (1½hr from the hut). Note that if there is good snow cover on this upper section, and no waymarks are evident, you're advised to veer north towards the top of the slope, then swing round to the right to gain the pass. The pass makes an interesting viewpoint; looking back Piz Buin is seen in profile as a sharp pyramid.

The descent into Val d'Urezzas is steep at first on (possibly) snow-patched shale, then over a chaos of boulders before both the gradient and the terrain ease as you approach the decrepit alp hut of Marangun d'Urezzas at 2273m, reached about 1hr from the pass. Now follow the left bank of a stream down to Alp Urezzas above a little plain at the confluence of Vals d'Urezzas and Urschai where the way forks. (Note: a very fine alternative route used by the Tour of the Silvretta diverts here into Val Urschai, eventually crossing Pass Fütschol and descending the Austrian flank to the Jamtal Hut.)

Branch right into Val Tasna. This is reached through a narrow cleft where you come to the grey stone buildings of **Alp Valmala** at 1979m, about 20min from the path junction. Drinks are available here, and there's a choice of onward route. One option is to cross the bridge behind the alp buildings and walk down-valley on a track to the mouth of the valley where you come onto a minor road leading to Ardez. The second (and preferred) option remains on the west side of the valley where a path – the Via Engiadina once more – leads to Ardez through pasture and forest; a charming end to the walk, with route options that are either signed or obvious at all junctions. ▶

This descent path – the preferred option – is fully described in the reverse direction in Route 94.

Above the Tuoi Hut the Furcletta affords views of mountains on the Swiss/Austrian border

ROUTE 94

Ardez (1464m) – Alp Valmala (1979m) – Ardez

Start	Ardez (1464m)
Distance	14km (8.7 miles)
Height gain	515m (1690ft)
Height loss	515m (1690ft)
Grade	2
Time	3½–4hr
Location	North of Ardez

Between Ardez and Ftan Val Tasna is a partly wooded pastoral valley of great charm. Route 93 made a descent through the valley after crossing the Furcletta, but this walk (which reverses much of the last section of that route) is an opportunity for visitors staying in Ardez to discover its magic. It exploits the best of the views and samples the variety of its landscapes, climbing above Ardez to sneak into the valley through its west flank larchwoods. Out of the woods there are steep pastures easing towards Alp Valmala, then on the return we go through neat meadows as trim and enticing as a parkland, and end the walk along a balcony overlooking the Engadine.

Begin by the side of the handsome 16th-century church in Ardez where a sign indicates the route of the Via Engiadina up a narrow lane between houses. At a crossing lane go ahead along a walled path rising between fields; this leads to a dirt road which makes a left-hand hairpin after about 100m (note the track branching from it at this point, for our return walk comes this way). Remain on the road for another 5min, then take a footpath rising above its right-hand side. After topping a minor ridge the path brings you back onto the road at a junction. ◄

Note that the continuing road, which swings left here, is the one to take for Chamanna Cler and Val Tuoi.

Turn right on a track, but a short distance along this leave the track for a waymarked path slanting above it across the wooded hillside. From open sections between the trees fine views are afforded across and along the

Engadine. About 35–40min from Ardez emerge to the open meadow of **Clüs** (1743m) where there's a junction of paths. Veer left and soon re-enter larchwoods. After easing among the trees the path steepens to gain another high meadowland with a small hut seen off to the right; this is **Plan Chamuera** (1816m), a good vantage point from which to study mountains on the south side of the Engadine.

Over the meadows the path then hugs the steeply sloping west wall of Val Tasna. At first clothed with coniferous forest, as the trees thin so you gain views to the head of the valley where the Augstenberg carries the Swiss/Austrian border. About 1½hr from Ardez come to the solitary hut of **Alp Tasna** (1896m) on an open slope of pasture with uninterrupted views up-valley. Then, 10min later, join a broader trail and continue up-valley.

The two stone buildings of **Alp Valmala** are reached after 2–2¼hr, and during the summer drinks and fresh cheese are for sale at the farm. ▸

Crossing a bridge by the alp buildings, join a track and turn right. The Via Engiadina path cuts above the

Immediately behind the alp the valley is briefly squeezed into a semi-gorge, with rough slopes and screes beyond: this is the way to the Furcletta and Pass Fütschöl.

Ardez on its green terrace above the Lower Engadine

track, but we ignore this and wander down-valley between neat pastures and past a few small huts.

OPTIONAL PATH

Note that about 30min after leaving Alp Valmala a path drops among trees to a bridge fording the stream. This option leads to a broad path on the right bank, which is later joined by the main route described.

About 40min from Alp Valmala, where the valley narrows, cross the stream on a fine wooden bridge, then climb briefly among trees to gain a broad path/track where you turn left.

Wander downstream with views across the Engadine to Piz Plavna Dadaint, its finger-like projections being a prominent feature. The way skirts an open meadow, and 15min after the bridge crossing, leave the track for a clear

Below Alp Valmala in Val Tasna

path slanting right. Contouring through woodland, in another 10min join a hillside track, which gives a fine balcony walk. Out of the trees there's a wonderful view of Tarasp Castle below, the Engadiner Dolomites as a backdrop. Shortly after this, pass the ruined building of Chanoua, and moments later gain sight of **Ardez**. Rejoin the outward route and wander down the slope to the church where the walk began.

Ardez village square

ROUTE 95

Ardez (1464m) – Chamanna Cler (2476m)

Start	Ardez (1464m)
Distance	6km (3.7 miles) one way
Height gain	1012m (3320ft)
Grade	2–3
Time	2½hr
Location	Northwest of Ardez

Although this route is described only as far as the hut, it's not necessary to return by the same path, for it's perfectly feasible to make a circular walk, as a glance at the map will indicate. As for the Cler Hut, this belongs to the Ardez Ski Club and is permanently locked, but if you wish to stay overnight, see details below.

The first part of the walk is the same as that for Route 94. It begins along the narrow lane rising beside Ardez church, continues on a walled path between fields, then comes onto an unpaved road. Following this uphill, 5min after turning the first left-hand hairpin take a path rising above the road on the right. This tops a rise and rejoins the road at a junction. Route 94 (to Val Tasna and Alp Valmala) breaks to the right, but we stay on the road curving left (part of the Via Engiadina) and follow this past **Chöglias**, shortly after which the dirt road finishes and a lesser track takes over. This twists up the hillside, heading northwest to reach the alp of **Murtera Dadoura** (2142m) where there's a crossing path. The right branch contours to another alp, Murtera Dadaint, while the left-hand route takes the Via Engiadina round a spur into Val Tuoi.

Continue ahead, climbing to **Alp Maranguns** (2303m) in a little over 2hr from Ardez. From here the Cler Hut should be seen above and to the northeast, and as you mount the final slopes to reach it, note the small tarns off to your left.

CLER HUT

Owned by the Ardez Ski Club, Chamanna Cler is unmanned and locked. Contact details for reservations and keyholder will be found on www.ski-ardez.ch/seite_chamonna.htm. The hut has places for 22, good self-catering facilities, a wood-burning stove and solar-powered lighting. The water supply is outside the building, where there are splendid views across the valley to the Engiadina Dolomites.

The Adam and Eve house in Ardez

The non-technical but mostly pathless ascent of the 3031m rock peak of Piz Cotschen, by its southeast ridge, makes a worthwhile outing from the hut – about 1½hr to the summit.

◄ Either return to Ardez by the same route in 2hr, or continue southeast from the hut on a descending path to Muot da l'Hom (2330m/30min), dropping steeply south from there to a track looping down the hillside to join the dirt road near **Chöglias** used on the outward route.

Allow 2–2¼hr from Chamanna Cler to Ardez.

Other walks from Ardez

Almost any path or track taken along the hillside terrace to east or west of Ardez will be rewarding so far as views are concerned, for this natural shelf, with its tree-rimmed meadows, makes a wonderful belvedere. More energetic routes go up through forest onto the south-facing hillsides; others delve into tributary valleys, invite along the Via Engiadina, or descend into the Engadine's pastoral bed. A few suggestions are given here, but consultation with the local map will give rise to many more.

- An easy walk descends to the River Inn close to its confluence with the Aua da Sampuoir, which comes pouring out of its wooded gorge-like narrows to the south. A minor road leads round to the hamlet of **Sur Enn**, then you continue westward along the edge of woods until another bridge takes you back to the north bank at **Giarson**, below Guarda (2¼hr). Either take the train back to Ardez, or walk up the hillside to **Guarda** and head east along the hillside track to **Bos-cha** and **Ardez**.

- Another route south of the Inn goes up through the **Sampuoir gorge**, then crosses to its east side and climbs to **Motta Jüda** (2147m). From here you slope down through forest to **Mottana** (1958m), to join a track looping down the hillside to **Valatscha**, a hamlet set on the edge of pastures. Now take a track heading west (up-valley) to **Aschera** and **Hof**, after which you recross the Inn back to Ardez. This circular walk will take about 5–5½hr.

- The crossing of the 2768m **Pass Futschöl** on the Swiss/Austrian border is frequently used by trekkers and climbers to connect the Engadine side of the Silvretta Alps with the north flank in Austria.

On that north side the DAV-owned **Jamtal Hut** (2165m/220 places, meals provision) makes a convenient overnight lodging, reached after a 6–6½hr walk from Ardez. Follow Route 94 to **Alp Valmala** in Val Tasna, then continue northward through **Val Urschai** to gain the pass in about 2½hr from Alp Valmala. Descend the Austrian flank for another 1½hr to reach the hut.

Walks from Scuol

This, the largest village in the Lower Engadine, has the added advantage for the casual walker of a gondola lift that swings up to **Motta Naluns** (2142m) for the start of some high paths on the north side of the valley. A sample of these high trails is given below.

- The **Via Engiadina**, met on so many of our walks, is immediately accessible from Motta Naluns. If this is followed across the hillside to the west it leads to **Alp Valmala** in Val Tasna, then south to **Ardez**.
- By following the **Via Engiadina** north then eastward from Motta Naluns, you come to **Sent**, just west of Val Sinestra, in 2½hr. The way continues into Val Sinestra, crosses the valley at **Hof Zuort** (refreshments) in 5hr, then returns down the east flank to reach **Vnà** and **Ramosch**, about 6½hr from Motta Naluns.
- The 2793m **Piz Clünas**, northwest of Motta Naluns, makes a wonderful viewpoint, and a steep zigzag path climbs directly to the summit after breaking away from the westbound **Via Engiadina**, in a little under 3hr from the gondola station.
- A very fine 6hr walk heads roughly north from the gondola station and takes a path to a saddle in a ridge linking Piz Nair and Piz Champatsch. Crossing the **Fuorcla Champatsch** (2730m/2hr) it then descends through the length of **Val Laver**, a feeder glen for the larger Val Sinestra which drains down to the Engadine below Ramosch. At **Hof Zuort** (refreshments) in Val Sinestra's upper reaches, take the right-hand path heading south; this leads to the

Via Engiadina which you follow down to **Sent** and on to **Scuol**.

- On the south side of the Engadine a 4hr walk (3hr if using postbus to the start) leads to the **Lischana Hut**, whose valley drains into the Inn a little east of Val S-charl. This is described from **San Jon**, which will be found under Route 96.

Val Sinestra walks

The Engadine's most northerly tributary of note is Val Sinestra, a long feeder valley whose entrance northeast of Scuol is guarded by Sent on the west flank, and Ramosch on the east, the two linked by the Via Engiadina, as has already been mentioned. Sent in particular is a sunny village that's popular with walkers, for there's no shortage of accessible paths nearby. While there's an abundance of local walks, only long routes are outlined here.

- An interesting route from Sent, Vnà or Ramosch, heads up-valley to **Griosch**, an alp at 1817m at the confluence of two valleys: the Chöglias and Tiatscha, reached in 2½hr from Sent. Branch left up the Chöglias stem to **Alp Chöglias** (3½hr) where a steepish climb begins in order to gain the pass of **Cuolmen d'Fenga** (Fimberpass: 2608m) which provides access to Val Fenga. A 45min descent then takes you down to the **Heidelberger Hut** at 2264m (5½–6hr). Although on Swiss territory, the hut is owned by the German Alpine Club (DAV), while the valley is geographically Austrian, and the border is just a short walk to the north (see above for information).

- Another long route (7¼hr) from Ramosch through the Val Sinestra leads to the duty-free resort of **Samnaun** by way of the 2848m **Fuorcla Maisas** and the Val Maisas. Samnaun is linked with the Engadine by a postbus route, so a return to base is straightforward.

- **Piz Arina** (2828m) stands above Ramosch and Vnà as a gatepost to the Val Sinestra. A walker's route winds up the long south and east slopes (first wooded, then grass) to gain the summit from the north in 5hr from Ramosch (3½hr for the descent).

VAL S-CHARL WALKS

Reached by a minor road from Scuol, the neat hamlet of S-charl gives access to several fine walks (Routes 97–100)

South of Scuol the long S-charl valley leads to some very fine walking country. With the national park boundary being drawn along the west bank of the Clemgia stream from Plan da Funtanas to its confluence with Val Mingèr northwest of S-charl village, then continuing along a ridge flanking Val Tavrü southwest of S-charl, one might predict its special nature. But although the park is accessible via Val Mingèr (see Route 83), some of the best walks are to be had in the Val Sesvenna tributary northeast of the village, and also in the Val S-charl's headwaters where trails lead over grassy saddles to the Ofenpass, Val Müstair and also into Italy. S-charl is a charming little village, reached by postbus from Scuol (car parking at the village entrance). Overnight accommodation is available in three hotels – see information above. One SAC hut is accessible from the valley: Chamanna Lischana stands high in the little Val Lischana (see Route 96), while trekkers can cross the Fuorcla Sesvenna above S-charl to visit the Sesvenna Hut in Italy (see Route 98).

ROUTE 96

San Jon (1389m) – Lischana Hut
(Chamanna Lischana: 2500m)

Start	San Jon (1389m)
Distance	5km (3.1 miles) one way
Height gain	1111m (3645ft)
Grade	2
Time	3hr
Location	Southeast of Scuol

This is a direct route to the Lischana Hut, steep at times as it climbs through the wildly romantic Val Lischana which is separated from Val S-charl by Piz San Jon and its extending ridges. The postbus from Scuol to S-charl passes the San Jon turning at a hairpin bend; there's also a marked parking place for visitors to the hut.

From the bus stop on the S-charl road, walk along the side road (unpaved) for a very short distance, then turn right on a track. This rises up forested slopes to the buildings of **San Jon** (a stud farm), at 1465m. Continue across a large clearing heading eastward, then fork right on a forest path that climbs steeply alongside a stream in the narrow **Val Lischana**. Using numerous zigzags the way progresses above the forest with Piz Lischana above to the left, and Piz San Jon ahead on the right-hand side of the valley. At last you reach the hut, which is set on a

LISCHANA HUT

Belonging to the Engiadina Bassa section of the SAC, Chamanna Lischana has places for 48 and offers a full meals service when manned. This is from July to mid-October. Reservations are essential at weekends Tel 081 864 95 44 www. lischanahuette.ch. Ibex, chamois and marmots are frequently seen nearby.

rocky knoll that makes an idyllic location with a tremendous view north across the Engadine to the Silvretta Alps.

A direct return to San Jon by reversing the upward route takes no more than about 2hr. The ascent of Piz Lischana (3105m/2hr) from the hut is for experienced scramblers only, with a fabulous summit panorama: the view extends to the Bernina and Ortler Alps (south), Bernese Alps and Tödi (west), the distant Zugspitze (north), and Ötztal Alps and far-off Dolomites (east).

ALTERNATIVE EXTENSION

Continuing to the head of Val Lischana, then descending to S-charl via the Fora da l'Aua and Alp Sesvenna, is a 5hr route for experienced trekkers. Another challenging route for trekkers breaks eastward across the Lais da Rims plateau to reach the upper Val d'Uina where you have the option of crossing Passo di Slingia into Italy, or of descending through Val d'Uina to the Lower Engadine at Sur Enn (5½–6hr).

ROUTE 97

S-charl (1810m) – Alp Sesvenna (2098m)

Start	S-charl (1810m)
Distance	3km (1.9 miles) one way
Height gain	288m (945ft)
Grade	1
Time	1hr
Location	Northeast of S-charl

This short and very easy walk quickly leads to a solitary alp hut with cattle byre attached, with Piz Cristanas looming above and behind it. Val Sesvenna is a gem of a little glen, with forest at its entrance and sloping pastures within. In early summer it's especially attractive when snow still lies on the mountains and flowers colour the pastures before cattle are taken up for grazing. Later, when the alp is inhabited, it's possible to buy milk or coffee at the hut.

Val Sesvenna, a charming valley that reaches behind S-charl

In the village square in S-charl a sign gives a generous 1¼hr to the alp. Begin by turning left along a track between houses, and pass a water trough. Walking on the right-hand side of the Sesvenna stream among pine and larch trees, in 20min you cross a rustic bridge to the west bank and continue up-valley. The gradient is mostly undemanding, but after 40min or so the way steepens on the approach to the alp. Behind the building, which looks directly down-valley to S-charl, **Val Sesvenna** is embraced by an attractive amphitheatre of mountains, of which the most striking is Piz Cristanas (3092m), rising above a fan of screes that sweep down to pastures rimmed with dwarf pine. The path curves right beyond the alp building to a trail junction at 2110m, and there are several pleasant sites nearby that would be ideal for a picnic.

OPTIONAL EXTENSIONS

From the 2110m path junction at Alp Sesvenna, the left fork climbs into the upper cirque to mount through the Fora da l'Aua to the Lais da Rims tarns (2¾hr), and continues on from there to the Lischana Hut in 1hr. The right-hand path goes into the eastern cirque and crosses Fuorcla Sesvenna into Italy – see Route 98.

ROUTE 98
S-charl (1810m) – Fuorcla Sesvenna
(2819m) – Sesvenna Hut (2256m)

Start	S-charl (1810m)
Distance	11km (6.8 miles)
Height gain	1009m (3311ft)
Height loss	563m (1847ft)
Grade	2–3
Time	4½hr
Location	Northeast of S-charl

East of Alp Sesvenna the 2819m Fuorcla Sesvenna is a saddle on the walling ridge of the upper valley carrying the Swiss/Italian border. An hour below the pass on the Italian flank the modern Sesvenna Hut, owned by the AVS (South Tyrol Alpine Club), makes an obvious destination – but don't forget to carry your passport and take some Euros to pay for refreshments or accommodation there. This hut is situated in the Valle di Slingia, which drains down to the Vinschgau.

Walk up to **Alp Sesvenna**, following directions given under Route 97. At the path junction just beyond the alp building, take the right branch, cross a stream and work your way along a reasonable path that keeps above the north bank of a second, larger stream. Although the upper part of the valley is rough and stony the way is clear, and leads without difficulty to the *fuorcla* in 2½hr from Alp Sesvenna. A small tarn lies below on the Italian side, and the descending path takes you past it. A larger tarn lies nearly 100m further down, but the way keeps well to the left of this, edging round cliffs where the path forks. The right branch cuts back to visit the tarn, but for the hut we continue down and reach it about 1hr from the pass.

To return to S-charl by the same route, allow at least 3hr.

SESVENNA HUT

The Sesvenna Hut (Schutzhaus Sesvenna or Rifugio Sesvenna) is a modern hut at a major path junction with a small tarn nearby, and views of the Ortler Alps to the southeast. The hut has 80 places and meals provision when manned; from mid-June to end October. For reservations Tel (0039) 473 830 234 www.sesvenna.com. (See *Walking through the Italian Alps* by Gillian Price, published by Cicerone.)

OPTIONAL EXTENSION

To make a rewarding two-day excursion, spend a night at the hut, and next day walk up-valley for 30min to cross back into Switzerland at the **Schlinig Pass** (Passo di Slingia: 2295m). Over the pass an easy trail slopes down into the Sursass pastures, then through the short but dramatic Uina gorge where a route cut in the rock is overhung and safeguarded with handrails and fixed cables. Below this the beautiful Val d'Uina is forested, but with open meadows at **Uina Dadaint** (1783m refreshments) and **Uina Dadora** (1499m). After 3½hr from the Sesvenna Hut you come to the Lower Engadine at **Sur Enn** below Sent. (Take the postbus up-valley to Scuol, and change there for S-charl.)

ROUTE 99
S-charl (1810m) – Alp Astras (2135m)

Start	S-charl (1810m)
Distance	7km (4.3 miles) one way
Height gain	325m (1066ft)
Grade	1
Time	2hr
Location	Southeast of S-charl

The long S-charl valley leads from forested narrows at its entrance near Scuol, to a hidden region of pastures and lush inner glens with tumbling streams, forests and remote alps. This walk takes us towards its head where a large moorland-like pasture gives a sense of space and openness. It's an easy, undemanding walk, but with opportunities to extend it for those who wish for more exercise.

Through the village wander up-valley, heading southeast on a broad track bordered on the left by forest. In 35min come to the meadows of **Plan d'Immez** where a path breaks left to visit Alp Tablasot; ignore this and remain on the track, which forks soon after. While the route to the pass of Cruschetta (or S-charlsjoch) branches left, we keep to the main track, avoiding the temptation to cross a bridge 2min later, but then crossing the next bridge over the **Clemgia** in a further 15min (2018m/50min from S-charl).

Over the bridge the track now rises, giving views across to alp buildings on the east side of the valley, and a little over 10min after crossing the stream you come out of a patch of woodland to an open stretch of pasture. In another 10min pass below **Alp Praditschöl**, a fine example of Alpine vernacular architecture, with shingle-roofed dwelling house, cattle sheds and milking parlour set above a slope of rock and grass. Continue ahead to

where the upper valley widens with a moorland-like quality, and at a junction of paths you come to **Alp Astras**, another collection of well-designed buildings in an enchanted setting. Look out for marmots here. (See Route 100 for a continuing route to Fuorcla Funtana da S-charl.)

Alp Praditschöl, on the way to Alp Astras at the head of the S-charl valley

To return to S-charl by the same route will require a little over 1hr, but this can be varied by taking an alternative path from Alp Astras across the valley to the alp buildings of **Tamangur-Dadaint**, then following this downstream. After visiting **Tamangur Dadora** further down-valley, it rejoins the main route where the track crosses the Clemgia bridge at 2018m.

ROUTE 100

S-charl (1810m) – Fuorcla Funtana da S-charl
(2393m) – Pt 2535m – Ofenpass (2149m)

Start	S-charl (1810m)
Distance	14km (8.7 miles)
Height gain	725m (2379ft)
Height loss	386m (1266ft)
Grade	2
Time	4–4½hr
Location	Southeast and south of S-charl

This is one possible extension of the walk to Alp Astras (Route 99). Of the three passes that cross the mountains above Alp Astras and give access to the Ofenpass/Val Müstair region, the Fuorcla Funtana da S-charl is the most westerly. The pass is served by postbus, making it easy to return to the Engadine in one direction, or Val Müstair in the other.

ALTERNATIVE ROUTE

An alternative to the Valbella route approaches the Ofenpass across the south flank of **Munt da la Bescha** (3½hr). Yet another option is to avoid the Ofenpass altogether, and instead make an eastward traverse above the Val Müstair slope, then return to Alp Astras and S-charl by way of the **Pass da Costainas**, thus creating a 7hr route.

Take Route 99 to **Alp Astras** (2hr) where you then choose the right fork at the path junction. It's a clear trail, easy and well defined, and it mounts the rough grassy hillside southwest of the alp buildings. After about 45min it brings you to the long trough-like pass of **Fuorcla Funtana da S-charl**. Just before reaching the actual pass, take a path on the right, which continues to gain height to reach a high point of 2535m below Piz Vallatscha. The path now descends along the south flank of Val Valbella, contours round the western end of Munt da la Bescha and drops down the partly wooded slope to the **Ofenpass**.

Other walks in the Val S-charl

Walking routes described above provide an example of opportunities available in and around the head of Val S-charl. A few more outline routes are suggested here; use these in conjunction with the local map to devise your own walks and tours.

North of S-charl **Mot Madlain** is a 2434m high point accessible in 2hr by a marked path, which begins at the car park on the outskirts of the village.

Southwest of the village **Val Tavrü** is worth visiting. With larch and pinewoods in its lower reaches, a path leads to Alp Tavrü at mid-height on its western slope, and continues from there up to **Mot Tavrü** (2420m) on the dividing ridge which carries the national park boundary. From here you overlook Val Mingèr (2hr up, 1½hr back).

A short and easy valley walk leads to **Alp Plazer** (2091m) in Val Plazer southeast of S-charl in 45–50min. But a much longer trek continues from there to cross the 2296m pass of **Cruschetta** on the Swiss/Italian border. On the Italian side a path continues down into Val d'Avigna which leads to Taufers, a short distance from **Müstair**. Crossing back into Switzerland a postbus will return you to the Engadine. Alternatively, you could spend the night in Müstair or Santa Maria, and next day return to S-charl across **Fuorcla Sassalba**.

Fuorcla Sassalba (2619m) is the most easterly of the three crossing points in the upper Val S-charl, and can be reached by a path from **Alp Astras** (see Route 99). The other crossing places are Fuorcla Funtana da S-charl and Pass da Costainas, already described.

APPENDIX A
Useful Addresses

Tourist Information
NB Details of offices in specific resorts are given at the head of each section

Switzerland Travel Centre
30 Bedford Street
London WC2E 9ED
Tel 0207 420 4934
https://switzerlandtravelcentre.co.uk

Swiss National Tourist Office
608 Fifth Avenue
New York NY 10020
Tel 212 757 5944

Graubünden Ferien
(Canton Graubünden Tourist Office)
Alexanderstrasse 24
CH-7001 Chur
Tel (0041) [0]81 254 24 24
www.graubuenden.ch

Swiss National Park
Chastè Planta-Wildenberg
CH-7530 Zernez
Tel (0041) [0]81 851 41 11
www.nationalpark.ch

Schweizer Alpen-Club
(Swiss Alpine Club)
CH-3000 Bern 14
Tel (0041) [0]31 370 18 18
www.sac-cas.ch

Map Suppliers
Cordee www.cordee.co.uk

Edward Stanford Ltd
7 Mercer Walk, Covent Garden,
London WC2H 9FA
Tel 0207 836 1321
www.stanfords.co.uk

The Map Shop
15 High Street, Upton-upon-Severn
Worcs WR8 0HJ

Tel 01684 593 146
www.themapshop.co.uk

Rand McNally Map Store
https://store.randmcnally.com

Omni Resources
PO Box 2096, 1004 South Mebane Street
Burlington NC 227216 20096
www.omnimap.com/maps.htm

NB Swiss maps can also be obtained from Swiss National Tourist Offices

Specialist Mountain Activities Insurance
BMC Travel & Activity Insurance
(BMC members only)
177–179 Burton Road, West Didsbury
Manchester M20 2BB
Tel 0161 445 6111
www.thebmc.co.uk

Austrian Alpine Club
Unit 43, Glenmore Business Park
Blackhill Road, Holton Heath
Poole BH16 6NL
Tel 01929 556 870
www.aacuk.org.uk
(Membership of the AAC carries accident and mountain rescue insurance, plus reciprocal rights reductions in SAC huts)

Snowcard Insurance Services
308–314 London Road
Benfleet SS7 2DD
Tel 01702 427 273
www.snowcard.co.uk

APPENDIX B
Bibliography

General Tourist Guides

The Rough Guide to Switzerland by Matthew Teller et al (Rough Guides Ltd) – Regularly updated, this is perhaps the best general guide to the country available at present.

Switzerland by Gregor Clark et al (Lonely Planet) – Frequent editions of this popular guide keep information up-to-date.

The Green Guide: Switzerland (Michelin Travel Publications) – Presented in gazetteer form with a wide range of illustrations, but with many inaccuracies.

The Alps by R.L.G. Irving (Batsford, 1939) – Long out of print, but available on special order from public libraries or via Internet book-search sites, this volume by a noted Alpine connoisseur contains passages of interest to visitors to the Engadine.

Mountains and mountaineering

Despite the numerous volumes dedicated to mountaineering that have been published in the last hundred years and more, surprisingly little in English has been devoted to mountains of the Engadine region. The following list is therefore rather small, but it contains a few books with passages of specific interest.

Adventures of an Alpine Guide by Christian Klucker (John Murray 1932) – Klucker was one of the most influential guides of the post-Golden Age era who lived in, and was buried in, Val Fex. This is his autobiography, with numerous references to local climbs, particularly in the Bregaglia.

Nanga Parbat Pilgrimage by Hermann Buhl (latest edition Bâton Wicks 1998) – The climbing memoirs of the great Austrian climber remembered for his first ascent (solo) of Nanga Parbat in 1953. This book also includes an account of his solo ascent of Piz Badile's Northeast Face.

Starlight and Storm by Gaston Rébuffat (Kaye & Ward 1968) – In his story of climbing the six great North Faces of the Alps, Rébuffat describes tackling Piz Badile in a storm.

The High Mountains of the Alps by Helmut Dumler & Willi Burkhardt (Diadem, London/The Mountaineers, Seattle 1993) – A beautifully produced volume, sumptuously illustrated with colour photographs and with an intelligent text depicting all the Alpine 4000m peaks. A section is devoted to Piz Bernina.

The Mountains of Switzerland by Herbert Maeder (George Allen & Unwin 1968) – A large-format book with splendid monochrome illustrations.

The Outdoor Traveler's Guide: The Alps by Marcia R. Lieberman (Stewart, Tabori & Chang, New York 1991) – With numerous fine colour photographs by Tim Thompson.

The Swiss Alps by Kev Reynolds (Cicerone Press 2012) – Comprehensive descriptions of each alpine district of Switzerland, with emphasis on walks, treks, climbs, huts and villages. The Engadine and neighbouring valleys are well covered.

The Mountains of Europe by Kev Reynolds (Oxford Illustrated Press 1990) – All the major mountain areas of continental Europe described, including the Bernina and Bregaglia Alps.

Bernina and Bregaglia – Selected Climbs by Lindsay Griffin (Alpine Club 1995) – The latest AC guidebook to the area, compiled by a noted authority.

Silvretta Alps by Jeff Williams (West Col 1995) – A very useful guide to these Austro/Swiss mountains. Most of the routes are from the Austrian side, but there's much to interest visitors in the Lower Engadine.

The Alpine 4000m Peaks by the Classic Routes by Richard Goedeke (Bâton Wicks 2nd ed 2003) – The title says it all; a well-illustrated guide that includes Piz Bernina.

Eastern Alps; the Classic Routes on the Highest Peaks by Dieter Seibert (Diadem 1992) – Includes peaks in the Silvretta, Albula, Bernina and Bregaglia Alps.

Walking and trekking

Walking in the Alps by J. Hubert Walker (Oliver & Boyd 1951) – Long out of print. Available on special order from some libraries, this is probably the best and most readable volume of inspiration to mountain walkers. Includes a fine chapter on the Bernina and Bregaglia Alps.

Walking in the Alps by Kev Reynolds (Cicerone Press 2005) – This second edition is illustrated with new maps and colour photographs throughout. It describes 19 regions of the Alps, from the Alpes Maritimes to the Julians of Slovenia, and includes, of course, much of the district covered by the present guide.

Classic Walks in the Alps by Kev Reynolds (Oxford Illustrated Press 1991) – A large-format book with some favourite Engadine and Bregaglia walks included.

Walking in Switzerland by Clem Lindenmayer (Lonely Planet 2001) – Strong on background information. Walks included in the Engadine region are well researched.

100 Hut Walks in the Alps by Kev Reynolds (Cicerone Press, 2014) – As the title suggests, a large selection of mountain huts across the Alpine ranges, some of which are also described in the present guide.

Trekking in the Silvretta & Rätikon Alps by Kev Reynolds (Cicerone Press 2014) –
A pocket-sized guide to multi-day routes among these lovely mountains. The Tour of the Silvretta strays into the Lower Engadine.

The Tour of the Bernina by Gillian Price (Cicerone Press 2015) – A worthy guide to a very fine 9-day hut-to-hut circuit of the Bernina massif, written by a well-known Cicerone author.

A Guide to Walks in the Swiss National Park by Klaus Robin (Swiss National Park 1995) – A handy pocket-sized guidebook with 20 walks in the national park. The text concentrates more on the flora and fauna than route descriptions, but is full of interest. On sale at the National Park Centre in Zernez.

Oberengadin and *Unterengadin* by Rudolf & Siegrun Weiss (Rother, München, 2002) – Two German-language guides to walks in the Engadine Valley; 50 routes in each.

APPENDIX C
Glossary

German	Romansch	English
Abhang	spuonda/costa	slope
Alp	alp	high pasture
Alpenblume	flur alpina	alpine flower
Alpenverein		alpine club
Alphütte	tegia d'alp	alp hut
Auskunft	infurmaziuns	information
Aussicht	la vista	view
Bach	ova/dutg	stream
Bäckerei		bakery
Bahnhof	staziun da viafer	railway station
Berg	munt/montagna	mountain
Bergell	Bregaglia	Bregaglia
Bergführer	guid da muntogna	mountain guide
Berggasthaus		mountain inn
Bergpass	fuorcla	mountain pass
Bergsteiger		mountaineer
Bergweg		mountain path
Blatt	charta topographica	map sheet

German	Romansch	English
Brot	paun	bread
Brücke	punt	bridge
Dorf	vischnanca	village
Drahtseilbahn		cablecar
Ebene	plan/plaun	plain
Feld	chomp/fuus	field
Feldweg	stradella/senda	meadow path
Fels	crap/grip	rock
Fereinwohnung		holiday apartment
Firn	vadret	snowfield
Fluss	flum	river
Fussweg	senda/via	footpath
Garni		hotel with breakfast included
Gasthaus/gasthof		inn/hotel
Gefährlich		dangerous
Gemse	chamutsch	chamois
Gestern	ier	yesterday
Gletscher	glatscher/vadret	glacier
Gletscherspalte	sfessa da vadret	crevasse
Gondelbahn		gondola lift
Grat	crasta, fil or spi	ridge
Graubünden	Grischüna	Graubunden
Grüss gott/grüetzi	allegra	greetings/hello
Halb pension	mesa pensiun	half-board
Haltestelle	fermada	bus stop
Heilbad		spa/hot springs
Heute	oz	today
Hirsch	tschierv	red deer
Hoch		high
Höhe		height
Höhenweg		high route
Horn	piz	peak
Hügel	muot, muotta or collina	hill
Hütte	chamanna/camona	mountain hut
Joch	fuorcla	col, pass or saddle

German	Romansch	English
Jugendherberge		youth hostel
Kamm	craista/cresta	crest/ridge
Kapelle	baseglia	chapel
Karte	charta topographica	map
Klamm	chavorgia	gorge
Kumme		coombe/small valley
Landschaft		landscape
Landstrasse	stradun	high road
Lawine	aviner	avalanche
Lebensmittel		grocery
Leicht		easy
Links		left (direction)
Massenlager/Matratzenlager		dormitory
Moräne		moraine
Morgen	damaun	tomorrow
Munstertal	Val Müstair	Val Müstair
Murmeltier	muntanella	marmot
Nebel		fog/low cloud
Nord	nord	north
Ost	ost/orient	east
Pass	fuorcla	pass
Pfad	senda	path
Puschlav	Poschiavo	Poschiavo
Quelle	funtana	spring/fountain
Rechts		right (direction)
Reh	chavriöl	roe deer
Rucksack	loulscha/satgados	rucksack
Sattel	fuorcla	saddle
Schlafraum		bedroom
Schloss	chastè	castle
Schlucht	chavorgia	gorge
Schnee	naiv	snow
Schweiz	Svizra	Switzerland
Schweizerische Nationalpark	Parc Naziunal Svizzer	Swiss National Park
See	lej/lai	lake
Seilbahn		cablecar

German	Romansch	English
Stausee		reservoir
Stein	*sass*	stone
Steinmann		cairn
Steinschlag		rockfall
Strasse	*via*	road/street
Stunde	*ore*	hour
Sud	*sid*	south
Tal	*val/vallada*	valley
Tobel	*vallun*	wooded gorge
Touristenlager		dormitory
Über	*sur/sura*	over/above
Unfall		accident
Unter	*suot/sot*	under/below
Unterkunft		accommodation
Verkehrverein	*turissem*	tourist office
Wald	*guaud*	forest
Wanderweg	*senda*	footpath
Wasser	*aua*	water
Wasserfall	*cas da aua*	waterfall
Weide	*pas-chura/pascul*	pasture
West	*vest/occident*	west
Wildbach		torrent
Zeltplatz	*campadi*	campsite
Zimmer-frei		rooms available

APPENDIX D
Route Index

Route		Grade	Time	Page
88	Zernez–Fuorcla Stragliavita–Ardez Station	3	7–7½hr	259
89	Lavin–Linard Hut	3	2½hr	263
90	Lavin–Chamanna Marangun	2	2–2½hr	265
91	Guarda–Tuoi Hut	2	2½hr	267
92	Guarda–Lai Blau–Guarda	2–3	5½hr	271
93	Guarda–Tuoi Hut–Furcletta–Ardez	3	7–7½hr	273
94	Ardez–Alp Valmala–Ardez	2	3½–4hr	276
95	Ardez–Chamanna Cler	2–3	2½hr	280
96	San Jon–Lischana Hut	2	3hr	286
97	S–charl–Alp Sesvenna	1	1hr	288
98	S–charl–Fuorcla Sesvenna–Sesvenna Hut	2–3	4½hr	290
99	S–charl–Alp Astras	1	2hr	292
100	S–charl–Fcla Funtana da S-charl–Ofenpass	2	4–4½hr	294

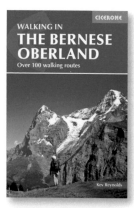
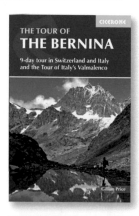

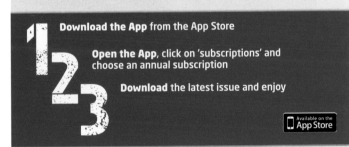

LISTING OF CICERONE GUIDES

SCOTLAND

Backpacker's Britain:
  Northern Scotland
Ben Nevis and Glen Coe
Cycling in the Hebrides
Great Mountain Days in Scotland
Mountain Biking in Southern and
  Central Scotland
Mountain Biking in West and North
  West Scotland
Not the West Highland Way
Scotland
Scotland's Best Small Mountains
Scotland's Mountain Ridges
Scrambles in Lochaber
The Ayrshire and Arran
  Coastal Paths
The Border Country
The Borders Abbeys Way
The Cape Wrath Trail
The Great Glen Way
The Great Glen Way Map Booklet
The Hebridean Way
The Hebrides
The Isle of Mull
The Isle of Skye
The Skye Trail
The Southern Upland Way
The Speyside Way
The Speyside Way Map Booklet
The West Highland Way
Walking Highland Perthshire
Walking in Scotland's Far North
Walking in the Angus Glens
Walking in the Cairngorms
Walking in the Ochils, Campsie
  Fells and Lomond Hills
Walking in the Pentland Hills
Walking in the Southern Uplands
Walking in Torridon
Walking Loch Lomond and
  the Trossachs
Walking on Arran
Walking on Harris and Lewis
Walking on Rum and the Small Isles
Walking on the Orkney and
  Shetland Isles
Walking on Uist and Barra
Walking the Corbetts
  Vol 1 South of the Great Glen
Walking the Corbetts
  Vol 2 North of the Great Glen
Walking the Munros
  Vol 1 – Southern, Central and
  Western Highlands
Walking the Munros
  Vol 2 – Northern Highlands and
  the Cairngorms

West Highland Way Map Booklet
Winter Climbs Ben Nevis and
  Glen Coe
Winter Climbs in the Cairngorms

NORTHERN ENGLAND TRAILS

Hadrian's Wall Path
Hadrian's Wall Path Map Booklet
Pennine Way Map Booklet
The Coast to Coast Map Booklet
The Coast to Coast Walk
The Dales Way
The Dales Way Map Booklet
The Pennine Way

LAKE DISTRICT

Cycling in the Lake District
Great Mountain Days in the
  Lake District
Lake District Winter Climbs
Lake District: High Level and
  Fell Walks
Lake District: Low Level and
  Lake Walks
Mountain Biking in the Lake District
Outdoor Adventures with Children –
  Lake District
Scrambles in the Lake District
  – North
Scrambles in the Lake District
  – South
Short Walks in Lakeland
  Book 1: South Lakeland
Short Walks in Lakeland
  Book 2: North Lakeland
Short Walks in Lakeland
  Book 3: West Lakeland
The Cumbria Way
Tour of the Lake District
Trail and Fell Running in the
  Lake District

NORTH WEST ENGLAND
AND THE ISLE OF MAN

Cycling the Pennine Bridleway
Cycling the Way of the Roses
Isle of Man Coastal Path
The Lancashire Cycleway
The Lune Valley and Howgills
The Ribble Way
Walking in Cumbria's Eden Valley
Walking in Lancashire
Walking in the Forest of Bowland
  and Pendle
Walking on the Isle of Man
Walking on the West
  Pennine Moors
Walks in Ribble Country
Walks in Silverdale and Arnside

NORTH EAST ENGLAND,
YORKSHIRE DALES
AND PENNINES

Cycling in the Yorkshire Dales
Great Mountain Days in
  the Pennines
Mountain Biking in the
  Yorkshire Dales
South Pennine Walks
St Oswald's Way and
  St Cuthbert's Way
The Cleveland Way and the
  Yorkshire Wolds Way
The Cleveland Way Map Booklet
The North York Moors
The Reivers Way
The Teesdale Way
Trail and Fell Running in the
  Yorkshire Dales
Walking in County Durham
Walking in Northumberland
Walking in the North Pennines
Walking in the Yorkshire Dales:
  North and East
Walking in the Yorkshire Dales:
  South and West
Walks in Dales Country
Walks in the Yorkshire Dales

WALES AND WELSH BORDERS

Cycling Lôn Las Cymru
Glyndwr's Way
Great Mountain Days in Snowdonia
Hillwalking in Shropshire
Hillwalking in Wales – Vol 1
Hillwalking in Wales – Vol 2
Mountain Walking in Snowdonia
Offa's Dyke Map Booklet
Offa's Dyke Path
Ridges of Snowdonia
Scrambles in Snowdonia
The Ascent of Snowdon
The Ceredigion and Snowdonia
  Coast Paths
The Pembrokeshire Coast Path
Pembrokeshire Coast Path
  Map Booklet
The Severn Way
The Snowdonia Way
The Wales Coast Path
The Wye Valley Walk
Walking in Carmarthenshire
Walking in Pembrokeshire
Walking in the Forest of Dean
Walking in the South Wales Valleys
Walking in the Wye Valley
Walking on the Brecon Beacons
Walking on the Gower

DERBYSHIRE, PEAK DISTRICT AND MIDLANDS

Cycling in the Peak District
Dark Peak Walks
Scrambles in the Dark Peak
Walking in Derbyshire
White Peak Walks:
  The Northern Dales
White Peak Walks:
  The Southern Dales

SOUTHERN ENGLAND

20 Classic Sportive Rides in
  South East England
20 Classic Sportive Rides in
  South West England
Cycling in the Cotswolds
Mountain Biking on the
  North Downs
Mountain Biking on the
  South Downs
North Downs Way Map Booklet
South West Coast Path
  Map Booklet –
  Vol 1: Minehead to St Ives
South West Coast Path
  Map Booklet –
  Vol 2: St Ives to Plymouth
South West Coast Path
  Map Booklet –
  Vol 3: Plymouth to Poole
Suffolk Coast and Heath Walks
The Cotswold Way
The Cotswold Way Map Booklet
The Great Stones Way
The Kennet and Avon Canal
The Lea Valley Walk
The North Downs Way
The Peddars Way and Norfolk
  Coast path
The Pilgrims' Way
The Ridgeway Map Booklet
The Ridgeway National Trail
The South Downs Way
The South Downs Way Map Booklet
The South West Coast Path
The Thames Path
The Thames Path Map Booklet
The Two Moors Way
Two Moors Way Map Booklet
Walking Hampshire's Test Way
Walking in Cornwall
Walking in Essex
Walking in Kent
Walking in London
Walking in Norfolk
Walking in Sussex
Walking in the Chilterns
Walking in the Cotswolds
Walking in the Isles of Scilly

Walking in the New Forest
Walking in the North
  Wessex Downs
Walking in the Thames Valley
Walking on Dartmoor
Walking on Guernsey
Walking on Jersey
Walking on the Isle of Wight
Walking on the Jurassic Coast
Walks in the South Downs
  National Park

BRITISH ISLES CHALLENGES, COLLECTIONS AND ACTIVITIES

The Book of the Bivvy
The Book of the Bothy
The C2C Cycle Route
The End to End Cycle Route
The Mountains of England and
  Wales: Vol 1 Wales
The Mountains of England and
  Wales: Vol 2 England
The National Trails
The UK's County Tops
Three Peaks, Ten Tors

ALPS CROSS-BORDER ROUTES

100 Hut Walks in the Alps
Across the Eastern Alps: E5
Alpine Ski Mountaineering
  Vol 1 – Western Alps
Alpine Ski Mountaineering
  Vol 2 – Central and Eastern Alps
Chamonix to Zermatt
The Karnischer Hohenweg
The Tour of the Bernina
Tour of Mont Blanc
Tour of Monte Rosa
Tour of the Matterhorn
Trail Running – Chamonix and the
  Mont Blanc region
Trekking in the Alps
Trekking in the Silvretta and
  Rätikon Alps
Trekking Munich to Venice
Walking in the Alps

PYRENEES AND FRANCE/SPAIN CROSS-BORDER ROUTES

The GR10 Trail
The GR11 Trail
The Pyrenean Haute Route
The Pyrenees
The Way of St James – Spain
Walks and Climbs in the Pyrenees

AUSTRIA

Innsbruck Mountain Adventures
The Adlerweg
Trekking in Austria's Hohe Tauern

Trekking in the Stubai Alps
Trekking in the Zillertal Alps
Walking in Austria

SWITZERLAND

Cycle Touring in Switzerland
Switzerland's Jura Crest Trail
The Swiss Alpine Pass Route –
  Via Alpina Route 1
The Swiss Alps
Tour of the Jungfrau Region
Walking in the Bernese Oberland
Walking in the Valais

FRANCE AND BELGIUM

Chamonix Mountain Adventures
Cycle Touring in France
Cycling London to Paris
Cycling the Canal de la Garonne
Cycling the Canal du Midi
Écrins National Park
Mont Blanc Walks
Mountain Adventures in
  the Maurienne
The GR20 Corsica
The GR5 Trail
The GR5 Trail – Vosges and Jura
The Grand Traverse of the
  Massif Central
The Loire Cycle Route
The Moselle Cycle Route
The River Rhone Cycle Route
The Robert Louis Stevenson Trail
The Way of St James – Le Puy
  to the Pyrenees
Tour of the Oisans: The GR54
Tour of the Queyras
Vanoise Ski Touring
Via Ferratas of the French Alps
Walking in Corsica
Walking in Provence – East
Walking in Provence – West
Walking in the Auvergne
Walking in the Briançonnais
Walking in the Cevennes
Walking in the Dordogne
Walking in the Haute Savoie: North
Walking in the Haute Savoie: South
Walks in the Cathar Region
The GR5 Trail – Benelux
  and Lorraine
Walking in the Ardennes

GERMANY

Hiking and Cycling in the Black
  Forest
The Danube Cycleway Vol 1
The Rhine Cycle Route
The Westweg
Walking in the Bavarian Alps

For full information on all our
guides, books and eBooks,
visit our website:
www.cicerone.co.uk

Walking – Trekking – Mountaineering – Climbing – Cycling

Over 50 years, Cicerone have built up an outstanding collection of over 300 guides, inspiring all sorts of amazing adventures.

Every guide comes from extensive exploration and research by our expert authors, all with a passion for their subjects. They are frequently praised, endorsed and used by clubs, instructors and outdoor organisations.

All our titles can now be bought as **e-books**, **ePubs** and **Kindle** files and we also have an online magazine – **Cicerone Extra** – with features to help cyclists, climbers, walkers and trekkers choose their next adventure, at home or abroad.

Our website shows any **new information** we've had in since a book was published. Please do let us know if you find anything has changed, so that we can publish the latest details. On our **website** you'll also find great ideas and lots of detailed information about what's inside every guide and you can buy **individual routes** from many of them online.

It's easy to keep in touch with what's going on at Cicerone by getting our monthly **free e-newsletter**, which is full of offers, competitions, up-to-date information and topical articles. You can subscribe on our home page and also follow us on **Facebook** and **Twitter** or dip into our **blog**.

Cicerone – the very best guides for exploring the world.

CICERONE

Juniper House, Murley Moss, Oxenholme Road, Kendal, Cumbria LA9 7RL
Tel: 015395 62069 info@cicerone.co.uk
www.cicerone.co.uk